"One of the most important books written on nutrition and health. Deville presents a powerful analysis of what is wrong with one of the major suppliers of our foods, the supermarket, and how you can protect yourself and your loved ones from this eminent danger. Everyone concerned with the health of their loved ones should study this most important book."

—Russell L. Blaylock, MD, Advanced Nutritional Concepts, LLC, visiting professor of biology, Belhaven College, Jackson, Mississippi

"A well-researched and reader-friendly book on the increasing dangers of modern factory food. A wake-up call to boycott supermarket food in favor of certified organic."

—Samuel S. Epstein, MD, professor emeritus, environmental and occupational medicine, University of Illinois at Chicago School of Public Health; chairman, Cancer Prevention Coalition; author of *Toxic Beauty*

"Nancy Deville's *Death by Supermarket* is a must-read for anyone interested in health and wellness. She has painstakingly researched the ugly realities of our food industry and exposes the real causes of the American health crisis."

—Maoshing Ni, PhD, DOM, Dipl. ABAAHP, cofounder of the Tao of Wellness and Yo San University, author of *Secrets of Longevity*

D1410013

DEATH BY
SUPERMARKET

The Fattening, Dumbing Down, and Poisoning of America

NANCY DEVILLE

GREENLEAF
BOOK GROUP PRESS

This book is intended as a reference volume only, not as a medical manual. The information given here is designed to help you make informed decisions about your health. It is not intended as a substitute for any treatment that may have been prescribed by your doctor. If you suspect that you have a medical problem, you should seek competent medical help. You should not begin a new health regimen without first consulting a medical professional.

Published by Greenleaf Book Group Press
Austin, Texas
www.gbgpress.com

Distributed by Greenleaf Book Group LLC

For ordering information or special discounts for bulk purchases, please contact Greenleaf Book Group LLC at PO Box 91869, Austin, TX 78709, 512.891.6100.

Design and composition by Greenleaf Book Group LLC
Cover design by Greenleaf Book Group LLC

Publisher's Cataloging-In-Publication Data
(Prepared by The Donohue Group, Inc.)
Deville, Nancy.
    Death by supermarket : the fattening, dumbing down, and poisoning of America / Nancy Deville. — 2nd ed.
    p. ; cm.
    ISBN: 978-1-60832-115-5
    1. Food industry and trade—Health aspects—United States. 2. Food industry and trade—Government policy—United States. 3. Obesity—United States. 4. Nutrition—United States. 5. Food habits—United States. 6. Convenience foods—Health aspects—United States. I. Title.
HD9005 .D47 2011
362.196/39800973   2010942467

Part of the Tree Neutral® program, which offsets the number of trees consumed in the production and printing of this book by taking proactive steps, such as planting trees in direct proportion to the number of trees used: www.treeneutral.com

Printed in the United States of America on acid-free paper

TreeNeutral™

11 12 13 14 15 16   10 9 8 7 6 5 4 3 2 1
Second Edition

For my grandma, Stella

Contents

Introduction

IN A RECENT FILM, after most of Los Angeles is destroyed by aberrant tornados, a climatologist warns the president of the United States that he must immediately enforce mass evacuations to save millions of Americans from an impending storm brought on by global warming. The president dismisses the urgency and refuses to take action. True to the climatologist's predictions, a devastating storm and accompanying ice age obliterate the Northern Hemisphere.

The epidemic of obesity in the United States is as ominous as tornados ripping across Los Angeles. Americans are the fattest people walking the earth today. In a population of 300 million, 68 percent of our citizens are overweight or obese. Some are so large they can't fly on airplanes, go to a movie theater, or otherwise function in society. New industries have sprung up to accommodate "people of size," manufacturing larger seats for restaurants, wheelchairs, and toilets; mega hospital beds; and XL coffins. It's gotten so surreal that we hardly blink an eye at people being hoisted around with cranes.

I believe that the American diet of processed, convenience, junk, fast, and otherwise industrialized "factory" food is the major contributing factor to our obesity epidemic. This diet is also responsible for our skyrocketing rates of degenerative disease. Yet because our medical community and government are not protecting us, the epidemic escalates, with millions of people on a trajectory that is certain to culminate in apocalyptic human tragedy.

The message we should be hearing is that if Americans stopped eating all factory-food products and ate only what I call "historic" real food we would calm the unnatural hunger that compels us to eat these injurious substances. Historic real food is organically produced meat, fish, poultry, dairy, vegetables, fruits, grains, legumes, seeds, and nuts that could (in theory) be picked, gathered, milked, hunted, or fished. By giving our bodies and brains the necessary nutritional building blocks found in real, living food, Americans would be healthy, sexy, and happy, with each individual fully realizing his or her unique physical and mental potential—we'd be as intelligent, tall, and physically and emotionally gifted as our genetics predispose us to be. This would dramatically reduce the number of patients flocking to obesity clinics, ERs, and shrinks' offices. As it stands, though Americans worship youth and beauty, we're aging more rapidly than we have to because we eat dead factory-food products instead of living, real food.

I initially held my beliefs about real food because of the influence of my grandmother, Stella, who taught me about real food. I also traveled the world from ages fifteen to twenty-two, before the American corporate invasion, and witnessed the healthy outcomes of populations that ate real food. Later, when I started writing on health, every subject I wrote about, whether weight loss, adrenal burnout, or Chinese medicine, had the common thread of stopping eating factory-food products and eating real food. But I also believe that our health and weight problems are not just because of factory food.

Before World War II much of our population suffered from malnutrition due to lack of food, which manifested in emaciation, depression, lowered IQ, disease, and premature death. Since World War II, our food chain has become permeated with factory foods, diets, and drugs; we're now suffering from a new type of malnutrition that manifests in obesity, depression, lowered IQ, disease, and—because we have medical means to keep people alive—long, lingering, ugly death. An unhealthy symbiotic relationship ultimately developed among our medical establishment; government; the food, diet, and pharmaceutical corporations; and us—American consumers. The food industry addicts us to their products, which make us fat, depressed, and sick. Then the diet and drug industries sell us products, "systems," and drugs that exacerbate malnutrition and disease.

The agencies that should be protecting us are complying with the corporations that are harming us. While the Food and Drug Administration (FDA) is supposed to be responsible for protecting public health by ensuring the safety and efficacy of the substances we ingest, the FDA has devolved into an incompetent and corrupt agency that's bought and paid for with payoffs and cronyism. In addition, our medical system has become a business that focuses on treating disease once it occurs with drugs, surgeries, and procedures. The majority of doctors in this system have no nutritional training, and the training that they do have supports the factory-food industry.

Since the government and the medical community aren't coming out against factory food, diets, and drugs, the public takes Madison Avenue's word for it that these substances are healthy and beneficial. And so we remain addicted to factory food, desperately dieting and taking drugs to try to fix the health problems caused by an unnatural factory-food diet.

Do Americans even care? Reportedly, the factory foods that have the worst nutritional value sell the most briskly. When it comes to suggesting health changes, health educators continue to set the bar lower and lower, ostensibly because Americans are too lazy to make any substantive changes. After fifteen years of research for the books I've written, I'm convinced that our fat and disease epidemic is no more our fault than it would be if we were caged lab rats being subjected to mind control, force-feeding, and bizarre experiments. That said, we've given in to the industries that have made us fat and sick without much of a fight. As a path of least resistance, we attempt to make ourselves feel better about our fatness, our dumb-and-dumberness, our unhealthiness, and our addiction to factory-food by adopting an affable camaraderie about our diet. We laugh to cope, but unfortunately, this dismissive attitude perpetuates our role as victims.

I want to make it perfectly clear that this book is not a condemnation for being fat, sick, or weak-willed. I also don't want to imply that eating and living in a healthy way is an absolute guarantee against illness; some of us will do our very best but still get sick. My purpose is to share with you what I've learned about nutrition and the influences of the food, diet, and drug industries so that you can make the healthiest choices.

There's a kind of division of the classes occurring that has less to do with money and more to do with personal choice. Increasingly, two distinct groups are emerging: the overweight, depressed, sick eaters of factory-food products, who constantly diet and rely on a cocktail of OTC and prescription drugs; and the eaters of organic, historic real food, who don't diet, avoid taking drugs, and are generally healthy, sexy, and happy.

What's about to happen in America is analogous to an apocalyptic movie. Picture a few survivors blinking at the devastation they have escaped and brimming with hope for a future utopia. You and your family could be numbered among the survivors.

All it takes to begin is turning the page.

PART ONE

How Factory Food Changed the Way We Live . . . and Die

CHAPTER ONE

America's Missed Opportunity for Utopia

FORTY YEARS AGO, ON the TV sitcom *Green Acres*, socialite Lisa (Eva Gabor) just added boiling water to prepare Dee Dee's "Dehydroficated" Mason Dixon Southern Fried Chicken Dinner for her husband, Oliver (Eddie Albert). This parody of the modern American diet presented back in the 1960s is a reality today. Instead of breastfeeding, we feed our newborns industrialized infant formula and wean them on toxic "kid foods" like Nabisco Teddy Grahams Clifford The Big Red Dog Cinnamon Graham Sticks, Danimals Swingin' Strawberry-Banana Flavored Yogurt, Betty Crocker Looney Tunes/Scooby Doo Fruit Flavored Snacks, X-Treme Jell-O Pudding Sticks, and Kool-Aid.

American children go off to school on breakfasts of Hostess Ding Dongs, Pillsbury Cinnamon Rolls, Cap'n Crunch, and Reese's Puffs. They eat Fritos and McDonald's for lunch, and snack on movie popcorn, Hot Pockets, Fat Free Pringles, Crystal Light Sugar Free Lemonade, Nickelodeon Fruit Snacks, and Coke.

Americans have evolved an "every man for himself" system for dinner, swinging through fast-food drive-throughs, 7-Elevens, and ampms, calling Domino's, or foraging in the kitchen for Kellogg's Eggo Buttermilk Waffles, Campbell's soups, Chef Boyardee Ravioli, and Lean Cuisine and Hungry Man frozen dinners.

Back when our country was founded, Thomas Jefferson idealized the family farm as the backbone of American democracy. But over the past one hundred years—accelerating after World War II—to increase profits, family farms and ranches have been taken over by behemoth corporations, and the production of poultry and meat has been industrialized. Livestock were moved from their natural habitats and were incarcerated in cramped, dark factories, pens, and cages to live short, miserable lives eating species-inappropriate food, being pumped with genetically modified growth hormones, and kept alive on drugs before being slaughtered in the cheapest (which often means the cruelest) ways. Since it's more profitable and less of a headache to ride herd on factory workers than it is manage the farms and ranches that historically fed us, the food industry developed "products" that have long shelf lives and can be easily shipped thousands of miles—unlike real, living food, which spoils and is difficult to transport.

Factory-food products are made, for the most part, from real food that is broken down in laboratories and factories, using heat and chemical solvents, into its basic components. The components are then mixed with colored dyes, preservatives, synthetic vitamins, and hundreds of other substances. Teams of chemists and "food flavorists" manipulate the chemical composition of recipes so the resulting products titillate taste buds and have appealing "bite characteristics" and "mouthfeel," along with a maximum shelf life. Although factory foods promise good health, beauty, and satisfaction, they lack the life-sustaining nutrients necessary to maintain healthy metabolic processes and are mostly foreign and toxic to human physiology. The heartbreaking reality is that rather than feeling sated by eating these products, the resultant unnatural hunger provokes people to binge insatiably.

Industrialized animal products (meat, dairy, fish, poultry, and eggs) that are produced in Concentrated Animal Feeding Operations (CAFOs) also contribute to obesity and ugly death. In CAFOs animals are deprived of sunlight, clean water, and space to move, swim, or lie down. They're fed species-inappropriate food (herbivores are fed soybeans and chicken poop, for example) and are injected with hormones, and because of the depraved conditions in CAFOs, they must be given antibiotics and hundreds of drugs to keep them alive long enough to fatten for slaughter. They're lonely, frightened, and crazed from birth to death. Since the way animals are treated and their nutrition determine the nutritional value of their meat, milk, and eggs, CAFO foods contain fewer of the life-sustaining nutrients necessary to maintain healthy metabolic processes. Because of the poisons in animal feed and the drugs animals are given, CAFO products contain toxins that can harm human beings.

On the other hand, real food (including humanely raised animal products) contains life-sustaining nutrients necessary to maintain healthy metabolic processes. Real food is recognized and utilized by human physiology. As I said in the Introduction, I learned this initially from my grandmother. Stella was a dark-haired beauty, a Polish immigrant who came through Ellis Island in 1911 and suffered her fair share of health problems as a result of inadequate early nutrition. In 1942, at age thirty-nine, Stella happened upon a "health" lecture, became a health-food devotee, and was henceforth labeled the family kook. When I was a child, I often found her in the basement, lying in the pitch black on her "slant board," blood rushing to her head as she meditated. She was notorious for her delicious cooking, juicing and canning homegrown vegetables, dispensing vitamin C capsules, and dog-earing pages in nutritional pioneer Adelle Davis's books for us to read.

Stella was an example of someone who started out with inadequate nutrition because her family was poor but regrouped later in life by providing her body and brain with the necessary building blocks of real, living food. By doing so, she was able to take advantage of her genetic gifts, such as was possible later in life. Among Stella's unique gifts were her physical beauty, strength, energy, and—her most remarkable quality—a positive attitude about life, despite hardship and tragedy. By giving our bodies and brains the necessary building blocks of nutrition, we could also take advantage of our genetic gifts, to the extent that is possible later in life. Future generations would benefit to a much greater extent in that adequate nutrition from conception on would allow them to fully realize their genetic gifts.

Our nation has a well-established superiority complex in which we see ourselves as the richest, most macho, most technologically advanced nation in the world. The truth is that we're number one in the world in obesity[1] and that we're falling way behind in world health. We're ranked fiftieth in life expectancy. In a 2009 World Health Organization (WHO) comparison, the United States ranked twenty-ninth in the world in infant mortality and 68 percent of adults were overweight or obese.[2] (WHO is a United Nations agency dedicated to global health.)

In addition, although studies have demonstrated that tall people enjoy a positive bias in society, get promoted faster in their careers, earn more money, and are better than short people in relationships and politics, American men are not growing taller as are other men around the world. American women are actually shrinking. According to John Komlos, Ph.D., the leading expert in the field of anthropometric history, which tracks how populations around the world have changed in stature, the average adult height attained by a population is a historical record of the overall nutrition of that population. Dr. Komlos's twenty years of research has documented the height of almost a quarter of a million people from the 1700s to the present.

"Americans were the tallest people in the world until right after World War II, which was a reflection our healthy eating habits," Dr. Komlos told me. "Because of our poor diet, Americans have gone from being tallest in the world—one to three inches taller than Western and Northern Europeans—to being towered over by the Dutch, Swedes, Norwegians, Danes, British, and Germans by one to three inches. Today, Americans are, on average, the same height of the men and women of the Czech Republic."[3] In other words, Americans are now the same height as the citizens of an Eastern European country that has been economically repressed and nutritionally deprived for hundreds of years. (The average American man is five-foot-nine, and the average woman five-foot-four.)

In addition to reversing our growth spurt, our industrialized diet has resulted in more American kids being at higher risk for a host of health problems, including precocious puberty and neurological disorders, such as attention deficit hyperactivity disorder (ADHD) and attention deficit disorder (ADD)—diseases characterized by inattention, impulsivity, and hyperactivity; and autism, a disorder of mental introversion, aloneness, inability to relate, repetitive play, and rage reactions. Type 1 diabetes, an autoimmune disorder of absolute insulin deficiency, is on the rise in children.[4] Also occurring more frequently in children are the degenerative diseases formerly associated with aging: cancer, heart disease, and type 2 diabetes, a chronic disorder of carbohydrate metabolism formerly known as "adult onset" diabetes.

In all age groups, there is an alarming increase in frightening, incurable autoimmune conditions—of which there are a hundred—such as Hashimoto's thyroiditis (chronic inflammation of the thyroid gland), lupus (progressive ulcerative skin disease), Crohn's disease (chronic inflammation of the intestines), rheumatoid arthritis (chronic inflammation of the joints), Graves' disease (overactive thyroid), myasthenia gravis (progressive muscular weakness), interstitial cystitis (chronic inflammation of the bladder), and Sjögren's disease (in which white blood cells attack moisture-producing glands, causing numerous health problems). Autoimmune conditions occur when the immune system loses the ability to distinguish between normal healthy cells and destructive foreign invaders and attacks healthy cells. People who develop autoimmune conditions are often condemned to a lifetime of chronic pain, the despair of being characterized as hypochondriacs, and the plight of being guinea pigs at the hands of doctors who don't know how to help them.

Millions of factory-food eating Americans today suffer from lack of what I call "happy" neurotransmitters (chemicals that carry messages between cells). Imbalances of these neurotransmitters cause the unnatural hunger that drives us to eat injurious substances. Neurotransmitter imbalances can also result in problems such as ADD, ADHD, insomnia, exhaustion, depression, obsessive or even suicidal thoughts, panic disorders, anxiety, rage, agitation, anorexia nervosa, bulimia, and zero sex drive.

Because we've deteriorated to this degree, Americans are dying excruciating deaths, drugged up and tethered to monitors with beepers going off in impersonal hospital rooms where strangers walk in and out.

On her deathbed at age ninety-seven, Stella's skin glowed and was virtually wrinkle free, and her hair was radiant. When a nurse came in to check her vitals, Stella demonstrated her famous bicycle kick exercise. The next day she died peacefully. At her eulogy, she was compared to the subject of an 1858 Oliver Wendell Holmes poem on old age called "The Deacon's Masterpiece" about a one-horse carriage that survived one hundred years in perfect shape and then on its last day disintegrated into a heap of sawdust. Holmes writes about an ideal life of good health and peaceful death that few Americans experience today. But Stella did, largely because she ate real food.

Even though my grandma died a relatively peaceful death, she still died in a hospital. I was there for her last hours with my nephew, James. We sat on either side of her bed the entire night, talking to her, being with her, remembering things about her. It was one of the profound experiences of my life. Just as Grandma influenced me about living, she also influenced me about dying, because I was sorry that she died in a hospital. In the years since her death in 2001, I've thought a lot about the correlation between the effects of the big three—factory food, diets, and drugs—and the way we die. I believe that by eating real, living food, by using drugs extremely judiciously, and by not dieting, more people would be healthy enough to stay at home attending to business as usual, instead of being wheeled into "assisted living," a euphemism for "waiting for death." Being healthy means we could live our old age and then die of old age peacefully in a celebratory experience at home, surrounded by loved ones. That's the way we are meant to leave this world.

This is something to think about, as death from degenerative diseases has risen spectacularly in the last hundred years. And dying from a degenerative disease is not like the pretty, soft-focus pharmaceutical commercials you see with Grandpa fishing with his grandchildren and Mom gardening with her daughter in idyllic settings with poignant music and perfect hair and makeup. Dying of a degenerative disease is torture that ravages the family as it brings its victim down.

Historically, people didn't suffer and die on a massive scale from degenerative diseases. Prior to the year 1900, hygiene—the basic practice of cleanliness—was an advancement yet to be "discovered." Raw sewage ran in city streets, contaminating drinking water. Doctors with filth under their fingernails blew their noses during surgery. People and their habits were essentially dirty. Prior to the year 1900, the primary cause of death was infectious diseases.

In the late 1850s, French chemist and bacteriologist Louis Pasteur promoted the "germ theory of disease": All infectious diseases have a causative agent, such as a bacteria, virus, fungus, or parasite. The discovery of microorganisms precipitated scientific advancements, such as the use of personal hygiene, antibiotics, sanitation, and refrigeration, which systematically eradicated many infectious-disease plagues. In addition, for the first time in the history of humankind, a population as vast as ours was gaining the capacity to produce enough life-sustaining meat, fish, poultry, dairy, vegetables, fruits, grains, legumes, seeds, and nuts to feed our nation. At the turn of the twentieth century, the United States was poised to evolve into a utopia filled with healthy, strapping people. But this didn't occur. Instead obesity and degenerative disease rose throughout and are now epidemic.

There are current statistics that demonstrate our epidemic of degenerative diseases, but we've become numb to numbers on pages. We haven't become inured to the fear of disease, however. More than fifty years ago, Adelle Davis wrote in *Let's Eat Right to Keep Fit: The Practical Guide to Nutrition Designed to Help You Achieve Good Health Through Proper Diet*

(1954), "Statistics can tell so little. The number of new cancer cases discovered each year tells nothing of the fear and dread in the hearts of millions of Americans who already know that some day they themselves will suffer from the disease."[5]

The more immediate focus should be why are we experiencing this radical rise in degenerative diseases?

Beginning a hundred years ago, as medical advancements in fighting infectious diseases developed, two factors thwarted our potential for utopia. First, we didn't take advantage of the perfect opportunity to thrive with fewer infectious diseases by eating real food. As factory food usurped real food in our food chain, more people started dying of degenerative diseases.

Factory food isn't the only contributing factor to the epidemic of obesity and disease. There are industrial chemicals and solvents, volatile organic compounds, exhaust, radiation, heavy metals, cigarette smoke, and pharmaceuticals, among other toxic insults, as well as genetic predispositions, bacteria, viruses, and other biological causes. But these other factors wouldn't have the same devastating impact on our health if we were eating an exclusive diet of real food. Eating real, living food—containing protein, fats, cholesterol, vitamins, minerals, trace minerals, and enzymes (catalysts necessary for internal chemical reactions)—fuels cellular processes, imparts energy for the muscles and the brain, supplies the building materials for the ongoing replenishing of cells, tissues, muscle, and bone, and keeps endocrine systems, including our immune system, functioning optimally, to at least give our bodies a fighting chance.

The second factor that thwarted America's potential for utopia was that Pasteur's germ theory of disease unfortunately influenced our medical community to drop the pursuit of disease prevention. Beginning in the nineteenth century, chemicals with drug actions were isolated from plants, and increasingly drugs were made by chemical synthesis. Our medical community became convinced that the newly discovered drugs were the most advantageous modality with which to practice medicine (i.e., combat germs and other disease-causing agents). Nutrition as "standard of care" (accepted modes of medical care), which had been accepted doctrine from the time of Greek physician Hippocrates (the "father of medicine," 460–377 B.C.), was unilaterally rejected by modern medicine, which has virtually ignored the impact of nutrition on the building up or breaking down of the body and shifted its focus to treating disease after it occurs—primarily with drugs.

The medical community's dismissal of nutrition as standard of care in favor of a drug approach was the first step in our becoming a nation of factory-food eaters because it encouraged people to abdicate responsibility for their own health and place utter trust in the medical community. As we became a nation of drug takers following the advice of the medical community—which had shunned nutrition—the old wisdoms of food and nutrition were lost. Today few people remember their grandmothers advising them what to eat or drink to prevent or correct illness. That's because most grandmothers did not learn the simple truths about nutrition from *their* grandmothers.

Our reliance on doctors to tell us what to do and the accompanying acceptance of drugs provided a natural segue for our acceptance of chemical additives to our food supply. Fifty years ago, DuPont sold us on "better living through chemistry," and many people today do not see a problem with ingesting factory-food products made from ingredients that they can't pronounce, much less explain what they are. As Americans increasingly adopted a chemicalized diet that was mostly foreign and toxic to our physiology, we also took over-the-counter (OTC) medications and prescription drugs to treat the resulting chronic conditions and diseases. It's proven to be a bad mix. Yet, because of the marvels of modern medicine, people are living longer—with tubes hanging out of them and beepers going off.

The fact that medicine abandoned the research, teaching, and employment of nutrition as a medical modality was an important factor in the rise to power of the factory-food industry. As our food culture shifted from the real foods produced by Thomas Jefferson's ideal small family farm to factory foods emblematized by Dee Dee's "Dehydroficated" Mason Dixon

Southern Fried Chicken Dinner, American brains have actually mutated from healthy brains constructed of cells made out of healthy biochemicals to abnormal brains made out of molecularly damaged fats. These unhealthy brains are also neurotransmitter-imbalanced, which results in unnatural appetites. The World Health Organization (WHO) politely referred to our bingeing as "excess intake" and linked mass gorging to our epidemic of obesity and degenerative diseases of aging. What WHO called the "malnutrition of excess" created a market for the diet and drug industries to flourish.[38]

Heroin, cocaine, caffeine, refined white flour, and sugar are all white, powdery, highly addictive substances. Sugar happens to be a socially acceptable addiction, and it's one ingredient that keeps us eating factory-food products.

PART TWO

Unnatural Hunger

CHAPTER TWO

Socially Acceptable Sugar Addiction

IN 1984, RIGHT AFTER the release of Arnold Schwarzenegger's *Terminator*, my childhood friend Mary Jane took her two-year-old daughter, Rosemary, to the dentist. To M.J.'s horror, Rosie was diagnosed with "bottle mouth," which in simple terms meant that her baby teeth were rotting out as a result of too much sucking on bottles of juice. In order to save her permanent teeth from the damage that would ensue if her teeth were left to decay any further, under anesthesia Rosie had her front teeth ground down to nubs and capped in silver. After the trauma of the ordeal began to wear off, I taught Rosie how to say "terminator baby."

Like my friend M.J., millions of Americans think they are doing the healthy thing by handing their babies bottles of juice. Families say grace over breakfasts of Count Chocula, Ho Hos, and Kellogg's Chocolate Chip Cookie Dough Pop-Tarts because it's socially acceptable to be addicted to sugar.

Sugar is a white, crystalline stimulant that offers zero nutritional value. Since refined white sugar is devoid of the vitamins and minerals necessary to digest and metabolize itself, your body ends up depleting vitamins and minerals from your diet or from internal stores in order to digest it. A short explanation of macronutrients and micronutrients might help explain why depleting vitamins and minerals is a bad thing.

Macronutrients (proteins, fats, and carbs) provide energy and are the materials that are used in the breaking down and building up metabolic processes that go on continually within your body.

Micronutrients (vitamins A, B, C, D, E, and K; minerals, such as calcium and phosphorous; and trace elements, such as iron, zinc, and manganese) are the essential cofactors for metabolism to function. In other words, your body cannot properly utilize macronutrients without micronutrients.

The vitamins A, D, E, and K are classified as fat soluble because they dissolve in fat before being absorbed in the bloodstream. Fat-soluble vitamins that are not immediately used are stored in the liver, and because they can be stored for a rainy day, they do not need to be consumed daily. B complex and vitamin C are water-soluble vitamins and are easily washed out of the body through urination, and so they must be consumed every day. The vitamins A, C, D, E, and K are antioxidants that neutralize free radicals in your body. (See page 50 for more on free radicals.)

If you eat a lot of sugar and don't eat a lot of foods containing, say, B vitamins every day (meats, whole grains, legumes, green leafy veggies, dairy, citrus, and so on), you'll become depleted of B vitamins and can ultimately suffer from a burning sensation on your tongue, wrinkles surrounding your lips, exhaustion, gastrointestinal problems, thinning, graying hair, and depression. These are only some of the problems that occur as a result of the vitamin and mineral depletion caused by overconsuming sugar.

Eating sugar also depletes your body of antibodies, which roam your body, fighting every cold and flu that goes around. Sugar is cancer fuel and fertilizer, causes type 2 diabetes, causes plaque to accumulate in the coronary arteries, and fuels unnatural hunger.

Unnatural hunger is the result of neurotransmitter imbalances, and these imbalances can begin at conception.

Our brains are 60 percent fat. From conception to birth human beings need essential fatty acids for proper brain formation.[6] (Essentially fatty acids are discussed on page 112.) Also imperative for proper brain formation from conception to birth is cholesterol.[7] (Cholesterol is covered starting on page 101.) Equally crucial for brain formation and development are amino acids, which are the chemical building blocks used to make cell membranes, tissues, enzymes, antibodies, hormones, and neurotransmitters.[8] There are twenty amino acids that are important for human metabolism. Ten of these can be produced within the body and are called nonessential. Two are conditionally essential, which basically means that age, stress, geography, and any number of factors can determine whether or not your body can make these or make them in the correct proportions. Eight essential amino acids are required for life but not made in the body. Amino acids are obtained by eating protein such as eggs, dairy, fish, poultry, and meat.

Healthy neurotransmitters are crucial for happiness. Here's how they work: Your endocrine system generates hormones, which comprise the chemical communication system that controls every function in your body. Your nervous system is actually an endocrine gland that generates impulses (chemical messages) and conveys these messages by jumping from neuron to neuron. Synapses are gaps between neurons, which are jumped by the chemical messengers called neurotransmitters. This jumping of the gaps is known as the "firing" of a synapse, a process through which your brain choreographs the complex orchestra of speech, hearing, sight, emotions, and trillions of metabolic functions that comprise human physiology. A healthy brain will have a healthy supply of the neurotransmitters, such as dopamine, which acts as a stimulant (you feel energized); endorphins, which are your brain's pain-killer and pleasure chemicals (the pains of life are diminished and you instead feel a sense of joy); serotonin, which is responsible for a sense of well-being (you feel high on life); and gamma amino butyric acid (GABA), which promotes a sense of calm (you feel calmly in control).

If a pregnant woman eats a high sugar, chemicalized diet of factory-food products instead of eating a diet of real, living food that includes essential fatty acids, cholesterol, and amino acids, her baby's brain won't get the building materials it needs, and that baby isn't likely to be born with a healthy brain.[9] In addition to having a brain made out of unhealthy building materials, the baby's brain will not be flooded with happy neurotransmitters.

Breastfeeding is the next step in the process of brain development and neurotransmitter production. Breast milk is real, living food for babies. But most Americans aren't breastfed, or are only briefly. And if breastfed by malnourished factory-food eating mothers, these babies are receiving the same poor-quality nutrition. Most are fed factory formula. Instead of being raised on a diet of real food, most American kids are fed substances that are permeated with sugar. From conception on, the majority of Americans' brains don't get the essential fatty acids, cholesterol, and amino acids necessary to build healthy brain cells and make neurotransmitters. So we are set up for lifelong brain neurotransmitter imbalances.

When brain neurotransmitters are in short supply, you're more prone to suffer from all the neurological problems we reviewed on page 7. Accompanying these symptoms are addictions to sugar, drugs, and stimulants like caffeine, alcohol, and nicotine. The reason we have these addictions is because we learn very quickly that consuming those substances makes us feel better temporarily.

Every visit to a restaurant or market is an anthropological research expedition for me as I observe what people eat. In a university cafeteria, I sat down to a lunch of steak, potatoes, and vegetables. An obese woman next to me was eating her lunch, which consisted of a small bowl of fruit salad and a Rice Crispy square. Fruit, while healthy, is all sugar, and so, obviously, is a Rice Crispy square. I couldn't help imagining the binge that woman was destined to go on later in the afternoon.

This is what happened inside that woman's body after she consumed that all-sugar lunch: Eating sugar triggers the pancreas to secrete the "nutrient-storing" hormone insulin. The secretion of insulin stimulates an excessive "rush" of stored neurotransmitters in the brain.[10] Thus the woman experienced the infamous sugar high. But also, since excess sugar damages cells, insulin's primary directive is to stow all that sugar away into cells. Now there was not enough sugar in her bloodstream to satisfy her brain's need for an ongoing drip of sugar, so her brain demanded more sugar. At the same time, her neurotransmitter rush ended, and unless she had superhuman self-control she was guaranteed to binge, as the craving for more sugar was intense. Meanwhile, all this stress alerted her adrenals to release the stress hormones adrenaline and cortisol. These chemical messengers mobilized sugar into her bloodstream to be utilized by her body and brain during this time of stress: Adrenaline released glycogen, sugar that is stored in her liver and muscles for immediate fuel needs, and cortisol began breaking down her lean muscle mass (muscle and bones) to convert it into sugar. All this internally generated sugar, along with the sugar she most likely binged on after lunch, propelled her back into her sugar high. But this dangerous influx of sugar into her bloodstream again triggered the secretion of insulin, which immediately stored this new sugar away into cells. The woman's blood sugar crashed again.

This roller coaster operates for some people all day long.

You might think that since eating sugar facilitates an excessive rush of stored neurotransmitters in your brain, continually eating sugar is a permanent solution to keeping your brain supplied with happy neurotransmitters. But the fact is that brain neurotransmitters are finite and will eventually become depleted if you don't eat the foods necessary to make more. Unfortunately, the brain doesn't say to you, "Please feed me food so that I can make more neurotransmitters." The brain is focused only on its immediate needs, and so it screams, "Give me sugar!" Thus you're led around by what I call your dumb pet—your brain—which demands sugar (or stimulants). In a futile attempt to balance your brain neurotransmitters, your body desperately extracts whatever minute amount of nutrients it can from your factory diet. And your doctor will likely be happy to write you a prescription for antidepressant selective serotonin reuptake inhibitors (SSRIs) that supposedly inhibit the disposal of serotonin from the brain, thus leading to longer-lasting normal levels of serotonin. (Antidepressants have been shown to be nothing more than placebos, which I discuss in *Healthy, Sexy, Happy*.)[11]

Eating refined grains is the same thing as eating refined white sugar. A perfect example of how much we love refined white flour products is our nation's love affair with cereal. In fact, a new restaurant chain called Cereality Cereal Bar and Café is rolling out across the country, featuring dozens of cereals, milk and soy options, and toppings like marshmallows and M&Ms, which will be served by pajama-uniformed "cereologists" while the Cartoon Network plays on TV monitors. David Roth, a cofounder and the president of Cereality, said, "The ubiquity of Starbucks is what we aim for."[12]

The fact that cereal franchises are springing up is alarming since young people already have so many strikes against them when it comes to building healthy brains. The brain isn't fully formed at puberty but continues to develop and mature until the age of twenty-four.[13] This means that college students who graduate after four years of eating cereal, sodas, chips, and other sugary garbage for breakfast, lunch, and dinner are going to have lesser brains than those who suck it up and figure out how to forage for real foods that contain brain-healthy nutrients.

Americans overeat refined grains not because we have a stupid gene that other cultures don't have. Rather, our culture is oversaturated with these products. Consider that every single culture on the face of the earth has a version of fried dough (here it's the doughnut). In Japan, where American *donhnatsu* franchises have proliferated, they also eat traditional *age pan*—a deep-fat-fried blob with sweet fillings. In Mexico it's *churro,* fried dough in a long, serrated breadstick shape rolled in sugar. In India, it's *papad,* a deep-fried, crispy, spicy, thin dough round. The difference is that in other countries real food is a prevalent part of the diet (although the world is rapidly catching up to the United States in factory food consumption). In the United States, refined grains are readily accessible; they're easy to eat, good tasting, and addictive.

Grains weren't part of the Paleolithic (hunter/gatherer) diet for millions of years and weren't eaten by humans until 10,000 years ago when agriculture first developed. Prior to that time, humans consumed carbs in relatively indigestible forms in nuts, berries, and roots. In other words, grains are a relatively recent addition to our food chain and physiology, and refined grains are brand-new.[14] Ten thousand years seems like long enough for human physiology to adjust to whole grains as part of the diet. Food companies capitalize on the belief that whole grains are part of a healthy diet. For example, Post, which produces Honey Bunches of Oats, Pebbles, Post Toasties, and Honeycomb, and also makes "healthy" cereals like Shredded Wheat and Raisin Bran, actually bills their cereal company as "whole grain experts for over 100 years." And refined grain products are accepted as "whole grain." We've also been told by food manufacturers that products like Eggo Homestyle Waffles and Sunshine Krispy Saltines, and cereals like Kellogg's Frosted Flakes, Post Banana Nut Crunch, and Rice Krispies are good for us because they are made from "enriched" grains (i.e., refined flour). In the immortal words of Adelle Davis, "Such flour is 'enriched' just as you would be enriched by someone stealing 25 dollars from you and returning 99 cents."[15]

So-called enriched flour is typically made from genetically modified grain with its coarse outer husks, which are rich in vitamins, minerals, and fiber, removed. The resultant stripped flour is combined with synthetic vitamins and minerals that were created in a laboratory.

Real foods contain the perfect ratios of naturally occurring vitamins, minerals, trace minerals, enzymes, amino acids, and fatty acids that are necessary to maintain healthy metabolic processes. This perfect ratio is never duplicated by food manufacturers. Instead, synthetic vitamins are added to factory foods in arbitrary amounts.

And then most cereals are manufactured in a process called extrusion that subjects grains to extreme pressure at high temperatures, rendering the proteins in the grains into neurotoxins (brain cell damaging compounds), including in "health food" cereal.[16]

In the 1960s, the hippie, baby-boomer generation was into natural foods and nourishing grains like barley, brown rice, whole grain buckwheat, corn grits, couscous, millet, oats, polenta, quinoa, rye, whole grain semolina, whole grain wheat, wheat germ, and wild rice. These youthful idealists reintroduced Americans to cool recipes like granola. Factory-food manufacturers immediately sensed a market like a shark senses blood in water. They glommed onto the concept of "natural" and hit the ground running with it. Since the first hippie girl made a batch of granola, factory-food purveyors have been offering their factory-food junk to a public eager for natural foods.

For example, today we have refined grain products that are marketed as healthy and have natural-sounding names like Kellogg's Nutri-Grain Yogurt Bars, which imply that the product is nutritious. The Nutri-Grain website proclaims, "Eat Better all Day" and "More of the Whole Grains Your Body Needs."[17]

In addition to genetically modified enriched wheat flour, Nutri-Grain Yogurt Bars contain high-fructose corn syrup (highly addicting, man-made sugar), partially hydrogenated soybean oil (a trans fat), natural and artificial flavor (MSG), mono- and diglycerides (partially hydrogenated oils), and many other toxic ingredients.

The Cheerios campaign claims that whole grains (in Chocolate Cheerios, for example) are healthy for your heart. The website features "Video Love Stories" with attractive, sophisticated "real people" and exclamations like "Love your heart so you can do what you love!" and "Oats: Superfood for your heart."[18]

In addition to their claims of "enrichment," refined, sugary cereals are notorious for claiming to have fiber. In 1984, the Kellogg Company, with the endorsement of the National Cancer Institute, launched a campaign for All-Bran cereal, which supposedly reduced the risk for certain types of cancer. This campaign was the first time a factory-food company used a "health" claim to market a product. Since that time, food makers have had the assistance of the FDA and the American Heart Association (AHA), as well as other "health" agencies, in selling us on the merits of their refined-grain cereals. (The AHA is a national voluntary health organization whose mission is to reduce disability and death from cardiovascular diseases and stroke.) Claims like the one for Kellogg's All-Bran—"A simple way to help your body work a little better"—sound convincing because we know that we need fiber.

Normal elimination is once or twice a day. Primitive humans likely didn't have problems with constipation because their rough, fibrous foods stimulated peristalsis, which is the organized, rhythm-like movement that moves foodstuffs from the mouth through the digestive system to elimination. But since refined food products immediately turn into soft, smooth, slippery, sugary sludge upon entering your system, there's no stimulation to get peristalsis moving. Refined-grain products contain toxins, such as the above-mentioned nerve-damaging protein fragments created by the extrusion process, and chemical additives and ingredients. Compounding this problem is the fact that many people today have undiagnosed sensitivities to the grains in these products because we have simply eaten too many refined grains and they have become toxins to our bodies. So you've got a double whammy. Toxins in the factory food you eat sit in your colon, where they can be reabsorbed through your intestinal walls, a condition called leaky gut. Those toxins must go somewhere. Fat cells are storage repositories for, among other substances, toxins. Since many toxins are fat soluble, they permeate and are stored indefinitely in your fat cells, where they kill and damage cells.

If you pay attention to your body, it will tell you that eating sugar doesn't feel good. In his book *It's Not About the Bike: My Journey Back to Life*, Lance Armstrong said, "In one of the first pro triathlons I entered, I made the mistake of eating badly beforehand—I downed a couple of cinnamon rolls and two Cokes—and I paid for it by bonking, meaning I ran completely out of energy. I had an empty tank. I was first out of the water, and first off the bike. But in the middle of the run, I nearly collapsed. My mother was waiting at the finish, accustomed to seeing me come in among the leaders, and she couldn't understand what was taking me so long. Finally, she walked out on the course and found me, struggling along."[19]

Lance Armstrong, who is arguably one of the most impressive athletes to have ever lived, was brought down by cinnamon rolls and Cokes.

Sugar is sugar, whether you eat a candy bar or a bowl of cereal. But there is a worse addiction than sugar and refined grains. On January 31, 2004, a *New York Times* article proclaimed, "The Last Grain Falls at a Sugar

Factory." American Sugar Refining, an operation that had been in business since the 1880s in Brooklyn, New York, was closing. But the closing of that sugar plant was like closing down a marijuana farm (sugar) because of an increased demand for heroin (high-fructose corn syrup). In other words, we went from a bad habit to an out-and-out lethal addiction, as you'll read next.

CHAPTER THREE

Addicted to High-Fructose Corn Syrup

"IN MY OPINION, Shape Up! products can play an important role in the support of an individual's physiology, which is often disrupted during the nutritional changes associated with weight loss," TV psychologist Phil McGraw said on his now-defunct website shapeup.com. "Thirty years of work with obesity have taught me that psychological, lifestyle, and physiological balance are all essential to lasting success. Shape Up! can contribute to that balance."[20]

Dr. Phil entered into a licensing deal for Shape Up! products in 2003 with CSA Nutraceuticals[21] and made so much money that in the fall of 2004 he was able to purchase a Beverly Hills home for $7.5 million in cash.[22] He writes in his book *The Ultimate Weight Solution: The 7 Keys to Weight Loss Freedom*, "So if you truly want to manage your weight, you must program your environment in every possible way to avoid difficult foods, binge foods, and reminders to eat . . . toss this stuff out, feed it to the garbage disposal, take it to the Dumpster, or at least get it out of your sight. Do this now, do this right away, so that it is impossible to fail. Begin today to reprogram your environment and set yourself up for success."[23] Nevertheless, in the two years that his Shape Up! Chocolate Peanut Butter, Oatmeal Raisin, Fudge Brownie, and Chocolate Toffee Crunch bars were on the market his followers consumed high-fructose corn syrup (HFCS), a factory-made sugar that's not found in nature and that can provoke a binge-prone person to frenzied binging. The products were quietly removed from the market as the rumblings of discontent grew over the bogus claims.[24]

Likewise, since more people have become aware that HFCS creates health problems, there's been a significant decline in overall consumption. It appears that the closing of American Sugar Refining may have been premature, as people aren't actually eating less sugar but rather are now eating more refined white sugar instead of HFCS. In response, the HFCS industry is frantically trying to change public perception about HFCS and has even petitioned the FDA to be allowed to market it as "corn sugar," in hopes of duping people into believing that it's "natural," so OK to eat. They've launched "Sweet Surprise" propaganda, and if you Google HFCS you'll see the tag line, "HFCS is nutritionally the same as sugar." In one of their commercials, a lovesick guy fumbles around for words when asked by the attractive object of his affection why he's so afraid of HFCS. The message is, "You dummy, HFCS isn't bad for you. It's just sugar!"[25] Just in case anyone ever implies that you're dense because you don't want to consume HFCS, here are the facts.

High-fructose corn syrup (HFCS) registers to the taste buds exactly like cane or beet sugar in sweetness and taste. Eighty percent of HFCS is extracted from genetically modified corn and is made in 16 chemical plants in the corn belt (Iowa, Indiana, Missouri, Nebraska, South Dakota, Minnesota, Ohio, Wisconsin, most of Illinois, and parts of Kansas) using enzymatic fermentation, fungus, and chemicals. It's then pumped into tanker trucks and dispersed to manufacturing plants that make factory-food products. Since its introduction in the 1970s, the consumption of HFCS has risen more than 1,000 percent.

Like sugar, fructose has no nutritional value, and so it must rob your body of nutrients in order to be metabolized (so it's true that HFCS is nutritionally the same as sugar!). However, fructose is more rapidly metabolized than sugar and ends up stored in the liver, which is why researchers are recognizing that HFCS produces exactly the same results as the force-feeding of geese: fatty livers analogous to *paté de foie gras*, clinically referred to as "non-alcoholic liver disease." The introduction of HFCS in the 1970s parallels the 47 percent spike in type 2 diabetes and the 80 percent increase in obesity in that same time period. Lab rats given access to HFCS gained significantly more weight than those with access to table sugar, even when their overall caloric intake was the same. The HFCS-fattened rats grew fat tummies and had increased triglycerides—both of which are symptoms of the "metabolic syndrome" (insulin resistance/obesity/type 2 diabetes, hypertension, and abnormal blood lipids).[26] But we're not lab rats with measured caloric portions, and HFCS is hard to eat in moderation because it confuses natural satiety.

The reason so many people have fallen victim to HFCS is because it's so much cheaper than refined white sugar, making it possible for food manufacturers to glut the market with products made with HFCS. Because HFCS has permeated our food chain, making it convenient to consume, it has contributed to unnatural hunger like no other food additive on the market.

Overweight bingers are not the only HFCS consumer targets. Optimal sports and integrative medicine factory foods—the latest spin-off in the "natural" factory-foods market—are blatant exploitations of people's interest in the emerging field of integrative medicine and in products like Balance Bars, Carnation Instant Breakfast Bars, PR Ironman Triathalon Bars, Trader Joe's Performance Bars, All Sport Body Quencher, and Powerade, all part of an ironic quest for good health and optimal athletic performance.

The food industry implies that we are getting the benefits of herbs when we consume alternative medicine products that contain herbs along with HFCS, such as Snapple Atomic and SoBe Courage drink, which contain ginseng and guarana, and Balance Nutritional Bars Honey Peanut Plus, which contain ginseng. But drinking, say, Snapple Ginseng Tea, which contains HFCS along with small amounts of hibiscus and ginseng, is not the same thing as taking the Chinese medicinal herbs hibiscus and ginseng in appropriate doses to treat a particular illness or to promote optimal wellness.

The fact that Chinese medicinal herbs are mixed with HFCS is an insult to this incredible 4,000-year-old medicine. Chinese medicine is energy based and centered on the concept of wholeness and balance. When you go to a doctor of Chinese medicine, he or she is truly interested in all the reasons your energy is imbalanced. In fact, one of the reasons Chinese medicine is so popular with Americans is that, while studies show that Western M.D.s interrupt within eighteen seconds of asking the patient to explain his or her problem,[27] doctors of Chinese medicine will listen raptly to a nonstop, graphic monologue about a person's poo, pee, snot, farts, and so on. All symptoms are important. After diagnosing a problem, the doctor designs an individualized herbal formula created especially to rebalance that person's energy system.

This simple explanation of a complex and dynamic medicine should be enough to demonstrate why factory products containing herbs are not the same as using herbal medicine to treat a particular illness or to promote health and wellness, and furthermore only serve to put your energy system out of balance. Incidentally, doctors of Chinese medicine don't just hand out herbs. A treatment plan always includes changes to one's diet. For Americans this always includes counseling to stop eating factory food, especially food containing HFCS.

"Emotional eating" and "emotional triggers" are terms bandied about by weight-loss psychologists. Emotional eating refers to bingeing in an attempt to assuage one's emotions. Emotional triggers are upsetting events or experiences that "trigger" emotional eating.

I believe that saying we're overeating because of our "emotions" is totally missing the larger picture. Rather, emotional eating is the result of eating factory-food products instead of real, living food. Years of consuming sugar and not eating enough real, living food has resulted in modified brains. Adding to this problem, these modified brains are chemically imbalanced. Brains that are made up of unhealthy building materials and that are deprived of healthy, happy neurotransmitters understandably go haywire, demanding that people gobble everything in sight in an insane attempt to satisfy the brain's needs for sustenance.

As much as someone might hate themselves for having an addiction to sugar, it's not the result of a weak will. It's a normal physiological response to an imbalanced diet that's heavily weighted with sugar.

In the nineteenth century, dairy cows were fed the distillery slop left over after the refining of whiskey. Prohibitionist Robert Milham Hartley likened distillery cows to alcoholics. At first, he wrote, the cows resist eating the slop, but ultimately, "generally learn to love the nauseous slush as men acquire a relish for intoxicating drinks. Eventually, indeed, they become voraciously fond of this kind of food; and if they fail of their usual supply, they will paw and rave and indicate all the unhappiness of the drunkard who is deprived of his accustomed drams."[28]

Like the addicted dairy cows of old, modified, neurotransmitter-depleted brains are permanently on code red, so that people paw and rave and act out extreme anxiety if they don't have their sugar fix.

Emotional triggers are the result of "conditioned response." The classic study of conditioning was conducted by Russian physiologist and experimental psychologist Ivan Petrovich Pavlov, who discovered the conditioned response. Pavlov began by ringing a bell (conditioned stimulus) and presenting his dogs with food. At first, the dogs salivated at the sight and scent of the food (unconditioned response). But after a number of trials the dogs salivated as soon as the bell was rung (conditioned response), even without the presentation of food. It took a very short time for Pavlov to detect the conditioning of his dogs to the bell.

Reinforced conditioning for sugary factory-food products begins in infancy and continues through childhood and adulthood. For many, eating sugar is associated with alleviating (however fleetingly) any type of pain. Because many brains lack feel-good neurotransmitters, these individuals feel pain a lot. They crave, feel insecure, unconfident, tired, cranky, depressed, obsessive, and so on. And because some have conditioned their brains to associate ingesting sugar with a temporary high that makes them feel so much better, that Pavlovian bell is always ringing. Thus we are an unnaturally hungry society that's "conditioned" to knee-jerk react to any type of pain by ingesting horrendously unhealthy junk.

Binge eating should be addressed first by eating real, living food so that, cell by cell, a new, healthy brain can form. At the same time, real, living food will replenish happy brain neurotransmitters. Purging our culture of sugary factory-food products and making real, living food abundant, affordable, and convenient (including organically produced protein, fats, and cholesterol) would stop the cycle of so-called emotional eating for most people.

In the Introduction I said that by avoiding factory food and eating only real, living food we would stem the number of patients flocking to obesity clinics, ERs, and shrinks' offices. Taking these steps would also dramatically reduce our prison population. This is a bold statement for some to swallow, as many people don't believe that food can affect us that much or don't believe that food can do what antidepressants can do.

One out of every 142 Americans is in prison. One out of every 32 is either in prison or on parole from prison, according to a report from the Bureau of Justice Statistics.[29] Known juvenile offenders were involved in about 1,043 murders in the United States in 2006, which is 10 percent of all murders.[30]

Consider that the majority of Americans aren't gestated or brought up on real, living food that would provide them with the crucial nutrients their brains and bodies need to develop. Instead, many women consume soft drinks and eat chemicalized, HFCS-laden factory-food products during pregnancy, don't breastfeed at all or long enough, and then feed their children sugary, synthetic, dead factory products. Consequently, we're a nation that doesn't have the healthy brains we were genetically predisposed to have. On top of that, we don't give our unhealthy brains the nutrients necessary to produce happy neurotransmitters. Some neurotransmitter-imbalanced people self-medicate on sugary, chemicalized factory-food products. Others act out, cutting themselves, smoking cigarettes, abusing drugs, being sexually promiscuous, and otherwise directing their pain toward themselves. Some neurotransmitter-imbalanced people project their pain outward, and their rage lands them in prison, where their chemical imbalances are further cultivated on a diet of the cheapest, most noxious substances in the American food supply.

What if the entire population of the United States—including drug addicts and prisoners with the potential for rehabilitation—stopped eating all factory-food products and ate only real, living food that provides amino acids, essential fatty acids, cholesterol, and other nutrients necessary to create healthy brains and to make healthy, happy neurotransmitters? It would be a utopian society.

Unfortunately, the government and some of our most trusted health agencies have gotten behind the sugar industry, as you'll read next.

CHAPTER FOUR

The Government's Role in the Sugar Industry

CARDIOVASCULAR DISEASE IS THE leading cause of death for men and women in the United States. According to the Centers for Disease Control (CDC), nearly one quarter of all Americans have some form of cardiovascular disease, and each year about 912,500 Americans die of heart disease. (The CDC is a government agency whose mission is to prevent and control disease, injury, and disability.)

The American Heart Association publishes guidelines for preventing heart disease and strokes on their website. Recommendations include eating a "heart-healthy," low fat, low cholesterol diet to reduce current risk and to prevent major risk factors from developing. To assist us in eating such a diet, the AHA sells their "American Heart Association Tested and Approved" heart-check mark to factory-food makers. For a product to qualify to bear the AHA heart-check mark, it has to meet the FDA criteria for a "healthy" food: It must be low fat, low cholesterol, low trans fat, and low sodium, and contain a minuscule amount of the daily value of one of six nutrients: vitamin A, vitamin C, iron, calcium, protein, or dietary fiber.[31]

When I contacted the AHA, I was informed that the heart-check mark was created "as a first-step in building a heart-healthy lifestyle. The mark continues to be an easy and reliable tool in selecting heart-healthy foods. Most importantly, it comes from the most respected source for health and nutrition." According to the AHA, 92 percent of shoppers say the heart-check mark influences their decision to purchase a food. Of third-party programs, the AHA heart-check mark is the most respected by consumers. Sixty-eight percent of consumers believe that the heart-check mark is backed by very strong or somewhat strong research. (The same percentage of Americans are overweight or obese.) If a consumer perceives that the nutrition symbol is backed by research, he/she is more likely to purchase the product. Fees to obtain the heart-check mark are $7,500 per product and $4,500 for annual renewals.[32] Factory-food makers get a discount if they enroll more than twenty-five products.[33] According to the AHA, the heartcheck mark is a powerful marketing tool that fulfills shoppers' needs—"with it on your packaging and in your promotions, the heart-check mark can help move your product."[34]

The AHA website offers a list of hundreds of factory-food products bearing the trusted AHA heart-check mark, such as Smart Beat Smart Squeeze Nonfat Margarine Spread, General Mills Cheerios, Cocoa Puffs, Cookie Crisp, Corn Chex, Count Chocula, Healthy Choice Low Fat Ice Creams, Chocolate Moose Milk Chocolate Drinks, Malt-O-Meal Frosted Mini Spooners, Honey Graham Squares, Honey Nut Toasty O's, Kellogg's Frosted Mini-Wheats Big Bite, Kellogg's NutriGrain Cereal Bars, and Pop-Secret 94% Fat Free Butter Microwave Premium Popcorn.[35] So if you're among shoppers who say the heart-check mark influences your decision to purchase a product, you trustingly eat up all that refined white flour, chemical flavoring, factory milk, aspartame, MSG, industrially processed soy, hydrogenated fat, colored dye, and, most of all, refined white sugar and high-fructose corn syrup.

Eating sugar results in the secretion of insulin. Chronic high insulin levels are implicated in every single degenerative disease, including type 2 diabetes, cancer, and heart disease.

On January 12, 2005, the Health and Human Services Department (HHS) issued the federal nutritional guidelines, which are issued every five years. (The HHS is a government agency founded to protect the health of Americans.) The guidelines affect what goes into school lunch programs, government dietary education such as the U.S. Department of Agriculture

(USDA) food guide pyramid, factory-food labeling, and the Supplemental Nutrition Assistance Program (SNAP), which doles out food stamps. (The USDA is a government agency founded to help farmers and ranchers and to keep our animal food products safe.)

The panel that composed the guidelines reviewed scientific evidence, submitted by an advisory committee, that linked sugar to obesity and demonstrated that eating sugar reduces the consumption of nutritious food. The panel chose not to include the specific guideline "Reduce added sugars" watering it down to "Choose carbohydrates wisely for good health." [36] This tepid admonishment fell on deaf ears, and we all know what happened to public health in the ensuing five years.

Given that the main concern of the writers of these guidelines appears to be more about navigating the political waters of factory-food lobbyists (including factory ranchers), the 2010 guidelines were such a yawn that they never even made the press. Basically what they reiterated was that Americans were fat, sick, and depressed and needed to do something about it. They proffered up their old food pyramid—the one with all the carbs as the largest daily food requirement. And since "healthy" carbs are products like heart-check-bearing boxes of Chocolate Cheerios, we will undoubtedly not see any changes in public health as a result of the 2010 guidelines. [37]

The International Obesity Task Force estimates that one billion people worldwide are overweight or obese, including 22 million overweight or obese children under the age of five. Way back in 2003 the World Health Organization recognized this alarming worldwide epidemic of obesity and the accompanying degenerative diseases of aging as being attributable to "malnutrition of excess." A group of internationally respected scientists attempted to address this problem by drafting a global strategy on diet, physical activity, and health entitled "The Expert Consultation on Diet, Nutrition and the Prevention of Chronic Diseases." [38]

The simple strategy focused on cutting down on sugar consumption and factory food, and replacing those items with real food. They also mentioned limiting advertising directed toward children. When the Sugar Association read these suggestions they threatened to use "every avenue available to expose the dubious nature" of the WHO report and pressured members of Congress to get the United States to threaten to withdraw $406 million in contributions to WHO.

Senators Larry Craig (R-ID) and John Breaux (D-LA), cochairmen of the Senate Sweetener Caucus, asked (Bush appointee) Health and Human Services secretary Tommy Thompson to insist that the WHO "cease further promotion" of the report. Trade associations for the sugar, corn-refining, and snack food industries questioned the report's legitimacy and asked Mr. Thompson to do something about it.[39]

Rather than support WHO's simple strategy, which might have actually helped a few people, including children, Thompson had his department issue a line-by-line, twenty-eight-page critique accusing the organization of shoddy sugar research. He demanded that the WHO "cease further promotion" of their report. In short, Thompson didn't allow the WHO to release the report to the mainstream media so that regular people could read that eating too much sugar is making us fat and sick.

Not long after the WHO report, the CDC issued a report in the *Journal of the American Medical Association* that obesity may soon overtake tobacco as the leading cause of preventable death in the United States. In response, at a March 12, 2004, news conference, Thompson had the gall to say, "Americans are literally eating themselves to death."[40] He proceeded to write to Dear Abby: "I know you care passionately about individuals taking steps each day to improve the quality of their lives. Please help me spread the word about improving the health of millions of Americans . . . Please encourage your readers to see for themselves how small steps can lead to big health benefits . . . eating only half portions of dessert can add up to giant steps on the path to a healthier life . . ."[41]

This from a man who sided against the American people so that the sugar industry would not lose profits. (Since the CDC warning, obesity has overtaken tobacco as the leading cause of preventable death in Australia.)[42]

The Food and Agriculture Act of 1977 stated, "Congress firmly believes that the maintenance of the family farm system is essential to the social well-being of the Nation and the competitive production of adequate supplies of food and fiber. Congress further believes that any significant expansion of non-family owned, large scale corporate enterprises will be detrimental to the national welfare." Nonetheless, the government paid out $75,835,175,775 in subsidies to the corn industry between 1995 and 2009.[43]

Eating sugar is detrimental to our health and supports corporations that harm humans, animals, and the planet, but should we completely give up sugar? As I said, my grandma, Stella, taught me a lot about living and dying. She was a health advocate, but she wasn't a zealot. Her motto was, "Do your best and don't worry about the rest." She would never want to rob her family of life's pleasures. Eating healthfully means eating real, living food, not living like a monk. A delicious dessert, a glass of wine, or a beer lend pleasure to life, and it's only making matters worse that we're made to feel guilty about indulging. It is better to eat a balanced diet of real, living food, and then indulge in moderation on occasion. If you're going to have dessert, have a real dessert. Sugar from time to time is not going to kill you, but factory dessert products will.

Brown sugar and turbinado are to white sugar what wheat bread is to white bread. But if you decide you want to bake your own desserts, there are a few healthier alternatives to refined white and brown sugar. Old-fashioned sugars like maple sugar and molasses contain minerals and are delicious in traditional recipes such as gingerbread and cookies. Unrefined honey contains healthy enzymes (see page 147 for more on enzymes) and antioxidants (which neutralize free radicals) and is a healthy addition to a balanced diet—and it can be purchased from family-owned suppliers. Sucanat and Rapadura are dehydrated cane sugar juice; they also contain minerals and are thus superior to refined white sugar. *Stevia rebaudiana*, a South American herb, is a new popular sugar substitute that has the same science-fictiony aftertaste as aspartame but doesn't kill brain cells. Stevia is 200 times sweeter than sugar but doesn't trigger an insulin response or have any calories or carbs. (There are no long-term studies on stevia, so moderation is suggested.)

Dark chocolate is loaded with flavonoids, which are plant compounds that keep cholesterol from clumping in your blood vessels and inhibit other responses that lead to heart attack. Dark chocolate containing 70 percent cocoa contains more flavonoids than any other flavanoid-containing food (green tea, black tea, red wine, or blueberries).

Alcohol is derived from grain and fruit, which are carbs. Alcohol is toxic to cells and increases insulin levels, so drinking excessive amounts of alcohol accelerates aging. But unless you're a recovering alcoholic or otherwise have a problem with alcohol there's no reason not to enjoy an occasional beer or glass of wine.

Commercial beers are made with ingredients from genetically modified organisms and city water, and are pasteurized (heated to kill microorganisms), which also kills life-giving enzymes. They have a shelf life of four months. Unpasteurized "live" beer actually provides healthy enzymes (although it's likely also to be made with city water). Even so, it's surprisingly nutritious food, as long as you don't drink a keg of it. Look for microbreweries that serve fresh, live (raw) beer on tap. You can take it home, and it will last three days in the fridge.

Sooner or later we'll have more organic wine choices than we currently do. Non-organic wines, especially California wines, which are grown with boron-containing fertilizer, are contaminated with fluoride. However, red wine does contain the highest amount of the polyphenol (a plant compound) resveratrol, which is concentrated in the grape skins and made available by the alcohol in wine. Resveratrol has been found both to be a cancer-preventative agent and to improve cardiovascular health. (Resveratrol is perishable when exposed to light and air, and so dark, corked bottles help preserve it.)[44]

Of course, you would have to drink twenty bottles a night to get the same antiaging results that lab monkeys got with resveratrol. In my book

Healthy, Sexy, Happy I go into greater detail about the benefits of added supplementation, including resveratrol. But the point I'm making here about food isn't to eat 300 oranges to get your vitamin C or a bale of spinach to get your vitamin A. The point is to eat a balanced diet of real, living food, as nature has packaged nutrients together and these packages all work in harmony. For instance, a steak and a baked potato lathered in butter, along with a green salad and a glass of red wine, are satisfying; moreover, the nutrients in this meal work synergistically.

Enjoying small amounts of sugar in the form of desserts, wine, and live beer in an otherwise balanced diet of real food is not going to kill anyone, but eating HFCS and white sugar on a regular basis will. Unfortunately, HFCS and white sugar aren't the only poisonous additives in our food supply. Monosodium glutamate (MSG) has virtually permeated our food chain, and millions of Americans are unaware that they are eating this brain-damaging flavor enhancer every day.

PART THREE

Science-Fiction Food Additives

CHAPTER FIVE

MSG Keeps Us Coming Back for More

WHO HASN'T BITTERLY COMPLAINED about the obnoxiousness of TV ads? Even though we hate commercials—and it's safe to say that no one really believes advertisers have our best interests in mind—we continue to consume their products. That's because factory food is addicting.

Factory foods, which are extolled as tasting good and being satisfying, affordable, and convenient, are in nearly every kitchen pantry, refrigerator, freezer, desk drawer, locker, purse, briefcase, backpack, and glove compartment in America. What does it mean to be satiated? To many it means tasting a yummy flavor and experiencing instant gratification. But factory-food is designed to make you want to eat more. And wanting to eat more is the polar opposite of being satisfied. How does the factory-food industry get you to want to eat more? The primary addicting ingredient is sugar, but the deal clincher is the flavor enhancer monosodium glutamate (MSG).

MSG, made from the seaweed *kombu* (sea tangle), has been used for thousands of years by Japanese cooks to enhance the taste of foods. After World War II, military officials heard through the grapevine that American GIs were raving that Japanese military rations were truly edible, even delicious. The military, interested in learning how to improve the palatability of military K-rations, met in 1948 with factory-food executives to discuss the flavor enhancer MSG. At this meeting, they learned that this additive enhances any flavor it's added to. If you want a cheeseburger to be more beefy and cheesier, add MSG. If you want ice cream to be creamier, add MSG. If you want chicken broth to be richer, add MSG. And so the light bulbs went on. Food execs understood that they could boil spaghetti noodles to mush, add some crummy sauce made from nutrient-deficient, tasteless tomatoes, and let their concoctions languish for months in a tin can if they added some handy-dandy MSG to spark up the flavor. Since that watershed meeting, the food industry has continually increased the quantity of MSG added to factory fare so that today it permeates our food chain.

But right after military and food bigwigs met in 1948, scientists began to note freaky experiments that should have halted the addition of MSG to our food supply. In one of the original experiments, conducted by a Japanese scientist in 1950, MSG was repeatedly injected into a dog's brain. Each time, the dog fell down convulsing uncontrollably. The conclusion: The amino acid glutamate caused the dog's neural cells to become overexcited, firing out of control.

John W. Olney, M.D., is a neuroscientist and researcher at the Washington University School of Medicine, where he is researching the potential role of excitotoxicity in chronic neuropsychiatric disorders such as schizophrenia and Alzheimer's disease.[45] Thirty-five years ago, Olney conducted experiments on glutamate and aspartate (aspartame) and dubbed these amino acids "excitatory amino acids" or "excitotoxins" because they excited neural (brain) cells to death.

After the food industry glommed onto MSG as the panacea for their bland fare back in 1948, they started adding it to baby food. More and more studies appeared showing the alarming health hazards of MSG and aspartame, Olney took notice. His own studies on MSG repeatedly confirmed that MSG caused severe damage to the neurons of the retina of the eye as well as massive destruction of neurons in the brain, including the hypothalamus, which regulates most endocrine glands and numerous systems that determine growth, the onset of puberty, and our circadian rhythms.

"I testified [before Congress] on many occasions," Dr. Olney emailed me. "Thirty-five years ago when [food companies] were dumping large amounts of MSG into baby foods that were ingested by babies throughout the world. Babies are vastly more sensitive to the neurotoxic effects of MSG than are adults, so it was a matter of urgency to get them to stop adding MSG to baby foods."[46] Dr. Olney's testimony before Congress resulted in MSG being removed from baby foods in 1969. Still, nothing was done to remove MSG from the rest of our food supply, so pregnant women have continued ingesting it—despite Dr. Olney's repeated experiments that demonstrated brain damage in the offspring of pregnant monkeys who were fed MSG.

Russell Blaylock, M.D., a board-certified neurosurgeon, made use of more than 500 scientific references to illustrate how MSG and aspartame cause serious neurological damage in his book *Excitotoxins: The Taste that Kills*. I asked Dr. Blaylock, "What made you pursue the subject of excito-toxins, which is outside the realm of conventional medicine?"

Dr. Blaylock replied, "Actually excitotoxins are within the realm of conventional medicine. Excitotoxins are considered the central mecha-nism for most neurological diseases, and are covered in all texts of neuro-science. It has just taken physicians so long to catch up, and most still have never heard of excitotoxins. Physicians are not known to keep up with new discoveries outside their field of expertise."[47]

I emailed Dr. Blaylock, "But if neuroscientists understand the damag-ing effects of MSG why did MSG receive FDA approval in 1959?"

Dr. Blaylock explained, "One of the reasons it is so difficult to con-vince skeptics and the FDA about the toxic effects of MSG and other food-borne excitotoxins is that the effects can be subtle and major damage may take years or even decades to manifest. Long periods of accumulative dam-age by excitotoxins are generally necessary to produce observable clinical effects on behavior, memory, and learning. We now know that in the case of the infant brain some of the injuries can be immediate, and some may not appear until later developmental milestones are scheduled to appear."[48]

As far as the general public is concerned, there are two major miscon-ceptions about MSG. First, when most people think of MSG, they think of fragile individuals who suffer from MSG sensitivity, known as "Chinese restaurant syndrome." But MSG affects everyone to a lesser or greater degree, and as Dr. Blaylock said, the effects of MSG may not be apparent for decades.

Equally important is that people believe they have a choice whether or not to ingest MSG. But this is a delusion brought to us by the FDA, which bent to the Glutamate Association, making it possible for factory-food manufacturers to add monosodium glutamate to products in concentrations less than 100 percent without having to notify the consumer on the label. (The Glutamate Association was formed to provide communication among its members, industry, and the government about the "use and safety" of glutamates.) This means that you could be regularly ingesting a product that contains an ingredient that is 99 percent MSG. To give you an example of how you unwittingly and regularly ingest MSG, just think back to your last Chinese restaurant experience. Many people understand that MSG isn't healthy—though they could not tell you why exactly—and they know enough to ask the waiter in Chinese restaurants if there is MSG in the food. Although the waiter will tell you no, they do not add MSG to the food, that isn't necessarily true. If the restaurant used, say, ready-made chicken broth, you are likely going to get MSG in your food as MSG is added to most chicken broths today. At home, if you make tuna salad with Bumble Bee Tuna, you may be ingesting MSG as this product contains vegetable broth, which often contains MSG. If you ate the celebrity doctor's nutritional weight-loss bars I talked about in chapter 3, you ingested glutamate, as they contained soy protein isolate, which is an ingredient that contains naturally occurring glutamate.

According to Blaylock, additives are often euphemisms for MSG. Additives that always contain MSG are hydrolyzed vegetable protein, hydrolyzed protein, hydrolyzed plant protein, plant protein extract, sodium caseinate, calcium caseinate, yeast extract, textured protein, autolyzed yeast, and hydrolyzed oat flour. Additives that frequently contain MSG are malt extract, malt flavoring, bouillon, broth, stock, flavoring, natural flavoring, natural beef or chicken flavoring, seasoning, and spices. Additives that may contain MSG or that can be high in naturally occurring glutamate are carrageenan, enzymes, soy protein concentrate, soy protein isolate, and whey protein concentrate.[49]

To understand how MSG and aspartame affect your brain, you must first understand the basics of brain chemistry. As we saw in our discussion of brain chemistry balance in chapter 2, your body's chemical communication system controls bodily functions. It has been said that a butterfly flapping its wings in Shanghai affects weather patterns in Los Angeles. That's what neurological activity is like, as one neuron firing impacts countless other neurons in the exquisitely complex, interconnected circuitry of your nervous system.

However, once a synapse has fired and accomplished its task, your brain has mechanisms to deactivate neurotransmitters to prevent the synapse from firing over and over uncontrollably and burning itself out.

Amino acids are the chemical building blocks the human body uses to make protein. When they're slightly altered by metabolic processes, they are classified into different categories or groups. One such group is the acidic neurotransmitters, to which glutamate and aspartate belong. Your brain naturally contains low concentrations of both. In fact, glutamate is the most common neurotransmitter in your brain. Glutamate and aspartate are excitatory neurotransmitters that stimulate your brain. Other neurotransmitters act as inhibitors. A combination of excitatory and inhibitory neurotransmitters results in balanced brain chemistry.

All cells and neurons in the human body are guarded in a lock and key fashion. This lock and key system enables the trillions of actions within the human metabolism to operate in an orderly fashion. In other words, everything goes where it is supposed to go. Hormones go where they are supposed to go, sugar goes where it is supposed to go, neurotransmitters go where they are supposed to go, and so on. In your brain, neurotransmitters are the keys that activate receptors (the locks), which allows entry into the neurons so that the neurotransmitters can fire synapses.

Excess glutamate and aspartame in your brain will facilitate a cascade of chemical reactions that result in the rapid and uncontrollable firing of synapses—culminating in brain cell death. Your brain has regulation systems to rid itself of the excess, but this system requires high levels of energy. Lack of energy is the outcome of dieting, extreme exercise, and hypoglycemia (which occurs when blood sugar levels dip too fast and too low because of eating too much sugar or as a result of going hungry).

Let's say you eat a diet heavily weighted in factory food containing MSG. You drink diet drinks as well as coffee and iced tea laced with NutraSweet. You eat very few fruits or vegetables (antioxidants). You either don't take supplements or you take an inferior drugstore, supermarket, or big box brand. Since blood levels of glutamate remain high for three hours after ingestion, if you eat three meals plus snacks containing aspartame and MSG, you will have high glutamate blood levels all day long, resulting in the above-mentioned cascade of chemical reactions that end in neural death.

"Once this cascade of destruction is triggered . . . the whole process proceeds with the explosiveness of a nuclear chain reaction," Dr. Blaylock writes.[50] Specifically, in addition to neurons firing to death, free radicals also reproduce like crazy, bouncing around and further damaging brain cells and destroying neural connections.

Free radicals have been written about extensively in recent years, but let's review. Molecules consist of a positively charged nucleus and negatively charged electrons that orbit the nucleus in pairs. Free radicals are molecules with a missing electron. When an electron is lost, the molecule becomes extremely reactive and is referred to as a "free radical" because it frantically seeks electrons to pair up with its unpaired electrons. Free radicals ravage the molecules in your body, stealing electrons from complete molecules. This process, called oxidation, is essentially a domino effect of molecules becoming free radicals and further rampaging to obtain paired electrons, causing more free radicals. Free radicals kill cells, damage DNA, cause chromosomal damage, create arterial plaque, accelerate aging, and are the key factor in almost every degenerative disease, including brain diseases such as Parkinson's and Alzheimer's.

Free radicals are produced in your body through normal, healthy metabolic processes and are regularly eliminated by antioxidants (also known as free radical scavengers). Antioxidant vitamins A, C, D, E, and K are allowed through your blood-brain barrier and can be obtained by eating food or by taking quality supplements.

Your brain is a chemical laboratory where all actions are tightly scripted. Because your brain's life or death depends on tight controls, your body has a blood-brain barrier that allows desirable substances in and bars toxic substances from entering. But, said Dr. Blaylock, "The blood-brain barrier is not fail-safe. It can be weakened by numerous factors including excessive physical stress, elevated core body temperatures, infection, trauma, head injuries, and certain drugs and metals, as well as the conditions of aging, such as hardening of the arteries, diabetes, hypertension, poor blood oxygenation, and tumors. When the blood-brain barrier is weakened it can be breached."[51]

According to Blaylock, because of the many factors that weaken the blood-brain barrier, people have, at one time or another, a porous blood-brain barrier. When your blood-brain barrier is porous and you ingest MSG or aspartame, they pass readily through to brain. Also, said Blaylock, even if your blood-brain barrier is not weakened, if there is chronic prolonged exposure to a flooding of MSG or aspartame, excitotoxins will ultimately seep past the blood-brain barrier to the brain. If excitotoxins are in even a minute overconcentration in the brain, they cause brain cells to become excited to death.

Consider the fact that if a pregnant woman ingests MSG or aspartate her blood levels can reach high enough concentrations to cross the placenta barrier—or the placenta barrier can be breached if there is a defect. Dr. Blaylock said, "MSG does most of its damage during the last trimester of pregnancy and the first two years after birth in humans. This is when the infant brain is undergoing its normal fluctuations in concentration.

An excess of glutamate during critical neuronal migrations can cause significant developmental dysfunction—many of which are delayed until later in life." Exposure in the womb and in the first few years of life may affect brain development, resulting in autism, learning disorders, hyperactive behavior, or even schizophrenia. Moreover, as Dr. Blaylock said, these effects may not be evident until puberty or early adulthood.

I asked Dr. Blaylock if MSG has been used for thousands of years in Japan, why they are not having the same neurological problems as Americans? Dr. Blaylock explained: "For several reasons. One, the Japanese consume a diluted form of MSG and less volume. Unlike Americans, they also eat a diet that is known to reduce excitotoxic injury—such as a diet high in flavonoids [compounds with therapeutic effects found in fruits and vegetables], foods that are high in omega-3 fats, which directly block excitotoxicity, as well as magnesium, which blocks the glutamate receptor, among other factors. Yet they are suffering from excitotoxic disorders, including Alzheimer's dementia, in increasing numbers."[52]

It's important to note that excitotoxins have a compounding effect on your brain. A fast-food meal adulterated with MSG from McDonald's, Wendy's, Taco Bell, or the like that's washed down with a Diet Coke containing aspartame will do compounded damage to your brain. For many it's hard to imagine eating a hamburger without drinking a diet soda.

CHAPTER SIX

Aspartame Poisoning: Urban Legend or Fact?

FUZZY THINKING, MEMORY LOSS, ringing in the ears, numbness and tingling of the extremities, blindness, multiple sclerosis, brain tumors, and, perhaps the most alarming, grand mal seizures suffered by commercial airline pilots—these and other serious neurological disorders were formerly nothing more than aspartame urban legend. Public attitudes have changed a lot in the past several years, and many people have an inkling that there is something amiss with aspartame. Still, even many of those who claim that aspartame is unhealthy couldn't really tell you why. I was one of those people until I started researching this book. When I did probe into the aspartame world, it was a short-click journey to innumerable, rather nutty Internet pages on aspartame that took me back to the good old days of trying to decipher the fine print on a bottle of Dr. Bronner's soap. Since then those sites have gone away, and numerous sites have sprung up to disclose the dangers of aspartame in a more reasoned manner.

Not everyone is buying in. For example, if you Google "aspartame controversy," Wikipedia will tell you, "The artificial sweetener aspartame has been the subject of several controversies and hoaxes since its initial approval by the U.S. Food and Drug Administration (FDA) in 1974. Critics allege that conflicts of interest marred the FDA's approval of aspartame, question the quality of the initial research supporting its safety, and postulate that numerous health risks may be associated with aspartame. The validity of these claims has been examined and dismissed. In 1987, the U.S. Government Accountability Office concluded that the food additive approval process had been followed properly for aspartame. Aspartame has been found to be safe for human consumption by more than ninety countries worldwide, with FDA officials describing aspartame as 'one of the most thoroughly tested and studied food additives the agency has ever approved' and its safety as 'clear cut'. The weight of existing scientific evidence indicates that aspartame is safe at current levels of consumption as a non-nutritive sweetener."[53]

Mainstream publishers aren't very interested in the subject of so-called aspartame poisoning either. The books that have been published on aspartame by small presses don't reach the masses, and the alleged problems with aspartame don't appear newsworthy to the media. In fact, doctors advocate the use of aspartame and use it themselves—for example, that box of free samples of sugar-free Metamucil in your doctor's office. Many bestselling diet books urge the use of aspartame, including the mega bestseller *The South Beach Diet: The Delicious, DoctorDesigned, Foolproof Plan for Fast and Healthy Weight Loss*, by Arthur Agatston, M.D. What's more, aspartame has the endorsement of the FDA, the CDC, the American Diabetes Association (ADA), the American Dietetic Association (ADA) and the majority of the medical establishment. (The two associations are, respectively, the nation's leading nonprofit health organization that provides diabetes research, information, and advocacy, and the nation's largest organization of food and nutritional professionals).

Yet despite these endorsements and the assertions by the aspartame industry and the FDA that we have nothing to worry about, reputable medical doctors and research scientists, hundreds of peer-reviewed research papers, mountains of empirical (anecdotal) evidence, and clinical experience tell a different story.

When aspartame first came on the scene, I asked a doctor friend of mine what he thought of it. He replied," It's just a couple of amino acids, so it's probably OK." This was partly true, but as it turns out, not that simple.

Dr. Blaylock told me, "Aspartame is a compound made from three components: phenylalanine (an amino acid), aspartic acid (an excitotoxic amino acid), and joined chemically by methanol, a toxic alcohol. When consumed, aspartame is metabolically broken down into its three component parts—all three of which are toxic to the nervous system as well as to all cells. In addition, further metabolism occurs, producing dozens of other potentially toxic compounds and even carcinogenic compounds.

"Three new studies have shown that the methanol component is metabolically converted into formaldehyde and formic acid, both powerful toxins, even in very small doses. Formic acid is the toxin that causes the intensely painful bite of the fire ant and blindness when methanol is ingested in sufficient quantities. [Think about alcoholics who ingest methanol to get drunk.] Formaldehyde is known to be a powerful cancer-causing agent, even in very small doses. In one of these studies it was shown that aspartame's formaldehyde accumulates near the DNA of cells, severely damaging this critical cell component. This can lead to neurodegenerative diseases and cancer.

"Because formaldehyde is tightly bound to the DNA and accumulates, drinking even one aspartame-sweetened drink a day can eventually lead to one of these diseases—especially in a cancer-prone person. Another new study found that aspartame dramatically increased leukemias and lymphomas in experimental animals in doses equal to that seen with human consumption of aspartame products. The highest intake of aspartame is in children and pregnant women, which would greatly increase the risk of these two highly malignant diseases in the children.

"There is also evidence that one of the other breakdown products, called diketopiperazine, is also carcinogenic and may account for the 4,700 percent increase in brain tumors seen in the original safety studies of aspartame. Combined with the formaldehyde, this would also explain the dramatic increase in breast, pancreatic, prostate, thyroid, liver, lung, uterine, and ovarian tumors seen in aspartame-exposed test animals."[54]

Considering that these factors are in addition to the excitotoxin effects outlined in the previous chapter, one would think that they would be enough to stop people from ingesting aspartame—or feeding it to children. But again, we have FDA approval, which still packs tremendous clout for many Americans.

The saga of aspartame began in December 1965, when a chemist at G. D. Searle discovered a substance that is two hundred times sweeter than sugar with no calories. Naturally, Searle was eager to get aspartame approved by the FDA. The goal was to get aspartame classified as an inert substance. The reason is that any compound that affects physiological systems is classified as a drug by the FDA, which means that it's subject to more demanding regulatory procedures than a food additive. But if a compound is shown to be inert, it's exempted from the ongoing safety monitoring imposed on drugs (such as it is). Factory-food manufacturers are not obligated to monitor adverse reactions associated with the additive, submit reports of adverse reactions to the FDA, or required to carry out additional research to confirm the additive's safety.

In November 1970 the popular artificial sweetener cyclamate was linked to cancer and yanked from the market. Saccharin was subsequently put under scrutiny, throwing the market wide open for the introduction of aspartame.

From that time on, numerous experts, including neuroscientist John Olney, informed the FDA of studies demonstrating the deleterious effects of ingesting aspartame. The drama that ensued over the next two decades involved independent researchers such as Olney, one dogged consumer interest attorney, and Searle's own researchers, as well as their legal and PR firms, an FDA task force, various FDA commissioners, Democratic and Republican senators, U.S. attorneys, grand juries, the then-president of Searle, Donald Rumsfeld, and the newly inaugurated POTUS Ronald Reagan in an incredibly convoluted story involving sloppy science of epic proportions, intrigue, self-interest, ambition, greed, and shenanigans, all too unwieldy for this book to cover in detail. The following is just a brief rundown.

There were efforts made by those concerned to halt FDA approval of aspartame, but it was granted FDA approval for limited use on July 26, 1974. It was approved specifically as a free-flowing sugar substitute, as tablets for sweetening hot beverages, and for use in cereal, gum, and dry bases (coating on products such as pills). And in 1983, the incredibly lucrative aspartame was FDA-approved for use in carbonated beverages and carbonated-beverage syrup bases. In 1985, Searle sold out to the chemical company Monsanto, which has a long and checkered history in the field of deadly chemicals. (Among its many affiliations was Monsanto's 1967 joint venture with I. G. Farbenfabriken, the manufacturer of a lethal nerve gas used in Hitler's Final Solution.)[55] After acquiring aspartame, Monsanto created the nutritious-sounding subsidiary the NutraSweet Company.

On June 27, 1996, the FDA removed all restrictions and authorized aspartame use in all products—even heated and baked goods, although studies had demonstrated that aspartame breaks down into free methanol in temperatures above 86 degrees Fahrenheit (like, say, when you cook no-cal Jell-O Pudding or leave a case of Diet Dr Pepper in your car).

Since the aspartame patent expired in the early 1990s, this fake sugar is now sold under the brand names Equal, Spoonful, and Equal-Measure, as well as generically, but the brand is essentially owned by NutraSweet. As with MSG, even those who want to avoid aspartame may be ingesting it in products like toothpaste, laxatives, wine coolers, vitamins, and prescription drugs.

By 1994, the Department of Health and Human Services had documented ninety-two adverse medical symptoms attributed to aspartame use, including anxiety attacks, arthritis, asthma, brain cancer, chronic fatigue, depression, insomnia, memory loss, migraines, numbness of extremities, seizures, tachycardia, tinnitus, vertigo, vision loss, and weight gain.[56]

In addition, aspartame use is thought to worsen or mimic the symptoms of Alzheimer's disease, arthritis, attention deficit disorder, chronic fatigue syndrome, depression, diabetes, epilepsy, fibromyalgia, lupus, Lyme disease, lymphoma, multiple chemical sensitivities, multiple sclerosis, panic disorders, and Parkinson's disease.[57]

Since the introduction of aspartame in the mid-1970s, the incidence of brain tumors has risen exponentially.[58] Evidence indicates that one particular type of brain tumor, primary lymphoma of the brain, may be associated with aspartame use. According to Dr. Blaylock, "It is a particularly nasty tumor with a high mortality rate."[59]

The medical establishment and the aspartame industry argue that the precipitous rise in the incidence of brain tumors does not correspond to the introduction and rise in use of aspartame, but rather it is due to better diagnostic techniques. Not true, Dr. Blaylock told me." The original studies by the G. D. Searle Company found a 47 percent increase in brain tumors in rats exposed to the highest dose of aspartame. My personal investigation, using the SEER brain tumor registry, found an increase in primary brain tumors, unexplained by better diagnosis or an aging population. Dr. John Olney, using the SEER tumor registry, also found an increase in malignant brain tumors in those consuming aspartame-containing diet products."[60] (The National Cancer Institute's Surveillance Epidemiology and End Results [SEER] program is considered the state-of-the-art brain tumor data base.)

Regarding the rise in brain tumors, Dr. Blaylock said, "As a neurosurgeon I see the devastating effects a brain tumor has, not only on its victim, but on the victim's family as well. To think that there is even a reasonable doubt that aspartame can induce brain tumors in the American population is frightening. And to think that the FDA has lulled them into a false sense of security is a monumental crime."[61]

Since the mid-1980s I have personally known several people who have been diagnosed with brain tumors. I wonder how many people you have known who have met the same fate?

So why do we use aspartame? Simply put, we want to be thin. Turn the TV on anytime, night or day, and you'll see beautiful, thin women with glossy lips drinking diet sodas. But really how many beautiful girls really do you see drinking diet sodas? None of the beautiful, thin women I know would so much as use diet sodas to remove the lime deposits on their shower doors. That's because diet sodas do not make you thin or beautiful.

Way back in 1983 Richard Wurtman, an MIT neuroscientist, researched the weight-loss effects of aspartame and concluded that using aspartame may actually result in cravings for foods high in calories and carbohydrates.[62] The reason is that although aspartame is calorie free, it triggers the release of insulin, which stows away sugar. If food is not forthcoming, hypoglycemia (low blood sugar attacks) and severe hunger follow.[63]

In 1986, after tracking 80,000 women for six years, the American Cancer Society documented that the women who used artificial sweeteners gained more weight than those who avoided them.[64]

One of the biggest quandaries in the obesity issue today is that many people are obese on normal amounts of food. Aspartate has been established as an excitotoxin that causes neurons to fire out of control until death. Numerous studies on excitotoxins in mice (closest to humans in glutamate and aspartate sensitivity) have concluded that the hypothalamic damage caused by MSG and aspartate resulted in the test subjects and their offspring being shorter than normal in stature and obese on normal amounts of food.[65]

Now that's depressing. But if packing on more pounds doesn't get you down, the use of aspartame just might. Excessive levels of the amino acid phenylalanine in your brain cause serotonin to dip. And if you recall from our discussion of neurotransmitters, serotonin is the one that gets you high on life. Without enough serotonin in your brain, it's depression *plus* carb craving.[66] And it's not just cravings that cause fat. Aspartame metabolizes into formaldehyde, which degrades cellular structures, including collagen, which means if you drink diet drinks or otherwise use aspartame you'll eventually have a lot more cellulite.

Brain tumors, Lou Gehrig's disease, severe mental retardation, seizures, multiple sclerosis, obesity on normal amounts of food—to date, studies continue to confirm that aspartame is a dangerous, neurotoxic substance that should never have been released into our food chain and should be illegal to give to pregnant women and children.[67] How in the world does a substance like aspartame even get FDA approval?

CHAPTER SEVEN

FDA-Approved Death by Supermarket

MY GRANDMA, STELLA, SET an admirable example and was a major influence on my lifelong attitudes about nutrition, but growing up I didn't always take her seriously. One of the reasons she didn't get the credit she deserved for being so ahead of her time in her views about nutrition might have had something to do with her somewhat apocryphal presentation. Like her word-to-the-wise story about a friend of hers who murdered her husband by feeding him nothing but hot dogs. We used to roll our eyes back whenever we heard that one.

About the time Grandma was telling us about the hot dog murder, forensic science was just beginning to develop. Today we have DNA testing, advanced computerization, and laser-light-scattering technology to help solve murders. You would have to be extremely dense to try to murder someone using arsenic or cyanide. But police agencies and the FBI aren't concerned if you feed your family carcinogenic, neurologically damaging, toxic food products, as long as the ingredients are approved by the FDA, the agency that is billed as "the Nation's Foremost Consumer Protection Agency." Today, millions of Americans are unwittingly killing their families by supermarket—with FDA approval.

Factory foods are manufactured or raised with toxic substances that have either received FDA approval or these substances have slipped through the cracks. There are many reasons for the lack of strict monitoring. First, policing the food industry takes money. In 1996, Michael Friedman, M.D., deputy commissioner of the FDA, testified, "Given the current constraints on government resources, it is unlikely the FDA will ever have sufficient resources to inspect, sample, and analyze more than a small percentage of all food products, domestic as well as imported." Friedman went on to say, "The current system generally relies on detecting and correcting problems after they occur rather than preventing them in the first place."[68]

Then there's the virtually meaningless FDA status Generally Recognized as Safe (GRAS)—the one granted to MSG way back in 1959. When first launched by Congress in 1958, GRAS status was granted to additives that already existed in the food supply based on unmonitored, inadequate, hit-or-miss surveys and nonexistent follow-up. After the initial structuring of the GRAS list, for a manufacturer to obtain a GRAS status for an unapproved substance, a formal petition was required by the FDA that provided evidence supporting the safety of the substance.

In 1997, the FDA decided that GRAS food ingredients would no longer be required by law to go through the same "review" process described above. Now factory-food manufacturers must only notify the FDA that such and such additive is GRAS and provide some evidence that the FDA can then file in a drawer. This eliminated pesky paper shuffling for the FDA and allowed the agency to "gain increased awareness of ingredients in the nation's food supply and the cumulative dietary exposure to GRAS substances."[69]

Although drug companies are required to report adverse reactions to the FDA, food companies are not required to report adverse reactions to GRAS additives to the FDA. So we don't really know which GRAS additives are problematic. But let's say that some GRAS substances are safe, some are moderately safe, some are safe in small amounts, and some are toxic, especially when accumulated in your body with prolonged use. But we are not just eating one little thing that is GRAS every day. We're bombarding our bodies with GRAS substances over the prolonged period of a lifetime.

The FDA has fallen into a truly sorry state of disorganization, ineptness, and corruption that ultimately affects many other decisions rendered by the FDA regarding food products, diet products, and drugs. In recent years, our nation has been rocked by the scandalous realization that the FDA might be too lackadaisical about drug approvals, many of which are now conducted in impoverished countries on indigents and malnourished infants, which has led to the unleashing of dangerous drugs onto the market that generate billions of dollars of profits for drug companies. For example, the FDA allowed the painkillers Vioxx, Celebrex, Bextra, and Aleve on the market although these drugs increase the risk for heart attack and stroke. In 1999, the *New England Journal of Medicine* reported that arthritis sufferers dying each year from the side effects of nonsteroidal anti-inflammatory drugs numbered up to 16,500—the same number as were dying from AIDS. In addition, more than 100,000 people were hospitalized every year due to gastrointestinal problems associated with these drugs.[70] Of the 25 million Americans who took Vioxx between 1999 and 2004, up to 4,600 of these—or their family members—sued the maker, Merck, claiming Vioxx caused strokes and heart attacks.

Samuel Epstein, M.D., is a professor emeritus of environmental and occupational medicine at the University of Illinois Medical Center in Chicago, an internationally recognized authority on cancer causes and prevention, and the author of 260 peer-reviewed scientific articles and eleven books on this subject. Dr. Epstein told me, "I urged the FDA to encourage the use of aspirin, which is a Cox-2 inhibitor and is as effective as Celebrex and all the other Cox-2 inhibitor drugs, but without all the dangerous side effects." But the FDA did not heed this warning.

Subsequent to the initial yanking of Cox-2 inhibitors from the shelves, we learned that FDA "drug advisors" were lobbying for some of these drugs to be returned to the market—despite their known problems. The press reported that ten of the 32 drug advisors to the FDA consulted in recent years for the drugs' manufacturers. Nine of these ten had voted to return the potential deadly Cox-2 inhibitors to the market. CBS reported, "If these ten 'experts' had not been drafted for the panel, neither Bextra nor Vioxx would have received enough votes to get the panel's thumbs up."[71]

The *New York Times* reported, "Researchers with ties to industry commonly serve on Food and Drug Administration advisory panels, but their presence has long been a contentious issue . . . Several of the panel members flagged with conflicts say most or all of the money from drug makers went not to themselves but to their universities or institutions." (An indirect route to their salaries, bonuses, and perks.) The *Times* also mentioned that shares of Merck and Pfizer soared after the panel's vote was announced.[72] You have to wonder if the nine FDA drug advisors also held stocks in Merck and Pfizer?

How did these drug advisors ultimately arrive at their conclusions that unsafe drugs should be re-released onto the market? In 2000 Merck found itself in an untenable situation when they were faced with the death of a 73-year-old participant in a clinical trial who had likely died of a heart attack. The woman's death, writes Merck's top scientist Edward M. Scolnick, M.D., in an email, "put us in a terrible situation." (As it turns out, in this twelve-week drug trial, called Advantage, eight out of 5,500 participants suffered a heart attack or sudden cardiac death.) The major issue appeared to be that Scolnick did not want the FDA to demand that Vioxx carry a warning for cardiac risks as it would then not sell as well as its competitor Celebrex, which did not warn of cardiac risk on its label. In fact, in other emails Scolnick "fiercely criticized the FDA and said he would personally pressure senior officials at the agency if it took action unfavorable to Vioxx."[73] And so Scolnick got his way and thousands of people were harmed.

In 2007, Merck reached a $4.85 billion settlement to resolve most of the roughly 50,000 lawsuits regarding Vioxx, apart from the $80 million deal the company cut with unions and insurers. By 2010, a shareholder lawsuit was still with the Supreme Court, and the company, in an attempt to appease shareholder derivative complaints against the company's officers, agreed to pay $12.5 million in legal fees and take steps to monitor the safety of its drugs.[74]

Perhaps the biggest head scratcher is Avandia, the blockbuster diabetes drug that hit the market in 1999 and became GlaxoSmithKline's top cash cow. By 2006 its annual revenue was $3.2 billion. By 2009, sales had dropped to $1.2 billion following a damning study published in the *New England Journal of Medicine* in 2007 which linked Avandia to a 43 percent increased risk of heart attack and a 64 percent higher risk of cardiovascular death than patients treated with other methods.[75]

Even though more than 83,000 users of Avandia experienced heart attacks due to side effects, instead of recalling the drug GSK developed another drug that could treat the condition caused by Avandia.[76] In fact, before Avandia's release, GSK had evidence that the drug causes the body to increase levels of a potentially deadly enzyme that the company's researchers connected to heart disease in their own studies. But rather than disclosing the problems with Avandia, GSK instead patented a diagnostic test to detect the enzyme and then proceeded to pour millions of dollars into research to create the new blockbuster drug that would inhibit the enzyme that allegedly prevented Avandia-caused heart attacks.

It took 1,354 cardiac-associated deaths from Avandia in 2009 for the FDA to intervene in late 2010 with regulatory action. Even then the FDA didn't remove Avandia from the market (although European regulators did). Instead the FDA imposed restrictions. Avandia couldn't be administered without the doctor first trying other less risky treatments. When proceeding with Avandia, the doctor is required to meet with the patient to discuss the risks, and the patient has to agree in writing to accept the risks.[77]

Meanwhile GSK continued to spin the risk benefit of Avandia, downplaying the risks even as they paid out $60 million to settle seven hundred lawsuits and thousands more lawsuits flooded in.[78]

David Graham, M.D., M.P.H., who has been with the FDA for twenty-six years, is currently the associate director for science and medicine in the

Office of Drug Safety. In November 2004, Dr. Graham appeared before the Senate Finance Committee and subsequently appeared on the *PBS Online News Hour* program to tell the country that the FDA was "incapable of protecting America from another Vioxx. Simply put, FDA and the Center for Drug Evaluation and Research (CDER) are broken."[79] (The CDER, a branch of the FDA, responds to written inquires regarding prescription and over-the-counter drugs.)

Another drug that is astonishingly not ringing any alarm bells is acetaminophen (the active ingredient in Tylenol). Because OTCs are FDA approved, most people blithely self-prescribe without pondering the prospect of acute liver failure. Partly as a result of the Cox-2 inhibitor debacle, Americans have been lulled into a false sense of security over the use of acetaminophen. A study in the December 2005 issue of *Hepatology* reveals that, because the FDA has not educated Americans about acetaminophen poisoning, most have no clue how easy it is to overdose on it. People with cluster symptoms can end up taking a variety of OTCs, all containing acetaminophen, without realizing they've reached or exceeded the maximum adult daily dose of 4,000 milligrams. Tim Davern, M.D., who is a gastroenterologist with the liver transplant program of the University of California at San Francisco and a coauthor of the above-mentioned study, commented on this scenario: "It's extremely frustrating to see people come into the hospital who felt fine several days ago, but now need a new liver."[80]

Autism spectrum disorder (ASD) is a disorder of mental introversion, aloneness, inability to relate, repetitive play, and rage reactions. In *Rolling Stone*, attorney and environmentalist Robert F. Kennedy writes, "Since 1991, when the CDC and the FDA had recommended that three additional vaccines laced with the [mercury-based] preservative [thimerosal] be given to extremely young infants—in one case, within hours of birth—the estimated number of cases of autism had increased fifteenfold, from one in every 2,500 children to one in 166 children." (The most recent data from the CDC puts autism at an average of one in 110 children, or 1 percent of children.)[81] Dr. Boyd Haley, an authority on mercury toxicity, was quoted in Kennedy's article, "You couldn't even construct a study that shows thimerosal is safe. It's just too darn toxic. If you inject thimerosal into an animal, its brain will sicken. If you apply it to living tissue, the cells die. If you put it in a petri dish, the culture dies. Knowing these things, it would be shocking if one could inject it into an infant without causing damage." Rep. Dan Burton, a Republican from Indiana, who oversaw a three-year investigation of thimerosal after his grandson was diagnosed with autism, stated in his House Government Reform Committee final report, "This epidemic in all probability may have been prevented or curtailed had the FDA not been asleep at the switch regarding a lack of safety data regarding injected thimerosal, a known neurotoxin."[82]

Although the FDA is now "working with drug companies" to reduce the amount of thirmerosol in vaccines, it has not stopped them from using it.[83]

In addition to Cox-2 inhibitors, acetaminophen, and thimerosal, the FDA failed to protect Americans from the serious risk of heart valve damage from the weight-loss miracle-in-a bottle Fenfluramine and Phentermine (Fen-Phen). The FDA failed to restrict the acne drug Accutane, even though it was known to cause Thalidomide-like birth defects when taken by pregnant women and is now known to cause liver damage, irreparable GI problems, and depression. The FDA allowed the sale of the cholesterol-lowering medication Crestor, even though it can lead to kidney failure.

The FDA didn't warn doctors and parents about the risk of suicide among children taking antidepressants. The use of antidepressants has tripled in the last ten years, and spending has increased by 130 percent. Antidepressants have obscenely high profit margins, as much as 569,958 percent in the case of Xanax.[84] Drug companies make so much money that they can handle the occasional lawsuit, even one as large as the Vioxx debacle, and still show a profit. SSRIs have not been pulled by the FDA even though they increase the incidence of suicidality.[85] Almost all of the homicidal and suicidal "school shooters" (the ones whose medical files haven't been sealed) had been taking psychiatric drugs, either SSRIs such as Prozac or psychostimulants such as Ritalin.[86] Studies have shown that 4 to 8 percent of people under the age of eighteen will become psychotic, suicidal, or homicidal from SSRIs.[87] These drugs continue to be prescribed and FDA approved, even though a review of twenty years of studies in the *Journal of the American Medical Association* in early 2010 concluded that antidepressants are no more helpful than placebos.[88]

The FDA's failings are not exclusive to the pharmaceutical industry, said Dr. Epstein, "Whether you want to look at it from the standpoint of indifference, conspiracy, or conflict of interest, the FDA poses a great danger to consumers. What's happening now with these drugs is symptomatic of the FDA."[89]

While the recent drug scandals may make it appear as if the FDA has all of a sudden sunk to an all-time low, it appears that this government agency has had problems for a very long time. Herbert L. Ley. M.D., FDA commissioner from 1968 to 1969, said, "The thing that bugs me is that the people think that the FDA is protecting them—it isn't. What the FDA is doing and what the public thinks it's doing are as different as night and day."[90]

Richard Crout, former director of the FDA's Bureau of Drugs, testified way back in 1976 that the FDA was in serious shape. "I want to describe the agency as I saw it. No one knew where anything was . . . There was absenteeism; there was open drunkenness by several employees . . . there was intimidation internally . . . People—I'm talking about division directors and their staffs—would engage in a kind of behavior that invited insubordination; people tittered in the corners, throwing spitballs—now I'm describing physicians; people would slouch down in their chairs and not respond to questions; and moan-and-groan, [making] sleeping gestures. This was a kind of behavior I have not seen in any other institution from a grown man . . . FDA has a long-term problem with the recruitment of personnel, good, scientific personnel."[91]

In June 2006, after reviewing the results of a fifteen-month inquiry he had initiated, Representative Henry A. Waxman (D-CA) said, "Americans have relied on FDA to ensure the safety of their food and drugs for 100 years. But under the Bush administration, enforcement efforts have plummeted and serious violations are ignored." Waxman was referring to a 54 percent drop in warning letters to drug companies and medical device manufacturers from 2000 to 2005. In addition, there was a 44 percent decline in seizure of dangerous products and a 65 percent decline in enforcement actions concerning devices such as implantable defibrillators and pacemakers.[92]

When it comes to our food supply, the FDA is greatly responsible for our evolution from a real, living food diet to a supermarket factory-food diet, but not solely responsible. Food additives would not be getting FDA approval in the first place if companies weren't applying for approval. It's widely known that Washington players hop from government positions to law firms to corporate positions to elected office and back again. Career advancement in Washington and the biotech industry (an industry with far-reaching implications in food production) is predicated on favors and back scratching. In researching this book, I found dozens of references to people who went from White House careers to positions at Monsanto, from Congress to Monsanto, from federal agencies to Monsanto and the biotech industry, and from Monsanto and the biotech industry to government employment. When decisions are made about public health and safety, career and financial interests often influence these decision makers.

The sad state of affairs concerning our food supply has been developing since the late 1800s as the food, diet, and pharmaceutical industries systematically cultivated a complex and inextricable web of relationships with (some, not all) FDA scientists and other researchers, administrators and attorneys, biotech attorneys, elected officials, government agencies, lobbyists, medical associations, medical and scientific journals, and doctors. This tangled, powerful network of relationships has influenced what you have been putting in your mouth and what you will put in your mouth in the future. The billions of dollars in profits racked up by these industries through the sales and consumption of their products wouldn't be possible if it weren't for tickets and invitations to sports events, operas, symphonies, theater performances, and invitations to prestigious movie premiers, lunches, dinner parties, birthday parties, weddings, golf games, and exotic vacations, as well as the honorariums, grants, donations, kickbacks, payoffs, and miscellaneous and sundry "favors" accepted by the support players listed above.[93]

Clearly, there are innumerable independently operating moving parts that buoy the activities of these industries. Not everyone involved is corrupt. Some people in government and industry are simply trying to make a living at their careers. And many Americans—including elected and appointed officials—still have a "better living through chemistry" mentality. We can only assume that at least some of our elected and appointed officials and their families are as much in the dark as we are. If they knew the facts about our food supply one can only hope that our elected and appointed officials would revise their current diversionary strategy of health-care reform to shift the primary focus instead to reforming the food supply that is causing so many people to need health care in the first place.

Industries have gained a powerful foothold in America because of the efforts of a relative handful of very wealthy, extraordinarily powerful, self-interested inside players, their paid-off henchpeople, and agencies such as the FDA, as well as the unwitting participation of millions of bit players and trusting consumers. So we can't really say that this is a conspiracy—except insomuch as it is a conspiracy to protect shareholder profits. Nevertheless, the end results (our epidemic of obesity and disease) are just as horrendous as if these contributing players had reconnoitered in a back room and agreed, "Let's get rich at the expense of Americans' health."

Corporations are able to market injurious substances like MSG and aspartame to Americans because of FDA approval. For example, the public is continually assured by the FDA that aspartame is an inert compound that does not affect physiological systems.

It might be useful to take the FDA's stance on aspartame in the context of its overall mentality about dangerous substances. A landmark study by the Institute of Medicine called "To Err Is Human" found that as many as 98,000 Americans die every year from preventable medical errors, and that is now thought to be a conservative number. Every year more than 700,000 Americans are killed from medical mistakes, including adverse reactions to prescription and over-the-counter medicines. In addition, 2.2 million are seriously injured. These are only the numbers that are reported to the FDA of people having in-hospital adverse reactions; the FDA estimates that only 1 to 10 percent of these incidences are reported.[95]

Is it any wonder that the FDA is not bothered that aspartame is one of two additives that have consistently generated the most consumer complaints of adverse reactions?[96]

However, given the mountains of empirical evidence and hundreds of peer-reviewed research studies that demonstrate the dangers of aspartame use, it appears that the FDA approval of aspartame may have been premature. Dr. Blaylock told me that the FDA handling of aspartame "is what one would expect of a federal regulatory agency. They have ignored all studies and complaints."[97]

Because it's no secret that factory food is a primary cause of many of our obesity and health problems, many stalwart Americans are turning to "health food." Instead of supplying us with real, organic food, factory-food makers have flooded the market with pretend "health food," like meat "analogs"—fake meat products made from soy. It may come as a shock, but everyone is not as "go soy go" as you may have been led to believe.

PART FOUR

Science-Fiction Food

CHAPTER EIGHT

The Dangers of Soy: Internet Paranoia—
or Fact?

WHEN I WAS FIFTEEN, in 1966, my family packed up and moved to a Navy base in Japan. Only twenty years after World War II, Japan was still a developing country. Kimono-swathed Japanese shuffled along on *geta*. Homes were made of rice paper and tatami mats. There was no such thing as fast food. I learned to navigate the train system to better eat my way across Japan in soba shops and sushi bars. Never once did I see a single Japanese sit down to a meal of soy. It's true that, along with their traditional diet, the Japanese ate a number of soy foods. But mostly I remember Japanese chopsticking teeny pieces of condiment-soy out of their soup.

Flash forward to the 1990s. All of a sudden soy hits the scene. Medical experts say that eating soy protein reduces your risk for heart disease by lowering cholesterol levels, the isoflavones in soy reduce or alleviate hot flashes in menopausal women, the isoflavones in soy prevent osteoporosis, and numerous components in soy have anticancer properties. A clever PR campaign by the soy industry massaged this message into the brains of busy Americans as, "Asians are healthier because they eat soy, soy, soy, and more soy." And I'm thinking, *Hmmm. Call me crazy, but that's not my recollection of the Japanese diet.*

Did those involved in soy have our best interest in mind when they introduced new, industrially processed soy foods into our food chain? Or could it be that behemoth purveyors of scary substances, like Monsanto—which produced Agent Orange for the Vietnam war and is now sunnily saturating Earth with the herbicide Round Up—those types of companies might have planted the planet with soybeans and now they've got to convince you to brush your teeth with it?

Since we're inundated with soy propaganda, it may come as a surprise to you that not everyone is upbeat about it. I can't say that I was entirely objective about soy as I launched my investigation. My biases were formed based on these five facts: One, I had lived in Japan and didn't witness evidence to back up the claims that the historical Asian diet was heavily weighted in soy. Two, Americans don't eat whole soy foods as Asians do; rather, they eat factory foods containing industrially processed soy. Three, 80 percent of these soy products are made from "Roundup Ready" soybeans created by Monsanto (soybeans genetically engineered to withstand the spraying of the weed and grass killer Roundup.) Four, the FDA, which has given its blessing to soy, appears to be inept and corrupt. And five, big businesses are notoriously more interested in shareholder profits than Americans' health. Nevertheless, my motivation was to get to the truth about soy.

The pro-soy camp comprises the soy industry, the food processing industry, some vegetarians and vegans, the powerful contingency of administrators at the FDA, soy researchers whose research is funded by the soy industry, and celebrities and celebrity doctors who endorse products and/or have written books endorsing soy as a health food.

To get a well-respected opinion from the soy supporters, I began by emailing Christiane Northrup, M.D., celebrity women's doctor and author of *The Wisdom of Menopause: Creating Physical and Emotional Health and Healing During the Change*, who at that time was a spokesperson for Revival, a company that manufactures high-isoflavone soy protein powders, energy bars, and other soy products. Dr. Northrup replied, "The health benefits are very well documented . . . [Soy] helps support nearly the entire body and its systems, including hormone regulation, breast health, the heart, the bones, the brain, and the colon and bowels." She went on to explain in how soy relieves menopausal symptoms.[98]

For a second opinion, I turned to Bradley J. Willcox, M.D., M.Sc., co-investigator of the Okinawa Centenarian Study and coauthor of *The Okinawa Program: How the World's Longest-Lived People Achieve Everlasting Health—and How You Can Too.* Dr. Willcox emailed me his opinion. "The best evidence suggests that adding more soy foods to the Western diet may reduce the risk of heart disease through beneficial effects of soy on cholesterol levels and artery health . . . Our studies suggest that soy may have contributed to [the Okinawan population's] overall health and that it may be implicated in their low risk for heart disease and hormone-associated cancers such as breast, prostate, and colon cancers."[99]

I looked to integrative medicine advocate and celebrity author Andrew Weil, M.D., whose word is gospel to many Americans, and he was also pro-soy, referring to the questioning of the safety of soy as "Internet paranoia."[100]

It all sounded convincing. But I decided to look into the anti-soy group. As it turned out, clinical nutritionist and soy expert Kaayla T. Daniel, Ph.D., C.C.N., had very different experiences with her soy-consuming patients. She told me, "About ten years ago I started reading newspaper and magazine articles with titles like 'The Joy of Soy' and 'Soy of Cooking,' but the hype didn't correspond with reality. I knew many vegetarians and vegans, most of whom were eating soy as their primary protein source, but very few of them looked healthy, and many complained about fatigue, brain fog, poor skin, hair loss, and other problems. Also, as a health educator I worked with people privately and in classes. I couldn't help but notice that many of the most health-conscious people ate and drank a lot of soy and were developing many health problems, particularly thyroid problems. This piqued my interest. If soy was so healthy, why were these people doing so poorly?"

Daniel's curiosity instigated four years of research that culminated in the book *The Whole Soy Story: The Dark Side of America's Favorite Health Food.* Dr. Daniel told me, "The health benefits of soy are not well documented. The studies are inconsistent and contradictory at best. Possible benefits are outweighed by proven risks. Hundreds of epidemiological, clinical, and laboratory studies link soy to malnutrition, digestive distress, thyroid dysfunction, cognitive decline, reproductive disorders, immune system breakdown, and even heart disease and cancer."[101]

Dr. Daniel didn't agree with Dr. Willcox. "The authors of *The Okinawa Program* claim that soy was the key to lowered cancer risk in Okinawans, but a careful reading of the text indicates that they came to that conclusion based on three possibly unrelated factors: the presence of some soy in the Okinawan diet, the lower incidence of cancer there, and the pro-soy findings from several unrelated but well-publicized studies, most of which were funded by the soy industry."[102]

Agreeing with Dr. Daniel are a number of scientists from the FDA laboratories of toxicological research whose research findings on soy have been ignored by the consumer protection division of the FDA; scientists whose research is not funded by the soy industry; scientists who are funded by the soy industry but whose findings get buried; clinical nutritionists and other nutritional experts; doctors of Chinese medicine; and authors of alternative health and wellness books; not to mention the unhappy ex-soy consumers who attribute health problems to eating soy, everything from weight gain to birth defects.[103]

Soy entered our radar screen in the early 1990s, but wasn't officially launched into our collective consciousness until almost a decade later. In response to a petition submitted to the FDA by Protein Technologies International on October 26, 1999, the FDA issued a press release: "FDA's conclusion is that foods containing soy protein included in a diet low in saturated fat and cholesterol may reduce the risk of CHD by lowering blood cholesterol levels." This claim was supposedly based on "evidence that including soy protein in a diet low in saturated fat and cholesterol may also help to reduce the risk of CHD," and on the statement that "scientific studies show that 25 grams of soy protein daily in the diet is needed to show a significant cholesterol-lowering effect. In order to qualify for this health claim, a food must contain at least 6.25 grams of soy protein per serving."

This authorization had been fought by two FDA toxicologists, Daniel

Sheehan, Ph.D., and Daniel Doerge, Ph.D., who were concerned about the inconclusiveness of the alleged cholesterol-lowering effect and also about known health hazards. On February 18, 1999, Drs. Sheehan and Doerge wrote a protest letter to the FDA, saying, "There exists a significant body of animal data that demonstrates goitrogenic [thyroid inhibiting] and even carcinogenic effects of soy products. Moreover, there are significant reports of goitrogenic effects from soy consumption in human infants and adults."[104]

Nevertheless, the FDA ruling urged consumers to eat soy: "Because soy protein can be added to a variety of foods, it is possible for consumers to eat foods containing soy protein at all three meals and for snacks."[105] As if Americans need to hear "MORE IS MORE," the factory-food industry aggressively proceeded to scream, "MORE IS MORE," as they blasted soy into the marketplace. A boisterously enthusiastic press initially spurred on a wholehearted, blanket acceptance of the health benefits of soy, and vegetarians, vegans, menopausal women, eaters of low carb factory-food products, mothers of infants, and those at risk for heart disease fell into step with the multibillion-dollar-a-year soy industry.

The pharmaceutical and supplement industries quickly followed with marketing campaigns for soy isoflavone supplements. Isoflavones are a type of phytoestrogen, which are plant compounds that have estrogen-like effects and are believed to have both estrogenic and antiestrogenic capabilities. In other words, they are thought to both fit into to the estrogen receptor sites and block estrogen receptors. Phytoestrogens can either inhibit or stimulate the growth of certain cells.

Before the early ninth century doctor and pharmacist were one and the same. The herbalist both prescribed and prepared medical compounds. Drugs at that time were one step removed from their plant sources. But in the late eighteenth century, pharmacology developed and introduced advances that enabled pharmacologists to isolate active ingredients thought to have the primary healing property for a given condition. Isolating the specific active ingredient responsible for a therapeutic effect has since been the focus of Western medicine. This mentality of isolating active ingredients from their whole-plant form drives the soy isoflavone supplement industry, which isolates isoflavones from the whole soybean and then markets them in supplement form as a panacea for preventing heart disease, cancer, bone loss, and the symptoms of menopause.

It's worth noting that isoflavones are a factor in the bitter taste of soybeans, and products such as soymilk taste much better with isoflavones removed. With this financial incentive to go to the trouble of removing the isoflavones, more companies have tried to sell the isolated isoflavones as supplements.

According to Dr. Daniel, isoflavones are "hormonally active substances," or "estrogen mimickers," that are endocrine disrupters which can cause thyroid damage, reproductive system disorders, and other problems. Isoflavones can lower testosterone levels, sperm count, and sex drive in men, "estrogenize" baby boys (resulting in tiny penises and breast development), and cause premature puberty in boys and girls, and in women they can disrupt menstrual cycles and cause infertility and vulvodynia (swelling and pain in the external genitalia). Boys born to soy-eating mothers can have a birth defect called hypospadias (the opening of their urethra is in the wrong place).[106]

In the past, women going through menopause bit the bullet and hoped for the best outcome in post-menopausal old age. The outcome ultimately depended on their genetic predispositions, lifelong diet, and lifestyle habits. Today women have four choices: One, bite the bullet and let menopause take its course. Two, use an equine-estrogen drug, such as Premarin. Three, use bioidentical hormone replacement therapy to replace the sex hormones that are no longer being supplied by the ovaries. And four, bite the bullet and use various alternative medicine modalities, including soy isoflavone supplementation, in an attempt to alleviate the symptoms of sex hormone decline and cessation.

Millions of boomer women have decided not to follow in their mother's footsteps of zero sex, male-pattern-like balding, hot flashes, facial hair, weight gain, emotional roller coasters, and insomnia, and have opted not to bite the menopause bullet. First they tried the lucrative equine-drug estrogens, erroneously billed as "hormone replacement." These drugs are made by extracting estrogen from the urine of pregnant mares and adding drugs, and therefore they cannot be "replaced" in a woman's body, which never made horse estrogen drugs in the first place. In fact, the horse-estrogen drug was never FDA approved as HRT, but rather was approved to alleviate hot flashes and to reduce bone loss. But in July 2002, an eight-year study by the Women's Health Initiative was halted early when researchers concluded that Prempro, made by Wyeth, didn't prevent heart disease or breast cancer; rather, it increased the risk for breast cancer, heart attack, stroke, and blood clots—and also it did not prevent Alzheimer's or memory loss. So millions of women decided against the horse-estrogen drug. (This study as well as bioidentical hormone replacement [BHRT] are covered more extensively in *Healthy, Sexy, Happy*.)

Since the definition of hormone replacement is replacement of the hormones lost when a woman's own sex-hormone production declines and ultimately ceases, some users of horse-estrogen drugs switched to BHRT. Bioidentical estrogen is synthesized in a laboratory from plant chemicals, mostly wild yams and sometimes soy, to match the exact molecular structure of the estrogens made by the human female body; it can therefore legitimately be referred to as bioidentical hormone replacment. Taking bioidentical estrogen that is synthesized from soy and prescribed in physiologically appropriate doses is not the same as consuming estrogen-mimicking soy products and isoflavone supplements. (Pharmaceutical companies don't study BHRT, as natural substances can't be patented and therefore do not produce the same extravagant returns on their research investment that drug companies have enjoyed with the sales of drugs.)

Many women feel that using BHRT is still "unnatural" and choose to bite the bullet through menopause with the help of various alternative approaches, including soy isoflavone supplements. Soy is the most concentrated dietary source of the phytoestrogen isoflavones genistein and daidzein. These phytoestrogens were touted as the natural way to replenish declining estrogen levels and were said to relieve menopausal symptoms such as hot flashes, as well as to decrease the risk of heart disease and osteoporosis. Although isoflavone supplementation is a booming business, studies have shown that soy isoflavone supplementation does not consistently alleviate hot flashes or other menopausal symptoms. And as Dr. Daniel said, when women use soy isoflavone supplementation during menopause they risk damaging their thyroid glands, which are already vulnerable in midlife women.[107]

I emailed Dr. Northrup again. "There appear to be many studies that dispute the claims that soy relieves menopausal symptoms and that, in fact, this claim is not authorized by the FDA."

She replied, "My position that [soy] relieves menopausal symptoms is based on my clinical experience with hundreds of women. The studies vary widely on what type of soy was used, how much was used, over what period of time, etc. I generally recommend soy powders made from whole soybeans that contain over 100 milligrams of soy isoflavones per day. Any dose that's lower than that doesn't give much benefit. But at doses of 100 to 180 milligrams day, you see a decrease in hot flashes, an increase in vaginal moisture, and also a nice effect on skin."

Dr. Daniel disagreed. "As a clinical nutritionist, I've seen many premenopausal and menopausal women who trace hypothyroidism, weight gain, depression, fatigue, poor skin, and hair loss to 'health food' regimens including 'natural hormone replacement' programs based on soy."[108]

But what about taking soy isoflavone supplements to ward off cancer and heart disease? Some studies on the cancer-preventative properties of soy suggest that soy isoflavones might ward off some cancers, but other studies indicate that soy isoflavones may actually increase the risk of cancer, especially breast cancer.

In fact, there is a growing uneasiness within the scientific community that soy isoflavone supplements and products are being marketed without iron-clad proof of the health benefits and, more important, in the face of potential health risks of consuming arbitrary amounts of isoflavones.[109]

When I attempted to question the safety of isoflavones with one celebrity doctor, the author of numerous books on supplements and other aspects of nutrition, as well as soy, he became defensive and argumentative, accusing the dairy industry of making up lies about soy. Another high-profile nutritionist also became hostile, and accused me of entering into my research with a bias against the FDA. I'd like to pause here and say that fifteen years ago I coauthored my first book, in which we endorsed soy without really researching it. I regret that and no longer endorse that book, and in I fact recently put my remaining thirty copies into recycling. I understand, though, how easy it is to get swept up in the excitement of new research—even though as I wrote that book and the two accompanying cookbooks in the back of my mind I was pondering my own experience in Japan. I sincerely believe that anyone who attempts to educate the public on nutrition has to admit mistakes. Because if I was swept away, then someone who's not spending their days reading and researching is not likely to question what the media is presenting in easily digested sound bites. In deference to the soy experts mentioned above, I chose not to name them, as my position isn't to pick fights but to arrive at a truth that will result in the best positive outcome for public health.

Regarding soy isoflavones, Mike Fitzpatrick, Ph.D., is an environmental scientist whose research on phytoestrogens led him to the conclusion that soy isoflavones disrupt the endocrine system. Fitzpatrick found that high daily doses increase the risk for hypothyroidism. "There is potential for certain individuals to consume levels of isoflavones in the range that could have goitrogenic [thyroid inhibiting] effects," Fitzpatrick writes. "Most at risk appear to be infants fed soy formulas, followed by high soy users and those using isoflavone supplements."[110]

Hypothyroidism currently affects up to 40 percent of our population—though many go undiagnosed—and the incidence of hypothyroidism is increasing. The thyroid is a small, butterfly-shaped endocrine gland located just below the Adam's apple. Every cell, tissue, and organ of your body is affected by the actions of the thyroid gland. Symptoms of low-functioning thyroid are anemia and bruising easily, weight gain and inability to lose weight, constipation, depression or extreme agitation/anxiety, dry skin, decreased sex drive, dull facial expression, droopy eyelids, emotional instability, fatigue, feeling cold, low body temperature, hoarse, husky voice, slow reflexes, impaired memory, brain fog, infertility, migraines, tinnitus, vertigo, muscle cramps, muscle weakness, puffiness in the face and hands, thinning, coarse, dry hair, and a yellow cast to the skin.[111] Hypothyroidism is a life-altering condition that is very difficult to reverse. If you develop hypothyroidism, you'll likely spend your life in an uphill battle with your weight and suffer the symptoms listed above, which can contribute to type 2 diabetes and heart disease.

Consuming soy isoflavones isn't the only cause of our rise in hypothyroidism. Fluoride, mercury, and other xenohormones (environmental estrogen mimickers) have also been implicated. But according to Fitzpatrick those "most at risk" are adults who consume a lot of soy products or soy isoflavone supplements and babies who are fed soy formula.

If isoflavone supplements are questionable, what about eating soy, and how much soy should we eat? We continue to hear that Asians have less disease because they eat a lot of soy. But how much soy do Asians really eat? In ancient times, farmers cultivated soybeans to instill nitrogen into the soil so that other crops would thrive. When they did begin to eat small amounts of soy, they subjected it to a long fermentation process to make foods such as miso and *shoyu* (soy sauce). Historically, Asians understood that it was imperative to soak and naturally ferment soy to rid it, at least in part, of naturally occurring antinutrients (compounds that decrease the nutritional value of the plant) and toxins (which serve to protect plants from annihilation by insect and animal predators). The fermenting process, aided by healthy microorganisms, deactivated or eliminated most antinutrients and toxins, improved the soybean's nutritional profile, made the resulting food item more digestible, and imparted disease-fighting microorganisms to the intestinal tract.

Naturally occurring antinutrients and toxins include allergens, which can cause a range of reactions from sneezing to death; lectins, which can affect the functioning of your immune system; oligosaccharides, which cause painful gas; oxalates, which block calcium absorption and contribute to kidney stones and, in women, the aforementioned condition called vulvodynia; phytates, which impair absorption of minerals; isoflavones (explained above); protease inhibitors, which interfere with digestion and stress the pancreas; saponins, which may lower cholesterol but also may damage your intestinal lining; and goitrogens, which damage the thyroid gland and can lead to hypothyroidism and cancer.

Since my experience in Japan was contrary to the claims of the soy industry, I felt it was important to understand where the claims that Asians ate a lot of soy were coming from. According to Dr. Willcox, "Our studies of the Okinawan population, who are among the world's healthiest and longest-lived people, show that adults consume between 60 to 120 grams per day [one to two cups] of soy (ten to one hundred times what Americans consume)."[112]

Dr. Daniel, however, said that there is inconsistent and contradictory data in *The Okinawa Diet Plan*, Willcox's subsequent book, regarding the consumption of soy products by Okinawans. In addition, she told me, "Although reported levels of soy consumption in China, Indonesia, Korea, Japan, and Taiwan vary from study to study, Asians eat small amounts of soy, as condiments in the diet, not as staple foods."[113]

Suffice it to say, there is much debate about how much soy Asians eat or don't eat, but everyone agrees that Asians are eating whole, mostly naturally fermented soy food condiments as part of a whole foods diet. In agreement was David Zava, Ph.D., a biochemist with twenty-five years of experience in breast cancer research and the coauthor of *What Your Doctor May Not Tell You About Breast Cancer*, who told me, "I believe [soy] should be consumed in the manner that Asians have consumed it for thousands of years—well complemented with animal protein and a broad variety of vegetables."[114] But what exactly comprised this whole foods diet historically eaten by Asians?

Since space doesn't allow the analysis of every single Asian diet, let's take a quick look at the Japanese diet as another example of the whole foods diet Asians historically consumed. While the Japanese traditionally ate more soy than Westerners (we ate virtually none until just recently) the traditional Japanese diet did not comprise soy, soy, soy, and more soy. The average Japanese consumes a diet of more than 100 biologically different foods per week. (In Western countries the recommended minimum is only thirty.)

The traditional Japanese diet includes *meguro* (raw tuna), *shiokara* (pickled squid guts), *kusaya* (dried fish), eggs, pork, beef, and chicken; white rice, linseeds and wholegrain bread, sesame seeds, *soba* (buckwheat noodles), *seitan* (seasoned wheat gluten), and *udon* (wheat noodles); bamboo shoots, eggplant, sweet potato, Chinese cabbage, seaweed, sea vegetables, shitake and matsutake mushrooms, ginger, broccoli, garlic, onions, lotus root, yam, taro, ginger, chicory, truffles, welsh onion, shallots, corn, sansai (garlic, bamboo grass shoots, and fiddlehead fern), green leafy vegetables, carrots, burdock root, diakon radish, and cucumber; *nankusu* (rice porridge); tofu, bean paste, bean curd, *nato* (fermented soy cheese), *okara* (pulp from soymilk), tempeh, edamame (steamed soy pods); azuki beans; toasted sesame oil, coconut oil, rice-bran oil, butter, talo, lard; wasabi, miso, curry, lemon, kuzu root, pickled ginger, sesame seed, mustard, rice based sake wine, dashi-stock and seasoning made from kelp and mackerel, *shoyu*, pickled plums, tea twig, brown rice vinegar, and tamari; sake, soy coffee, and ocha (green tea); and all types of fruits.[115]

This whole foods diet, which as you can see includes some soy, provides combined chemical or physiological effects on the human body. But Americans are most certainly not eating the whole foods that Asians traditionally ate. We are eating highly industrialized soy substances. Dr. Daniel writes, "The old-fashioned traditional products bear little or no resemblance to the modern soy protein products promoted by the soy industry and sold in grocery stores."[116]

My investigation revealed that modern industrialized soy is indeed science fiction. Aside from the naturally occurring antinutrients and toxins outlined in the previous chapter, like all foods subjected to industrialization, soy is adulterated with substances that are bad for humans. And most soy is genetically modified.

In *Seeds of Deception: Exposing Industry and Government Lies About the Safety of the Genetically Engineered Foods You're Eating*, Jeffrey M. Smith writes, "On May 23, 2003, President Bush proposed an Initiative to End Hunger in Africa using genetically modified (GM) foods. He also blamed Europe's 'unfounded, unscientific fears' of these foods for hindering efforts to end hunger. Bush was convinced that GM foods held the key to greater yields, expanded U.S. exports, and a better world . . . The message was part of a master plan that had been crafted by corporations determined to control the world's food supply. This was made clear at a biotech industry conference in January 1999, where a representative from Arthur Anderson Consulting Group explained how his company had helped Monsanto create that plan. First, they asked Monsanto what their ideal future looked like in fifteen to twenty years. Monsanto executives described a world with 100 percent of all commercial seeds genetically modified and patented. Anderson Consulting then worked backward from that goal, and developed the strategy and tactics to achieve it. They presented Monsanto with the steps and procedures needed to obtain a place of industry dominance in a world in which natural seeds were virtually extinct."[117]

They didn't count on Europeans, who were not going to have anything to do with GM foods. Furthermore, the United States was not going to control the world's food supply if the Europeans had anything to do with it. Meanwhile, as Europeans continue to fight genetic engineering of their food supply, U.S. companies have succeeded in getting government approval for forty varieties of genetically engineered crops and putting these genetically modified mutations into 60 percent of the factory foods Americans eat.

DNA is the unique blueprint of an organism. An organism relies on the information within its DNA to conduct every biochemical process necessary for its survival. Genes are the elements of the DNA that contain specific features or functions of the organism. For example, the genes within your DNA will dictate if you have blue eyes or brown, or if you will be stocky or lanky. In crops, DNA dictates whether a fruit or vegetable is wind resistant or loves hot sun, among other qualities.

Genetic engineering, which is also known as recombinant DNA technology, is a two-step process. Molecular biologists use enzymes to dissect specific genes from the structure of DNA in living organisms. They then insert vectors (such as viruses and bacteria) into these genes to create desired characteristics, and insert these altered genes into the DNA of the organism they wish to alter. They are essentially creating new genetic DNA, which will dictate if a crop will be frost-, bug-, or drought-resistant and so on. This new crop is now "genetically modified."

Genetic engineering has created corn that resists insect infestation, "Monsanto Roundup Ready" wheat and soybeans, and fruits and vegetables that have altered nutrient content and higher levels of antinutrients and toxins but don't rot. (Antinutrients are compounds that interfere with the absorption of nutrients.) It has instilled "antifreeze" genes into vegetables to extend the growing season and created genetic pesticides within the DNA of crops that essentially kill or ward off predators.

Humans, animals, birds, fish, insects, organisms, microorganisms, and so on have always lived and died in a seemingly random, but actually highly organized, pattern of coexistence. No one knows what altering the natural DNA of organisms will do to the natural food chain, our future health, or the environment. Genetic engineering occurs purely for the profit of big business. Small farmers do not need genetic engineering, and in fact, small farming thrives by using time-tested, old-fashioned methods of agriculture and animal husbandry.

Genetic engineering may be creating new and more dangerous toxins in our food supply, including allergens, and it may be contributing to human resistance to antibiotics. Genetically Modified (GM) foods are foreign to human physiology and have never previously existed on the face of this planet. No long-term tests have been conducted on GM foods, and the tests they have undergone are reminiscent of the flimflam review process the FDA uses to grant Generally Recognized as Safe (GRAS) status to food additives. Moreover, GM foods are not labeled, so you have no idea if you are eating genetically engineered organisms.[118]

Although we don't yet understand the repercussions of eating GM food, we do have some understanding of the dangers of unleashing these organisms into our environment. Genetically altered organisms and seeds are not stagnantly and obediently sitting where scientists assign them. They are carried by insects, birds, and wind into neighboring fields and beyond, and the pollen from genetically modified crops cross-pollinates with natural crops.

In the meantime, genetically modified organisms (GMOs) are not labeled, so you have no idea if you are eating them.[119] GMOs are suspected to increase the risk of food allergies and cancer, the creation of new, more virulent viruses, and antibiotic resistance.[120] Animals fed GMO feed refuse to eat it.[121] When force-fed GMO feed, animals develop stomach lesions and malformations of organs.[122]

Eighty percent of all soy substances originate as GM soybeans that are resistant to Monsanto's weed killer Roundup. When you eat a "Roundup Ready" soy product, you are eating both the genetic organism that made it resistant to Roundup and you are eating the Roundup. So when you eat a soy product or feed soy to your children, the most important question to ponder is, do you really want to eat something that is made by Monsanto? If you'd like to know more about GMO I recommend the documentary *The Future of Food*, which you can view on thefutureoffood.com.

Much of the U.S. soybean crop today is processed into oil that accounts for 80 percent or more of the edible fats and oils consumed in this country in the form of shortening, margarine, cooking oil, and salad dressings. When you see the term "vegetable oil," assume it is close to or all soy oil. Oil manufacturers use the chemical and heat processes described on page 109, which create oxidizing free radicals that are then deposited in your coronary arteries as plaque. When you see the word "partially hydroge-nated," bet on the fact that you are eating soy oil, which has been rendered into dangerous trans fats (described in chapter 12). Prior to recent manda-tory trans fat labeling, all fried foods in this country were fried in partially hydrogenated soybean oil.

Lecithin, extracted from soybean oil, is a natural emulsifier and lubri-cant used in many foods. As an emulsifier, it can make fats and water com-patible with each other as in, say, keeping chocolate and cocoa butter in a candy bar from separating. Because we have been told for decades that lec-ithin prevents a number of diseases, including brain aging, some consum-ers are also taking soy lecithin supplements, thinking it's a miracle food. But again we have the problem of the damaging processing of lecithin out of soybeans. Dr. Daniel writes, "Soybean lecithin comes from sludge left over after crude soy oil goes through a 'degumming' process. It is a waste product containing solvents and pesticide residue and has a consistency ranging from gummy fluid to plastic solid." In other words, the oil indus-try didn't know what to do with the massive amounts of sludge left over after refining soybean oil, so they came up with an industrialized process that could turn it into so-called "healthy" soy lecithin and put it into every conceivable factory-food product and many health-food-store products.

The chemical processing used to refine soy protein isolate—a very popular additive used to bulk up protein in products—infuses the soy pro-tein with known carcinogens, such as nitrites and nitrosamines, among other toxins. High-temperature processing denatures some of the protein, rendering it largely ineffective as a metabolic building material. While soy naturally contains aluminum (toxic to the nervous system and kidneys), processing imparts even more. Soy also naturally contains fluoride, and processing impregnates soy with extra doses of it, which may be play-ing a role in the epidemic of childhood neurological disorders, as well as hypothyroidism and osteoporosis. Soy protein isolate also contains minute residues of up to thirty-eight petroleum compounds[123] and is also often "enhanced" with MSG.[124]

On his website, Dr. Weil recommends one cup of soy foods, such as soy milk, per day. However, unlike all the wholesome ads we see for soy milk, my investigation revealed that soy milk is really a ghastly brew that few people would willingly drink without the added sugar that covers up the natural greasy, beany taste of soybeans. Also added is vitamin D_2, although, as internationally recognized biochemist and nutritionist Mary Enig, Ph.D., and Sally Fallon, president of the Weston A. Price Foundation (a nonprofit organization devoted to educating the public about nutrition), point out in their book *Eat Fat, Lose Fat: Three Delicious, Science-Based Coconut Diets*, "Research indicates that synthetic vitamin D_2 has the opposite effect of natural vitamin D, causing softening of the bones and hardening of soft tissues such as the arteries. The dairy industry used to add D_2 to milk but quietly dropped it in favor of D_3 when they realized how dangerous it was."[125]

Some brands of soymilk also contain canola oil, which is a chemical- and heat-processed monounsaturated fat that contains oxidizing free radicals, which cause coronary artery plaquing. Another additive often used to thicken soymilk is carrageenan, which is suspected to cause ulcerations and malignancies.[126] Soy milk naturally contains high levels of glutamate (an excitotoxin) and can contain hydrolyzed vegetable protein, an additive that always contains MSG. Soy milk must never be given to infants in place of formula as it is so deficient in vital nutrients that near fatal incidents have occurred. "The myth that soy is a health food has led many parents to believe that soy milk is a complete and nourishing food not only for adults but for babies and children," writes Daniel in her October 25, 2005, newsletter that discusses the possible link between soy milk and the death of three-month-old Brooklyn twins.[127]

Regarding the assertion that only fermented soy is healthy to eat, Dr. Weil writes, "That is simply not true. Some of the best forms of soy—edamame, tofu, and soy nuts—are unfermented and are much more likely to help you than hurt you."[128] (A very strange choice of words.)

According to Dr. Daniel, edamame, which are boiled green vegetable soybeans, are safe to eat—occasionally—since the soybeans are harvested young before developing mature levels of antinutrients and toxins. But she is concerned that many people today are "noshing on edamame like it's popcorn." Tofu is made by soaking and slow boiling soybeans, then curdling the resulting mash. Outside of monasteries, where a lowered sex drive caused by eating large amounts of soy was desirable, tofu has always been eaten in very small amounts in Japan. It is a distant choice after favored animal proteins like pork and seafood. Tofu has been studied here in the United States, and Dr. Daniel writes of one that found that "men and women who eat two or more servings of tofu per week in midlife are more likely to experience cognitive decline, senile dementia, and brain atrophy later in life than those who eat little or none."[129]

Weil recommends eating soy nuts, and Mireille Guiliano, author of *French Women Don't Get Fat,* suggests soy nuts as a snack when your flight is delayed or some such event occurs that allows traditionally nonsnacking Frenchwomen to eat between meals. According to Dr. Daniel, soy nuts are notoriously hard to digest and may cause cramps and flatulence, and they are among the soy foods that contain the highest level of isoflavones (phytoestrogens).

Fermenting does not remove the isoflavones, but Dr. Daniel believes fermented soy foods such as miso, *natto,* tempeh, and raw (unpasteurized), naturally fermented tamari or *shoyu* can be eaten regularly because such foods are typically eaten only in small amounts. Soy sauce is a classic example of the difference between traditional Asian soy and Americanized soy. Supermarket soy sauce is not the *shoyu* created by the traditional long, healthy fermenting process; rather, it's made by a fast, cheap industrial process that imparts chemicals, artificial dyes, and MSG.

The soy industry told us soy was a prestigious health food, and we bought that message. So instead of eating small handfuls of edamame, tiny pieces of tofu in our miso soup, a few sprinkles of naturally fermented *shoyu* on our meals of real food, Americans are consuming inordinate amounts of chemical-processed soy—and babies are now being fed soy formula instead of breast milk. Reading about babies and kids was the most disturbing part of the research I did on soy.

Eleven-year-old Kevin was a tall, slim and attractive all-American boy. His mother delighted in his articulate, quick wit. The joy his mother felt was dampened only by self-doubt and remorse over feeding his twin brother, Dennis (who was lactose intolerant), soy formula. Dennis had developed into a sluggish, underachieving, overweight, gawky adolescent with large breasts. Brittany had also fed her baby soy formula and agonized over her seven-year-old son's small stature. The kids at school were merciless about his small penis. Marc and Jennifer finally decided to take matters into their own hands when eleven-month-old Chrisy's pediatrician refused to see anything out of the ordinary about her developing breasts, pubic fuzz, and premenstrual spotting. The young parents were incredulous when they read that soy formula had estrogenizing capabilities.[130]

Although breast milk is real, living food for babies, today only about 60 percent of American mothers breastfeed their babies, and most stop breastfeeding by the time their babies are two months old. Breastfeeding, however, is a crucial step in your baby's ability to achieve his or her genetic gifts, and it is also the most important preventative measure for breast cancer for both mother and baby. Studies show that a woman's risk of breast cancer decreases by 7 percent for every birth she experiences, another 3 percent for each year under twenty-eight years old she is when that child is born, another 4.3 percent for every twelve months of her life that she breastfeeds, and yet another 23 percent if she was breastfed by her mother.[131] (Note that breast cancer is rising today in men.)

Other benefits of breastfeeding range from boosting your infant's immune system to boosting his or her IQ. No matter how much the baby formula companies try to paint a benevolent picture of vibrant health, they just do not have the goods.[132] Mother's first milk contains protein and mineral-rich colostrum that is vital for your baby's immune system. From then on, breast milk delivers good bacteria, immunoglobulins (a type of antibody), digestive enzymes, growth factors, hormones, and nonessential fatty acids—about 100 elements that are not contained in baby bottle formula—nutrients that are vital for the full development of your baby's brain.[133] The composition of breast milk changes over time. The ratio of nutrients on day one is very different from what it is eight to twelve months later. Baby bottle formula ratios are stagnant.

Chapter 2 reviewed the importance of developing a healthy brain, and brain development explodes in the first three months of life. This explosion is dependant on nutrition. Breast milk contains brain-healthy essential fatty acids (EFAs), which are crucial for neurotransmitter production and brain and nervous system development. Soy formulas either do not contain any EFAs or only trace amounts.[134] Breast milk also contains cholesterol, imperative for a baby's growing brain and nervous system. Soy formula contains no cholesterol. According to Dr. Enig, "Infants who don't get enough cholesterol in their diets during the first years when their brains are developing risk a loss of cognitive function.[135]

Breast milk also contains lactose, which is used for, among other things, brain development. "In reality, very few infants are lactose intolerant," Dr. Daniel writes, "although many are allergic to the processed proteins and other ingredients in milk-based formula."[136] In breast milk the balance of lactose and fats creates a healthy, happy baby with balanced brain neurotransmitters.

Soy formula, which incidentally is not "milk" but rather heat- and chemical-processed juice from a legume, possesses a number of problems: Soy formula is not as digestible as breast milk and may cause loose stools and gas. Soy estrogens from soy formula have been linked to rising rates of ADD/ADHD and learning disabilities. Soy formula contains high amounts of manganese, which can cause brain damage resulting in learning disorders, ADD/ADHD, and even violent behavior.[137] It may also contribute to the development of cancer [138] and thyroid damage.[139] As soy formula delivers to your baby the equivalent amount of estrogen of three to five birth control pills each day, it may contribute to precocious puberty in girls and delayed puberty or feminization in boys; and soy formula may contribute to the development of type 1 diabetes.[140]

A January 2006 study demonstrated that the isoflavone genistein can disrupt the development of the ovaries of newborn female mice, causing reproductive problems and infertility.[141]

Soy formula contains a natural protein called phytic acid that blocks the absorption of calcium, magnesium, iron, copper, and zinc. These minerals are important for brain health. Depletion of magnesium and calcium is associated with neurological malfunctions such as depression, anger, and learning disabilities, to name a few problems.

While American parents may find it confidence-inspiring to hear assurances from the soy industry that Asian babies have been raised on soy milk for centuries, as it turns out, this claim is false. Soy milk is a very recent aberration in Asia that was first promoted by well-meaning Seventh Day Adventist missionaries and subsequently by American soy industries attempting to infiltrate new markets. If you think questioning the potential health hazards of soy formula as nothing more than Internet paranoia, you have to ask yourself whether any scientists are ringing alarm bells about the health risks of breast milk? If not, then you have to ask yourself, is breast milk the very best food for my baby?

Real, living food for babies is breast milk. If you can't breastfeed, you can find recipes for healthy infant formula in Sally Fallon's cookbook, *Nourishing Traditions: The Cookbook That Challenges Politically Correct Nutrition and the Diet Dictocrats.*

Vegetarian or vegan women often rely on soy foods as an alternative to animal proteins during pregnancy and breastfeeding, and so finding out that soy is not a good alternative might be deflating. The logical next option would be rice and beans, which together form a complete protein. A complete protein contains an adequate proportion of all of the twenty essential amino acids. Although rice and beans together do make a complete protein, one cup of brown rice contains 5 grams of protein but also 46 grams of carbohydrate, and one cup of kidney beans contains 15 grams of protein but also 40 grams of carbohydrate. So eating two cups of the rice-and-bean combo provides a mere 20 grams of protein but packs 86 grams of carbohydrate. Unless you are an extreme athlete like some of the vegan

Ashtanga yogis I know or engage in comparable vigorous activity every day, 86 grams of carbohydrate is too much sugar entering the system at one meal. Equally important, rice and beans do not contain cholesterol, B_{12}, or ideal ratios of essential fatty acids.

Women who eat a vegetarian or vegan diet may want to consider making concessions during pregnancy and breastfeeding for the sake of their baby's optimal health and brain development. Drinking vitamin-, mineral-, enzyme-, and protein-rich natural, raw milk and eating organically produced eggs and cod liver oil as well as small fish such as herring, sardines, and anchovies for complete amino acids, cholesterol, and essential fatty acids will guarantee that your baby's brain is getting the nutrients it needs for proper formation and development. (Small fish feed on even smaller fish and so have not consumed as much mercury as, say, tuna or salmon.) As a baby's brain explodes in development in the first three months of life, I can't really see any alternatives to giving your body—and thus your baby's body—these essentially fatty acids for brain development.

There are many FDA scientists who don't believe that soy is healthy and who were against the FDA allowing factory-food producers to use soyhealthy claims on their packaging. In fact, in January 2006 the American Heart Association, after concluding a review of a decade of studies, announced that there was no evidence that soy affords us any of the purported miraculous health benefits, essentially debunking the FDA-approved cholesterol-lowering claim. From 1939 to 2010 there have been numerous unbiased studies demonstrating the deleterious health effects of soy.[142]

The fact that soy, soy, soy has permeated our factory-food chain should be enough to give anyone pause. We are no longer talking about thousands of factory-food products that scream SOY! on their labels. We're talking about virtually every factory food on the market today. Today it's nearly impossible to find a loaf of supermarket bread, a can of tuna, or any other supermarket product that doesn't contain a refined soy ingredient. Is it just me, or is the wholesale takeover of livestock feed, the infant formula market, and the factory-food supply not just a little bodysnatcherish? Over the past fifty years, Americans have been force-fed factory foods made out of bizarrely refined substances, and now the medical establishment mentality of isolating active ingredients from their whole plant form has resulted in our factory-food supply becoming permeated with bizarrely refined additives.

I've devoted a lot of space to soy because it's important for us to understand how virtually any substance can be slipped under our noses beneath the banner of "healthy" while we are busy living our lives. Industrially processed soy is not the first unhealthy substance to be foisted on Americans, and with billions invested in food technology it definitely will not be the last.

Consider that there are three types of phytoestrogens: isoflavones found in soy, coumestans found in clover and alfalfa sprouts, and lignans mainly found in flaxseeds. Flax contains the lignan phytoestrogens that, like isoflavone phytoestrogens, can dampen thyroid function. In addition, flax is highly prone to rancidity (caused by oxygen, light, and heat), which creates free radicals. Putting flax in products that are cooked or otherwise heated and that sit on the shelf is counterproductive to health. But if corporations get a news flash that Americans want flax—or anything else—they will begin to hammer us with every imaginable form of flax food product. Right now we already see things like flax milk, flax cheese, flax margarine, flax shortening, flax salad dressing, flax power bars, flax cereal, flax crackers, flax baked goods, and flax dog and cat kibble. If it were cheap enough, fast-food restaurants would undoubtably be frying French fries in flaxseed oil.

Going back in time to the inception of the food industry provides an understanding of the logical progression of the development of the factory-food, diet, and drug industries, and how Americans fell under their spell. It began early in the twentieth century when doctors, researchers, and our government recognized that we had an epidemic rise in heart disease.

PART FIVE

The Fat Fiasco

CHAPTER NINE

Fat Kills!

THE LARD CRISIS HIT Britain hard in the Christmas season of 2004. The supply of pork fat, traditionally used to bake the flakiest of holiday piecrusts, had run low due to a snafu with European Union production regulations. Prices for lard climbed 20 percent, and eBay bids were up to $18 per container. British Lard Marketing Board founder Tim Allen was quoted in *Newsweek*, "If you launched [lard] as a product now, no one would touch it because it's not healthy."[143] Such is the enduring sentiment of most of the developed world: Fat kills.

This belief began fifty years ago with the wholesale embrace of the so-called lipid hypothesis by the medical community: the belief that elevated blood cholesterol levels are a risk factor for heart disease and that blood cholesterol levels are elevated by eating cholesterol-laden foods and saturated fat. The lipid hypothesis vilified historically consumed saturated fats, promoted the consumption of processed polyunsaturated vegetable oils, and instigated the low fat diet. These three factors worked in concert to prime the marketplace to be receptive to the introduction of thousands of factory products into our food supply that dramatically increased the incidence of disease and obesity in our country.

Meanwhile, the French never stopped gorging on butter, cheese, and cream, which led researchers to coin the term "the French paradox." To researchers, it's a mystery why the French can consume so much dietary fat and be so thin and have lower heart-disease rates. The only solution they could come up with is that it must be all the red wine that the French drink.

But today not all Americans shudder at the thought of lard (pork fat, which is made up of 50 percent monounsaturated fat, 40 percent saturated fat, and 10 percent polyunsaturated fat). A growing faction of renegade researchers, clinical nutritionists, M.D.s, and naturopathic physicians would return Americans to the same diet—rich in organic saturated fats and cholesterol-laden foods—that we ate prior to the year 1900, when heart disease was virtually nonexistent in the U.S. Many of these rebels are followers of the obscure research of a little-known dentist named Weston A. Price.

Born in Ontario, Canada, in 1870, Price earned a degree in dentistry and immigrated to the United States in 1893, settling in Cleveland, Ohio. In his practice, he was continually taken aback by the crowded, crooked, rotten teeth of the children of the relatively well to do. Concluding that nutrition was most likely the problem, Price and his intrepidly sturdy wife, Florence, set out in 1931 on a difficult expedition to study the effects of nutrition on human health and disease by examining the indigenous diets of fourteen savage groups of people: Swiss alpine villagers, Gaelics in Scotland, Eskimos in Alaska, North American Indians, Peruvian Indians, the Melanesians and Polynesians in the South Pacific, African tribes, Australian aborigines, and the Malay tribe and the Maori of New Zealand. Whenever possible, Price also studied members of the primitive tribes who had been in contact with modernized white races.[144] The results of his ten-year study were published in his meticulously documented tome (with photographs, thank goodness) entitled *Nutrition and Physical Degeneration* (1939).

The long and the short of it was that the primitive people who ate historically indigenous diets almost always had all thirty-two, perfectly aligned teeth, and cavities were a rarity. The photographs of these native people show smiles out of *People* magazine. They were attractive, cheerful, robust, fertile, and free from mental, dental, and degenerative diseases. The photographs of native people who ventured out to live on white man's food—sugar, flour, pasteurized milk, hydrogenated vegetable oils, and other factory foods—were more reminiscent of the backwoods folks in the

1972 movie *Deliverance*. Without exception, primitive people who became civilized in their eating habits developed infertility problems and suffered with gnarly, rotten teeth, and rank gums, as well as infectious, mental, and degenerative diseases and obesity.

The diets that promoted robust health consisted primarily of foods that are forbidden by our modern medical establishment: fat, fat, and more fat, from the organ meat of wild or grass-fed domesticated animals, to insects (including such savory treats as fly and ant eggs), birds, sea mammals, guinea pigs, bears and hogs, the egg yolks of various birds, whole raw milk, cheese, butter, and other dairy products, as well as the more conventionally acceptable fish, shellfish, fish organs, fish liver oils, and fish eggs.

Price shipped twenty thousand food samples back to America for analysis, including deep yellow butter—a product of grass-eating cows—that was a prized food of many of the cultures studied. When Price analyzed the butter, he found it to be exceptionally high in fat-soluble vitamins, particularly vitamins A and D. (Without these fat-soluble vitamins, humans cannot properly utilize minerals or absorb water-soluble vitamins.) From grass-fed dairy products, fatty organ meats, and some seafood, Price also isolated another biochemical catalyst for the absorption and utilization of minerals—which was also an immune system enhancer—a substance that he dubbed with the Flash Gordonish name ActivatorX, which has subsequently been identified as containing vitamin K. In addition, his research determined that the savages consumed four times the minerals and water-soluble vitamins and about ten times the fat-soluble vitamins that Americans were eating at that time (roughly seventy years ago).

Francis Pottenger, M.D., had just finished his residency at L.A. County Hospital in 1930, the year before Weston and Florence Price set out on their journey. During the years the Prices trekked the globe, Pottenger engaged in parallel research and became known for his research on more than 900 cats, which he conducted between 1932 and 1942.

Pottenger compared the effects of two diets on cats. Cats that were fed diets of raw milk and raw meat had shiny, petable fur, sound bones, and good teeth, and were parasite free, healthy, fertile, and loveable. The cats that were fed cooked meat and pasteurized milk gave birth to weak, puny kittens. These cats were riddled with fleas, ticks, intestinal parasites, skin diseases, and allergies. The females were she-devils, the males meek and cringing. They had terrible bone structure, and in fact, Pottenger observed the same types of facial and dental degeneration in his cats that Price found in his civilized native people.[145]

Pottenger maintained, like Price, that where there is smoke there is fire. In other words, terrible bone structure and messed-up teeth indicate poor nutrition, just as sound bone structure and pearly whites indicate healthy nutrition. (This is not to say that, in this book, we're headed toward gnawing on raw meat, but only to point out that both Price's and Pottenger's research demonstrate that nutrient-dead foods—i.e., civilized diets—produce poor health, while untampered-with, real, living food produces robust health.) However, because of the prior rejection of nutrition as standard of care, neither Price's nor Pottenger's research made a lasting impression on the medical community. On the contrary, events unfolded within the American population that spurred the medical community in the opposite direction, so that dairy and meat would be vilified and factory fats that were made in laboratories would be glorified as health-giving.

From 1900 to the end of World War II, the rise in myocardial infarction brought the medical community together in an attempt to figure out the cause. Atherosclerosis is the stiffening of the coronary arteries combined with plaque, which is a coating on the artery walls. In some people with advanced atherosclerosis, arterial plaque becomes so thick and protruding that it blocks off the blood and accompanying oxygen supply to the heart, thus causing radiating discomfort called angina. If blood and oxygen flow to part of the heart is completely blocked, the part of the heart that is affected will die. This condition is known as myocardial infarction or a heart attack.

Today 2,500 Americans die of cardiovascular disease every day, an average of one death every thirty-four seconds.[146] Each year ten million Americans are disabled by cardiovascular diseases, including heart disease, stroke, and disorders of the circulatory system. Children now suffer from heart disease, a degenerative condition formerly related to aging.

Prior to 1900, when Americans ate butter, cheese, whole milk, red meat, beef and lamb tallow, chicken fat, and lard, heart disease caused only 9 percent of all deaths. Today heart disease causes 30.3 percent of deaths. The first reported incidence of myocardial infarction didn't occur until 1926. By then Americans' diets were changing rapidly, with factory foods infiltrating our food chain. But our medical community didn't use research like Price's and Pottenger's to determine ways to get Americans eating real foods again. Instead, they fixated on cholesterol as the culprit in the rise of heart disease and discouraged the consumption of historically eaten animal fats.

In 1953, when biochemist Ancel Keys, Ph.D., argued that heart attacks could be prevented by avoiding cholesterol-laden foods, the scientific community was primed to embrace this message.[147] Scientists had already observed that the incidence of heart disease was low in occupied Europe after World War II at a time when Europeans were eating less cholesterol (meat, dairy, eggs). Ignored was the fact that sugar, flour, alcohol, cigarettes, and gas were scarce after the war and so people were eating less sugar and refined white flour, drinking and smoking less, and walking more. Then there was the obvious fact that butter and other animal fats are yellow and viscous, just like the fatty deposits found in the arteries of autopsied heart attack victims. It stood to reason: Cut out the cholesterol from animal fat in your diet, and you would not have plaque in your arteries (even though it contains only an insignificant amount of cholesterol along with collagen, calcium, and other materials).

Keys arrived at his lipid hypothesis in his famous Seven Countries Study, in which he maintained that countries with the highest fat intake had the highest rates of heart disease.[148] Keys was accused of handpicking data from the countries that supported his hypothesis and ignoring those that didn't (data was available from twenty-two countries). And just as he ignored data from the countries that didn't support his hypothesis,

Keys ignored the fact that in 1936, pathologist Kurt Landé and biochemist Warren Sperry of the Department of Forensic Medicine at New York University conducted an extensive study that found no correlation between the degree of atherosclerosis and blood cholesterol levels.[149] These findings were repeated by Indian researchers in 1961, Polish researchers in 1962, Guatemalan researchers in 1967, and Americans in 1982.[150]

Lipid biochemist David Kritchevsky, Ph.D., was a young Russian immigrant in 1954 when he conducted studies that demonstrated that rabbits fed artificial cholesterol had elevated blood cholesterol levels while rabbits fed polyunsaturated vegetable oils had lowered cholesterol levels.[151] (Fats fall roughly into three categories: saturated, monounsaturated, and polyunsaturated. The polyunsaturated fats used in animal studies were extracted from soy and corn.)

Similar studies, also done on animals, were said to prove the lipid hypothesis. But by the late 1950s, scientists understood the flaws inherent in studies that force-fed plant-eating rabbits an artificial, species-inappropriate diet. Dr. Kritchevsky agreed that artificial cholesterol is an unnatural food for a rabbit and remarked, "Alexander Pope said, 'The proper study of mankind is man.' But I don't think the average guy would submit to a diet and let me tear his aorta out after six months. Animal experiments are just animal experiments." Nevertheless, animal experiments using inappropriate vegetarian test subjects were used to promote the lipid hypothesis.

It didn't take much to frighten people into believing that saturated fats caused heart disease. America originated with Puritanism, after all. Like sex (which feels good), if food tastes good, it must be bad. So millions of Americans stopped eating eggs and butter and pushed away their steaks.

Next came the instruction to eat polyunsaturated vegetable oils to lower your risk for heart disease. This pronouncement was easy to swallow too because polyunsaturated fats were found to lower cholesterol levels in animal studies. What was not understood at the time was that polyunsaturated fatty acids lower blood cholesterol because when these fatty acids, which are soft, are deposited into the cell membrane, the body must stabilize the membrane by pulling cholesterol, which is denser, out of the bloodstream and putting it into the cell structure. But because polyunsaturated fats were found to lower cholesterol levels in animal studies, the edible oil industry began heavily promoting polyunsaturated fats to the American public as heart healthy.

"The trouble is that science moves rather slowly, but promoters move quickly," Dr. Kritchevsky said. "If you published six papers that said horse manure is good for you, two days later it would be on the market." And so it was with polyunsaturated fat research. The edible oil industry hit the ground running with their polyunsaturated fats (and their wallets open to all government and health agencies that could help them promote these fats). Meanwhile science was left plodding slowly behind.

It's always been very difficult to introduce a new idea into the scientific community, said Dr. Kritchevsky. "You know there's an old saying that every new finding goes through three stages. First people say it's against the Bible. Then they say it's not wrong, but it's not important. Well, it's important, but we always knew it." And so researchers were not willing to pay attention to any new evidence that supported dietary cholesterol and discouraged the consumption of processed polyunsaturated fats. They had all the evidence they needed to support the lipid hypothesis, to continue to vilify saturated animal fats, and to promote the consumption of polyunsaturated vegetable oils.

Today the health benefits of small amounts of polyunsaturated fats as found in whole foods such as cold-water fish—cod, herring, mackerel, salmon, sardines, or fresh, nonrancid oils extracted from these fish—are well known. But the edible oil industry did not market naturally occurring polyunsaturated fats to Americans in small amounts. The oil industry manufactured and marketed factory fats made from polyunsaturated vegetable oils such as soy and corn and virtually inundated our food supply with these fats. Dr. Kritchevsky said that it wasn't "a scam where two guys got together in back of the poolroom and said, 'Let's do this.'" Rather, it was the unregulated self-interest of capitalism that got Americans eating dangerous polyunsaturated vegetable fats.

CHAPTER TEN

What Are Polyunsaturated Fats Anyway?

PRIOR TO 1900, VEGETABLE oil was processed out of its natural state (such as corn oil from corn) by small, slow, cold-temperature batch presses. But in the 1920s, industrialists realized that human-dependent, small batch cold-pressing was too slow and not profitable enough, so they switched to automated heat and chemical processes that produced high volumes of oil at a greater profit.

Unfortunately, these new processes did very bad things to oils. In simple terms, fatty acids are chains of carbon atoms with hydrogen atoms filling the available bonds. A fatty acid is considered "saturated" when all available carbon bonds are occupied by a hydrogen atom. Monounsaturated fatty acids lack two hydrogen atoms, and polyunsaturated fatty acids lack still more. The level of hydrogen atom "saturation" determines how stable, or resistant to rancidity, a fatty acid is when exposed to heat, light, and oxygen. Saturated fatty acids are the least likely to oxidize/go rancid (create free radicals), monounsaturated fatty acids are the second most stable, and polyunsaturated fatty acids are the most fragile under these conditions.

The heat and chemical processing of polyunsaturated oils goes like this: Seeds, kernels, fruits, and nuts are hulled and ground, which exposes their oils to air and light and begins the rancidity process, creating free radical oxidation.

After hulling, the pulp is cooked for up to two hours at high temperatures—creating more free radical oxidation. Subsequent pressing also exposes the oil to heat, causing a chemical reaction that essentially creates the same chemical constituent as plastic, varnish, and shellac. Another method of removing the oil from raw sources uses chemical solvents, which also infuses the oil with free radicals.

After the initial heat and chemical processing of vegetable oils, the oils are then often "de-gummed": Phosphoric acid (used in bathroom cleaners) and high temperatures to remove impurities and nutrients, a process that increases rancidity/free radical oxidation. To remove free fatty acids and minerals from the oil, sodium hydroxide (i.e., lye, which is also used in Drano and Easy Off oven cleaner) and high temperatures are used. Subsequent bleaching removes undesirable pigments from oils. At this point, the oils may possess pungent odors and tastes that must be removed through a high-temperature deodorizing process.

Some of these oils end up in row upon row of glistening, sanitary-looking cooking oils on your supermarket shelves. But much of this heat- and chemical-processed oil is partially hydrogenated. This process alters the molecular structure of the fatty acid by adding hydrogen atoms, changing the chemical structure from a "cis" shape that is recognized and utilized by human cells to a "trans" shape that is foreign and lethal to human physiology. Partial hydrogenation turns polyunsaturated vegetable oil into a hardened-butter-like product that holds up better than liquid oils in food-production processes and has a longer shelf life.

The industrialized fats that were introduced into our food chain were a far cry from the organic, saturated animal fats eaten by Price's native peoples. But these factory-polyunsaturated vegetable fats were touted as healthier than butter and other historically consumed animal fats. And in the minds of Americans, the word "polyunsaturated" became synonymous with protection against heart disease. However, back when scientists first decided the lipid hypothesis was the black-and-white answer to heart disease and began their campaign to eradicate saturated fat and cholesterol-laden foods from the American diet and to replace these fats with polyunsaturated vegetable oils, in their haste they overlooked one simple and very important fact: By the 1950s people had already, for personal economic reasons, significantly decreased consumption of butter and increased consumption of factory-polyunsaturated vegetable fats in the forms of oil, margarine, and shortening.[152]

In 1900, the average American consumed 18 pounds of butter per year but only 3 pounds of polyunsaturated vegetable fat in shortening and margarine. By the 1950s, Americans were eating 10 pounds of polyunsaturated vegetable fat and only 10 pounds of butter per year. [153] Americans had decreased their consumption of butter and increased consumption of polyunsaturated vegetable fats, and heart disease had increased correspondingly.

Some scientists questioned whether there might be a connection between the rise in polyunsaturated vegetable oil consumption and the rise in heart disease. But these rumblings were mere squeaks compared with the roar coming out of Madison Avenue—a din paid for by factory-fat makers who coined the slogan "Healthy for Your Heart" and whose sole interest was influencing Americans to eat factory-polyunsaturated vegetable oils.

Yet empirical evidence was mounting against the lipid hypothesis and the introduction of polyunsaturated vegetable fats. Empirical evidence is derived from observation. Let's say you notice that your flower garden does better with one fertilizer over another. You don't need a study to tell you what you see with your own eyes. Empirical evidence demonstrated that we had been healthier and had less heart disease before we traded our traditionally consumed diet that included saturated fats for a factory diet including factory fats. Still, the AHA launched the Prudent Diet in 1956, which encouraged Americans to replace saturated fats with polyunsaturated vegetable oils.

The expression "You are what you eat" aptly describes what happens when you eat any type of fat. "Dietary fat . . . is absorbed pretty much as it goes in and is then burned for energy, stored as adipose tissue, or incorporated into cell membranes and other tissues in just about the same form in which you ate it," write Michael Eades, M.D., and Mary Dan Eades, M.D., in their book *The Protein Power Lifeplan: A New Comprehensive Blueprint for Optimal Health.* "If you go out to a ball game and eat a hot dog, the next day . . . if you look in the mirror, the fat in the hot dog will be staring back at you, unchanged, in the lipid bilayers of your skin, in the whites of your eyes, and even in your brain. That's why it pays to be careful about the types of fat that you eat."[154]

Salad dressing, cheese "foods," deep-fried foods, vegetable cooking oils, imitation meat products, mayonnaise and mayolike products, fake sour cream and dessert toppings, margarine, movie and microwave popcorn, nondairy artificial cream products, soy spreads, and vegetable shortening are all examples of toxic factory fats. But just because food makers have processed polyunsaturated oils into poisons doesn't mean that you should avoid polyunsaturated fats altogether, because naturally occurring polyunsaturated fats are health-giving.

The two polyunsaturated fatty acids that are the most important for you to understand are linolenic acid (omega-3) and linoleic acid (omega-6). Omega-3 and -6 can't be made in the body and thus are referred to as "essentially fatty acids," or EFAs.[155]

Studies show that omega-3 promotes lean body mass, which means that including omega-3 fatty acids in your diet will help you burn fat and build muscle.[156] Omega-3 fats are essential to cellular health. Without omega-3 you will likely end up with dry skin, premature wrinkles, thin, brittle hair and nails, depression and other neurotransmitter imbalances, chronic constipation and a malfunctioning immune system, leading to muscle and joint pain and arthritis.

The ideal and traditional ratio of omega 3:6 polyunsaturated fatty acids is about 1:1-2. Today we consume a 1:10-46 ratio. Too high levels of omega-6 promote inflammation, and this high ratio of omega 3-6 has been shown to be a major contributing factor in the development of cancer and other degenerative diseases. Omega-6 is found in meat—but unfortunately it's too high of a ratio now that factory-raised animals are fed an unnatural diet of grains and soybeans. Like humans, they are what they eat, so when we eat them, we're eating too many omega-6s. Because we still need some omega-6 (and saturated animal fat), it's important to eat free-range, grass-fed animal *foods.*

Omega-6 is the precursor of gamma-linolenic acid (GLA), used in the production of prostaglandins, which are fatty acids that act as hormones. Prostaglandins are essential to the proper functioning of each cell and play a role in many biological processes, including regulating your immune system. Prostaglandins maintain homeostasis in your body—the body's adaptive responses that attempt to return the body from an abnormal state back to the status quo. GLA is an anti-inflammatory agent, inhibits the growth of some cancer cells, aids fat metabolism, and helps prevent rheumatoid arthritis, cardiovascular disease, high blood pressure, premenstrual syndrome, and neurological problems related to diabetes. The GLA oils black currant, borage, and evening primrose can be taken in supplemental capsule form.

Now that people are becoming aware of the health-giving properties of omega-3 fatty acids, factory-fat makers are jumping on the bandwagon to produce their factory omega-3 "spreads." However, it's important to note the distinction between factory omega-3 spreads and naturally occurring polyunsaturated fats. We now understand the fragile nature of the polyunsaturated fatty acids. These oils should be protected from heat, light, oxygen, and chemical processes. Just as when polyunsaturated vegetable oils were oxidized through heat and chemical processes, turning them basically into shellac, and those damaged fats were then partially hydrogenated, creating trans fats, omega-3 polyunsaturated fats are now being subjected to unnatural industrialization. Omega-3-fortified butter-like spreads like Smart Balance Omega Plus are not the same healthy polyunsaturated omega-3 fatty acids found in foods, no matter what the ads say, because manufacturing processes alter, reduce, or deaden the healthy biological properties of oils.

Processed polyunsaturated oils not to eat are corn, cottonseed, safflower, soy, and sunflower. Because of the heat/chemical/oxygen processing of oils, two other oils, canola and peanut, which are mostly monounsaturated fatty acids, should also be avoided.

Examples of healthy polyunsaturated fats are cold-water fish such as cod, herring, mackerel, salmon, sardines and their oils, flax seeds (in moderation), krill oil, marine plankton, and GLA oils (borage, evening primrose, and black currant).

My grandma was a believer in the power of healthy oils and chugged olive oil directly from the bottle every day and more if she needed to "fix herself." Olive oil is a monounsaturated oil. Monounsaturated fats lower LDL cholesterol in the blood, are necessary for healthy skin, maintain the structural integrity of neural membranes, and are high in the antioxidant vitamin E, which boosts immunity and provides protection against certain cancers, such as breast and colon cancer. Monounsaturated fats are more prone to the creation of oxidizing free radicals than are saturated oils when they are cooked, so it's best to eat monounsaturated foods and oils at room temperature, with the exception of olive oil, which can be used for cooking. Examples of healthy monounsaturated oils are almonds and their oil, avocados and their oil, cashews, fowl fat, hazelnuts and their oil, lard, olives and olive oil, peanuts and peanut butter, and pork (including bacon). (Saturated fat is the subject of chapter 13.)

It seems crazy in retrospect that anyone could be convinced that fats made in a laboratory were healthier than butter, a naturally occurring dietary fat that was historically eaten by humans. But as a friend of mine said, "Eighty percent of Americans believe that wrestling on TV is real." In other words, if there's enough pomp and press—or, in this case, studies—we'll go along.

CHAPTER ELEVEN

How Studies Influence Food, Diets, and Drugs

IN THE EARLY 1970s, I visited a friend who was going through medical school. He fixed himself instant Top Ramen for dinner and offered me some, too, but I declined. "I can't believe you're going to eat those chemicals," I said.

"The human body is made up of chemicals," he replied. That statement—from a medical student—blew my mind and has stayed with me all these years.

Modern medicine has advanced beyond our wildest dreams to a point where the impossible is now possible, and many brilliant, caring, hardworking M.D.s are able to perform seeming miracles on a daily basis. As extraordinary as medical feats are today, the advancements that are clearly obtainable in the near future boggle and excite the mind. To achieve this level of medical competence takes years of dedicated, tenacious hard work and sacrifice. However, nutrition is one area that most doctors have no experience with and should not lecture us about. Since Louis Pasteur's germ theory of disease influenced Western medical schools to reject nutrition as an important aspect of medicine, doctors haven't seen fit to learn about nutrition. And I say this with all due respect, as I have many doctor friends and am confident that most of them wouldn't profess to be qualified to give nutritional advice.

If a person wanted to go into the business of winemaking and become a vintner of fine wines, that person might end up at a school like UC Davis studying viticulture. The study of viticulture includes how and what to feed the grapevines in order to produce the best-quality grape. But somehow modern medicine has felt it unnecessary to understand—and teach—how and what to feed the human body to produce the best-quality human being.

After medical training, M.D.s are required to obtain continuing education credits every year. Other than these required courses, doctors learn from drug reps, medical journals, conferences and lectures, books, and the media. Sixty to 70 percent of nonsurgical continuing education comes to doctors via drug reps, referred to as "detail people," as in that's where docs get the details on which new drugs have hit the market, not about how to prevent patients from having to take drugs in the first place. (Now that the feds have squeezed pharmaceutical companies to knock off the gifts to doctors, this industry has cleverly turned to recruiting beautiful, sexy former cheerleaders as drug reps.)[157]

Very few doctors independently pursue an education in nutrition.

Nutritional information in medical journals is highly tainted. Nutritional research is often funded by the food industry. A 1996 survey disclosed that nearly 30 percent of university researchers investigating food products accepted funding from the food industry. Another survey demonstrated that 34 percent of the lead authors of 800 papers in molecular biology and medicine were involved in patents, served on advisory committees, and/or held shares in the companies that would benefit from their research. The *Journal of Nutritional Education* accepts financial contributions from eight corporate patron friends and four corporate sustaining friends, and the *American Journal of Clinical Nutrition* accepts financial assistance from twenty-eight companies and associations that support selected educational activities. Such sponsors are Coca-Cola, Gerber, Nestlé/Carnation, Monsanto, Proctor & Gamble, Roche Vitamins, Slim-Fast Foods, and the Sugar Association. In addition, drug advertising contributed $20 million per year to prestigious journals such as the *New England Journal of Medicine* and the *Journal of the American Medical Association*, which publish the supposedly latest nutrition research.[158]

A National Institutes of Health (NIH) survey demonstrated that 33 percent of U.S. scientists admitted that they engaged in "unethical practices" such as manipulating or hiding data, designing their studies to reach certain conclusions, or altering the conclusions of their studies to satisfy sponsors.[159] (The NIH is the primary federal agency for conducting and supporting medical research.)

With nutritional education coming from factory-food manufacturers, our medical community's collective consciousness has deteriorated to the point where diseased and injured patients in hospitals are served Ensure, Jello, Diet 7-Up, Better'n Eggs, Kellogg's Corn Flakes, and coffee with Coffee-mate Creamer and NutraSweet. Hospitals are also the new frontier for fast-food franchises.

Unfortunately, doctors are notoriously skeptical—to the point of scorn—of empirical evidence, which they refer to as "anecdotal." If you went into your doctor's office claiming that ingesting a certain substance caused you a health problem, he or she would not likely agree with you unless you provided evidence that that substance caused said symptoms. The evidence they want is at least one double blind, peer-reviewed study that is published in a peer-reviewed medical journal. A double-blind study means that neither the test subjects nor the researchers know what treatment the test subjects are receiving. At the conclusion of the study, the code is broken and the data analyzed. This method eliminates observer and test-subject bias. Peer-reviewed means that researchers of equal standing to the investigators evaluate the quality of study. Once a double-blind study is published in a peer-reviewed medical journal, the conclusions of the study are considered medical truth.

Over the course of fifty years, medical doctors have given Americans devastating nutritional advice about fats. This advice has encouraged Americans to eschew the historical human diet of real fat in favor of highly industrialized fats. Much of this advice was based on the results of studies.

There are many problems with studies. For one, it's only with absolutes that you can even begin to approach an absolute conclusion. The variables of human experience, genetics, and behavior automatically render results of human trials inconclusive, even if your test subjects were selected from a pool of virtually identical individuals, either male or female, sharing the same race, height, weight, dietary and exercise history, sleep patterns, cigarette and alcohol use, baseline cholesterol numbers, prescription and OTC medication use, sex lives, TV habits, golf scores, and number of children (alive and dead). You would still have to have a team of unbiased scientists from another planet examine the results because, again, human beings are flawed, and when they want to prove something they will go to nearly any length. When a researcher sets out to prove a hypothesis, he or she is looking for that proof of that hypothesis in the results of whatever study he or she conducts. Research protocols are not perfect, and data can be juggled or ignored, corners cut, and so on, so that a researcher is likely to get the results he or she is looking for, especially if they stand to make money from any ventures that rely on a hypothesis being correct. And scientists and doctors who have spent their entire careers hyping a hypothesis and perhaps have lucrative clinics, books, and other products based on this premise are not likely to back down from their original position.

I've cited studies throughout this book, but it's my opinion that nutritional studies should always be weighed against empirical evidence because there are just too many problems with studies. Again, most studies are paid for by the industries that stand to profit by the results of the studies. For example, over the past twenty years, soy symposiums where researchers present their findings have been funded by multi-billion-dollar soy-producing corporations and associations, including the Archer Daniels Midland Company, Monsanto, the Central Soya Company, the United Soybean Board, Cargill Soy Protein Products/Cargill Nutraceuticals, and the Illinois Soybean Association. Many of the studies presented are made possible by grants from these and other soy-producing corporations.

And it's not just the soy industry. Most scientists rely on funding from industries to do research. If they don't cooperate (i.e., provide research results that are consistent with the views of their benefactors), they have their funding (salaries) cut off.

Another problem with studies is that few doctors bother to read them. If they do, they most likely read the abstract, which is not as comprehensive as the body of the article. Ask your doctor why he or she supports avoiding saturated fat and cholesterol, eating soy, eating a low fat diet, taking statin drugs, or any other conventionally accepted doctrine that's floated today and he or she will likely say because of studies. OK, exactly what studies do you mean? I would venture to say that few doctors could legitimately say that they poured over the medical literature and analyzed the results of the pros and cons of the views they support.

At the same time, since the introduction of processed polyunsaturated fats there have been medical doctors and scientists who chose to stray from the status quo in search of deeper answers into the mysterious rise in heart disease.

CHAPTER TWELVE

Finally, Americans Are Told the Truth About Trans Fats

IN JULY 1971, Senator George McGovern (D-SD) announced the formation of the Select Committee on Nutrition and Human Needs, which would hold hearings on the relationship between diet and heart disease—and whose purpose was to prove that eating dietary saturated fat was as bad as cigarette smoking. McGovern declared that he would hear testimony only from those on the side of polyunsaturated vegetable oils. He didn't want to hear any testimony from scientists or representatives from the dairy and meat industries, who wanted to argue that eating meat, dairy products, and eggs might not be a contributing factor in heart disease.

Numerous scientists voiced skepticism and wanted to present opposing scientific papers and to encourage further discussion as to the real cause of heart disease. Nevertheless, it was ultimately McGovern's committee that, by 1977—having come to nowhere near unanimous conclusions—solidified the lipid hypothesis as official policy with the issuing of the USDA's mandate to eat less fat.

In May 1978, Mary Enig, then a biochemistry doctoral student at the University of Maryland, was scratching her head over the McGovern report. The committee had reached their conclusions in part because of their assumptions that the increased consumption of animal fats had caused the rise in heart disease. But Enig knew that the consumption of animal fats had declined steadily, while polyunsaturated vegetable fat intake had increased. In addition, Enig was aware of numerous studies that contradicted the committee's conclusions regarding the correlation between fat intake and breast and colon cancers. She poured over the USDA data that McGovern's committee had used and, when she finished her analysis, submitted her findings to *The Journal of the Federation of American Societies for Experimental Biology.*[160]

Enig's article claimed that the McGovern report had it all wrong about the correlation between dietary fat and cancer. She offered up data that demonstrated that the use of hydrogenated polyunsaturated vegetable oils predisposed consumers to cancer, but that animal fats provided protection against cancer. She claimed that the McGovern committee's analysts manipulated the data to get the results they wanted. Her article urged immediate investigation into the dangers of trans-fatty acids.

By the time Dr. Enig had reached her initial conclusions all those decades ago about saturated fats and trans fats, other researchers also understood the problems. Scientists continued to demonstrate that there was virtually no correlation between animal fat and other cholesterol-laden food intake and blood cholesterol.[161] Many studies concluded that thickening of the arterial walls is simply a natural, unavoidable process that has nothing to do with eating saturated fat and cholesterol.[162] Numerous scientists were also recognizing that total cholesterol numbers are meaningless. People with low cholesterol are more likely to have blocked arteries than those with high cholesterol.[163]

Mary Enig and her fellow researchers at the University of Maryland clocked thousands of hours in the lab analyzing the trans-fat content of hundreds of factory foods. The researchers found that shortenings used in cookies, chips, and baked goods contained more than 35 percent trans fat and that many baked goods and industrialized foods contained much more partially hydrogenated vegetable oil than their labels disclosed. Enig's analyses confirmed that (at that time) the average American consumed at least 12 grams of trans fat per day. (Today Americans eat an average of 6 grams of trans fats per day.)[164]

Enig's research concluded that trans fats interfere with the enzymes that neutralize carcinogens while increasing the enzymes that exacerbate the damage of carcinogens. Trans fats also increase (the so-called bad) LDL cholesterol and triglycerides, and lower (the so-called good) HDL cholesterol. Trans fats make blood platelets sticky, interfere with insulin actions, cause aberrant cellular structures, create free radicals, and lower immune response. These factors contribute to the development of insulin resistance, type 2 diabetes, hypertension, cancer, and cardiovascular disease. Trans-fatty acids lower cream volume in breast milk, and are linked to low birth weight; in men they decrease testosterone and increase levels of abnormal sperm, and in women they can shorten gestation. [165]

Trans fats also have a deleterious effect on the brain and nervous system. The human body doesn't reject trans-fatty acids as foreign but uses whatever fat it has on board to build cellular structures. And because trans fats can cross the blood-brain barrier, they are incorporated into brain cell membranes and are thus linked to neurodegenerative disorders such as multiple sclerosis (MS), Parkinson's disease, and Alzheimer's disease, as well as childhood neurological disorders such as ADD, ADHD, and autism.

Although Dr. Enig and other researchers came to these dire conclusions about trans fats, their findings were drowned out by the overwhelming support for the lipid hypothesis, which essentially diverted attention away from the dangers of trans fats and encouraged Americans to eat more factory-polyunsaturated fats. Because our medical and scientific community had endorsed polyunsaturated vegetable fats as heart healthy, promoters had already permeated our food chain with hydrogenated and partially hydrogenated fats (containing trans fats).

Since her early years as a graduate student, Dr. Enig has been a driving force in compelling the FDA to enforce the labeling of trans fats on products, which went into law on January 1, 2006. It is because of Dr. Enig that we are now aware of the dangers of trans fats. It's a telling commentary that although Dr. Enig has achieved some acclaim in the alternative health world for her efforts and contributions to Americans' well-being, she has nowhere near the household name status of Betty Crocker, that fictional character who has been used for decades to give science-fiction factory-foods a warm and fuzzy image.

It's highly likely that many food makers will continue to produce trans fat products—and that people will continue to consume those products. Even if labeling trans fats on products and banning trans fats in restaurants does make a small difference, this does nothing to hinder the marketing and sales of heat- and chemical-processed polyunsaturated vegetable fats that are just as much to blame for the epidemic of heart and other diseases.

Adding to consumer confusion is the fact that the medical industry and the government continue to categorize saturated fat together with trans fats as dangerous fats to avoid.

The truth may surprise you.

CHAPTER THIRTEEN

Saturated Animal Fat Is Good for You

WHEN I WAS 17, in 1967, I read *The Jungle* (1905), Upton Sinclair's exposé of the grisly and unhygienic conditions in the meatpacking industry. I felt reassured that public uproar after the publication of the novel had led to the passage of the Meat Inspection Act and other food-safety legislation, which I naively assumed had reformed the medieval slaughtering practices in the meatpacking industry. But thirty-eight years later, when I read Bob Dylan's memoir, *Chronicles, Volume One*, I was stopped cold. In 1961, Dylan migrated to New York City. He talks about a friend who had worked on the kill floor of an Omaha slaughterhouse. Dylan asked his friend what it was like, and he replied, "You ever heard of Auschwitz?"[166]

So why is it that we spend multi billions of dollars per year pampering our cats and dogs, and though we revile the imprisonment, torture, and brutal killing of innocent people, we accept the same treatment for the innocent animals that give us sustenance? As John Robbins explained in *Diet for a New America* (1987), all aspects of animal husbandry have taken a draconian turn in the last hundred years, as the food industry has operated with single-minded focus on one goal and one goal only: to save money. This means fattening up animals as cheaply as possible in as small a space as possible.

Although we may be able to compartmentalize our guilt over animal cruelty so we can continue to consume factory milk, meat, and eggs, ultimately the animals' horrible existence, garbage diet, drug intake, and gory deaths will come back to haunt us. The way an animal lives and its diet determines the nutritional value of its meat, milk, and eggs and, thus the consumers' subsequent health. It also explains why factory-raised saturated fat is almost as unhealthy as trans fat.

Factory animals are tethered, stalled, or otherwise tightly confined in dark factories or pens. They stand in their own waste and often drink water contaminated with, or are fed, their own or other animals' offal. [167] To save money on feed, animals are fed municipal garbage, stale cookies, poultry "litter," chicken feathers, and restaurant plate waste.[168] Concentrated Animal Feeding Operations (CAFOs), along with species-inappropriate feed, breed disease. (Species-inappropriate feed is composed of substances that the animal would not naturally eat and is not designed to digest and assimilate in a healthy way.) To treat these diseases, animals are given numerous drugs. According to cancer expert Dr. Samuel Epstein, "In the absence of effective federal regulation, the meat industry uses hundreds of animal feed additives, including antibiotics, tranquilizers, pesticides, animal drugs, artificial flavors, industrial wastes and growth-promoting hormones . . . The hazards of U.S. meat have retrogressed from the random fecal and bacterial contamination of Upton Sinclair's *The Jungle* to the brave new world of deliberate chemicalization."[169] It's not just the drugs and chemicals that animals are exposed to while living that we need to be concerned with. In a desperate attempt to prevent this meat from killing people it is routinely subjected to sanitizing processes, so CAFO meats also contain dangerous preservatives and disinfectants. Carcinogen and liver-damaging formaldehyde is used illegally to control bacterial growth on meat surfaces. Sodium tetraborate (used in Borax) is also used illegally in meat mixes. Chlorine, a known carcinogen, is used for microbial control of water in spin chillers in poultry slaughter. Hydrogen peroxide is used for bleaching cattle stomachs (tripes).[170] To kill *E. coli* and *Salmonella,* fatty slaughterhouse trimmings are liquefied in a centrifuge to extract the protein from the trimmings, blasted with ammonia gas, then flash frozen, producing a product referred to as "prime slime." This meat is routinely used in fast-food hamburgers, sold in grocery chains, and served in federal school programs.[171]

Although conventional wisdom is stuck on the belief that saturated fats are as unhealthy as trans fats, saturated fats and trans fats do not necessarily belong in the same sentence. Organically raised animal fat is a naturally occurring, historically eaten fatty acid with health-giving properties. Factory animal fat is almost as deadly as trans fats, but for a different reason: Because many toxins are fat-soluble, they permeate and are stored indefinitely in fat cells. When you eat factory-produced animal products, you are eating all the toxins that an animal consumed or was exposed to. Most trans-fatty acids are man-made aberrant molecules that destroy life. (There are naturally occurring trans fats in foods.) Because free radical oxidation generated by toxins is just as much a cause of heart disease as trans fats, you can say "factory-raised saturated animal fat and trans fat" in the same breath.

However, the medical community does not recognize the distinctions between organically raised saturated animal fat, factory-raised saturated animal fat, and man-made trans fats, and therefore continues to summarily campaign against "saturated fat and trans fat." (The uproar over trans fats has died down enough so that food makers can continue to add it to their products, listing partially hydrogenated fat in the fine print, and many consumers remain unaware.)

Historically, humans ate fat from organically raised animals in foods like butter, whole milk, cream, eggs, and meat. It's only been since World War II that saturated animal fats have been shunned by the medical community as a factor contributing to heart disease. But over the years, like Dr. Enig others questioned the campaign against animal fat. In the early 1960s, George V. Mann, Sc.D., M.D., Ph.D.—just as Dr. Weston Price did before him—took a team of researchers to Kenya to study the Maasai tribe, who virtually lived on milk, animal blood, and meat, and found that they did not suffer from heart disease.

Dr. Mann was a participating researcher in the most famous study of the causes of heart disease, the Framingham Heart Study.[172] This study has found no conclusive evidence that dietary fat contributes to heart disease. Dr. Mann said, "The diet-heart hypothesis has been repeatedly shown to be wrong, and yet, for complicated reasons of pride, profit, and prejudice, the hypothesis continues to be exploited by scientists, fundraising enterprises, food companies, and even governmental agencies. The public is being deceived by the greatest health scam of the century."[173]

During the mid-1980s you would have thought eggs were the spawn of Satan, but my grandma continued to refer to eggs as the perfect food. When I asked, "But Grandma, what about heart disease?" she replied in her Polish accent, "I don't know about that, honey" and fixed me a plate of eggs. She wasn't alone in her belief, because somewhere deep in our collective consciousness, Americans understood that eggs are a perfect food. Still the food industry tried hard to convince us—by using studies—that real eggs were bad for our health, but that weird science egg-like products out of a carton were healthy. And the condemnation of naturally occurring saturated fats is entrenched in our mind-set. For example, in *The South Beach Diet*, celebrity cardiologist cum diet doctor Arthur Agatston writes, "There is evidence now that immediately following a meal of saturated fats, there is dysfunction in the arteries, including those that supply the heart muscle with blood. As a result, the lining of the arteries (the endothelium) is predisposed to constriction and clotting. Imagine: Under the right (or rather, wrong) circumstances, eating a meal that's high in saturated fat can trigger a heart attack!"[174]

I contacted Dr. Agatston's office to obtain the study he used as "evidence" that "eating a meal that's high in saturated fat can trigger a heart attack." As it turns out, the study, "Effect of Single High Fat Meal on Endothelial Function in Healthy Subject," was published in the *American Journal of Cardiology* in 1997.[175] In this study one group was given a "high fat" meal of an Egg McMuffin, Sausage McMuffin, two hash-brown patties, and a noncaffeinated beverage (something from McDonald's). The other group was fed the "low fat" meal, which consisted of Frosted Flakes, skimmed milk, and orange juice.

I asked Dr. Enig for her opinion, and she explained that the subjects were tested for "endothelial function" by measuring the diameter change in the brachial artery after eating. Apparently there was a slight diameter change in the brachial arteries of the "high fat"–eating test subjects. However, Dr. Enig said, "For years we have been hearing that high fat foods raise so-called bad LDL cholesterol and blood pressure and therefore contribute to heart disease. But since that didn't happen in this study, the authors have declared that an inherently subjective measurement of 'endothelial function' is a better marker for heart disease. But was it saturated fat that caused the decline in endothelial function? Only 28 percent of the fat in the high fat meal was saturated. The rest was a combination of trans fats, monounsaturated, and polyunsaturated fat, any one of which or all together are the likely culprits in the decline in endothelial function." Dr. Enig explained that the high sugar meal did not likely contain MSG, whereas the high fat meal did contain MSG and that the presence of MSG also explained the decline in endothelial function.

To make the incendiary claim that saturated fat can trigger a heart attack, the researchers should have been able to cite other studies, said Enig. "As it becomes more and more obvious that cholesterol levels have little predictive value for heart disease—and that saturated fats in fact have little or no effect on cholesterol levels anyway—researchers are searching for other ways to demonize saturated fats."[176]

The lipid hypothesis, which has driven many Americans to fear eating saturated fats, has never been proven. In 1988 the U.S. Surgeon General's office embarked on a project to write the "final and definitive" report that would once and for all put any questions about the lipid hypothesis to rest. The plan was to gather all supporting evidence, have it bound nicely, have the requisite experts review it, and then publish it with pomp and circumstance. Unfortunately, the plan didn't go as smoothly as anticipated. After eleven years of active pursuit that consumed four project officers, no clear evidence could be found to prove the lipid hypothesis. The office killed the report without the pageantry.[177]

"The operative word is hypothesis," Dr. Kritchevsky told me. "The lipid hypothesis was a viable hypothesis until we learned more. The real sin here is that people [working in the field] who knew we were learning more wouldn't admit it because they were so comfortable with what was going on." (In other words, many researchers were receiving grants from the edible oil industry.)

The balanced diet that I'm talking about in this book—which will allow you to realize your genetic gifts—is comprised of the four basic food groups: protein, fats, nonstarchy vegetables, and carbohydrates. After protein, real, naturally occurring dietary fat is most important. Fatty acids make up 80 percent of our cellular structure and 60 percent of our brain. Fats are used to make neurotransmitters. Every cell membrane in your body is made up of fat. If you do not eat quality fats, your cells cannot function properly. Fats and cholesterol are used to make the hormones used by your endocrine system.

Fats slow down the absorption of food, so that you feel satisfied and can go for longer periods of time without feeling hunger. In fact, it's been our suppression of natural fats in our diet that has greatly contributed to our national unnatural hunger. "Suppression of natural appetites, such as eating processed fats instead of natural fats, leads to weird nocturnal habits, fantasies, fetishes, bingeing, and splurging," said Dr. Enig.[178]

Fats transport fat-soluble vitamins A, D, E, and K in your system and are necessary for the conversion of carotene to vitamin A, for mineral absorption, and for numerous metabolic processes. The antioxidant vitamins E, A, and D can't be absorbed into your bloodstream without the presence of fat in your intestines. That means that, in terms of antioxidants, which scavenge the free radicals that cause oxidation, all those dry salads we ate were for naught.

Eating a variety of fats every day is important because saturated, monounsaturated, and polyunsaturated fatty acids all provide different biological properties for the smooth operation of our metabolic processes.

Saturated fats provide energy for locomotion and metabolic processes and are the building blocks for cell membranes and hormones. Saturated fats strengthen your immune system, suppress production of tumors, and are necessary for your body to utilize essential fatty acids. Saturated animal fats from the meat and milk of pasture-raised, grass-fed animals contain conjugated linoleic acid (CLA), which has been shown to reduce the risk of atherosclerosis and cancer, and has the added benefit of increasing metabolic rate and burning fat. Saturated fats in organic animal products also contain enzymes (see page 147).

Saturated animal fat was not the only saturated fat to take a hit because of the lipid hypothesis. In the mid-1980s, the American Soybean Association (ASA), eager to increase the sales of soybean oil, sent "Fat Fighter Kits" to soybean farmers instructing them to lobby their elected officials about the dangers of tropical oils (palm, palm kernel, and coconut oil). Behind-the-scenes work by the ASA resulted in coconut oil being characterized as "poisoning America." An advertisement actually depicted a coconut as a bomb with a lighted fuse. Restaurants and factory-food manufacturers switched from healthy coconut oil to heat- and chemical-processed and hydrogenated soybean oil, and movie theaters switched from popping popcorn in "artery-clogging saturated" coconut oil to hydrogenated soybean oil, the deadliest oil on the market.[179]

Dr. Michael Eades told me, "Saturated fat, like coconut oil, has been vilified as 'artery-clogging,' but it's simply untrue. Polyunsaturated fats are easily oxidized and so we can say that they are, indeed 'artery-clogging.' But saturated fat doesn't easily oxidize so it doesn't collect in the arteries."

In *Over the Edge of the World: Magellan's Terrifying Circumnavigation of the Globe*, Laurence Bergreen writes of Magellan's sixteenth-century armada encountering tribes of healthy, beautiful, intelligent, fertile, coconut-eating Pacific islanders during their voyage. Bergreen writes of Magellan's reaction to the Philippine archipelago, "Perhaps they had found paradise . . . Each day Magellan fed coconut milk supplied by the generous Filipinos to the sailors still suffering from scurvy." With reverence, the expedition's chronicler Antonio Pigafetta's quill scratched out a description of the *cocho* (coconut) for all posterity to read. Bergreen writes that, "Pigafetta was so moved by the coconut's versatility that he declared, with some exaggeration, that two palm trees could sustain a family of ten for a hundred years."[180]

You have to wonder, if Pacific islanders historically ate coconuts, coconuts, and more coconuts, why then were they so breathtakingly healthy? Hawaiian islanders historically fit that same description and only became rotund and diseased after they eschewed their traditional diet—containing coconuts—and adopted the Westernized factory-food diet, including factory-processed vegetable oils.[181]

Coconut oil raises HDL cholesterol. It also contains antiviral and antimicrobial properties that have been found to be effective in combating viruses that cause influenza, measles, herpes, mononucleosis, hepatitis C, and AIDS; the fungi and yeast that result in ringworm, Candida, and thrush; parasites that cause intestinal infections, such as giardiasis; as well as bacteria that cause stomach ulcers, throat infections, pneumonia, sinusitis, rheumatic fever, food-borne illnesses, urinary tract infections, meningitis, gonorrhea, and toxic shock syndrome. No wonder Magellan's scurvy-suffering sailors indulged in coconut. Coconut oil is also thermogenic (fat burning—thus the body beautiful South Sea islanders). According to Dr. Enig, since allergies to coconut are caused by coconut proteins, coconut oil is probably safe for those who are allergic.[182]

A study in the *American Journal of Clinical Nutrition* in May 2010 demonstrated that vitamin D_3 is more effective in preventing flu than vaccines and antivirals.[183] In addition to Dr. Price's ten years of research on the benefits of fats such as whole, natural milk, there are numerous studies that prove the nutritional benefits of organic, raw, grass-fed milk, including those associated with vitamin D_3.[184] Natural vitamin D_3

prevents autoimmune diseases such as multiple sclerosis and rheumatoid arthritis and prevents osteoporosis.[185] Natural vitamin D_3 is also linked to improvement in mood and relief of symptoms of depression. Vitamin D_3 also modulates neuromuscular and immune function, reduces inflammation, and is necessary for bone growth and bone remodeling. Research has demonstrated that there is a seasonal correlation between Vitamin D_3 levels and influenza, as being in the sunshine means more vitamin D_3. The main source of vitamin D is conversion from sunshine. In food it's found in salmon, sardines, shrimp, whole milk, cod, butter, Activator X, and eggs. Among salmon, wild-caught fish have been shown to average significantly more vitamin D than non-organically farmed fish. The very best supplement to take for vitamin D_3 is Activator X, which is the butter made from whole, raw, living milk identified by Dr. Price.

Sources of healthy saturated fats are Activator X, beef, butter, cheese, cocoa butter, coconut, coconut butter and oil, crème fraîche, eggs, lamb, red palm oil, sour cream, whole coconut milk, and whole milk.

Protein is the primary food group, crucial both for survival and for healing from the malnutrition that is keeping Americans fat and sick. Only protein can provide your body with the amino acids necessary to build muscle, tissues, bones, and other structures. Protein is essential for growth, repair, hormone production, immune function, and every single metabolic process in your body.

Examples of healthy proteins are pasture-raised or wild-caught beef, buffalo, chicken, duck, eggs, game, lamb, pheasant, quail, squab, and turkey, as well as wild fish or shellfish. Beef and lamb cooked rare are good sources of enzymes. *Salmonella, Listeria monocytogenes,* and *E. coli O157:H7* breed in confinement but do not proliferate in pasture-raised animals. Never eat rare pork or chicken.

Because all fatty acids can produce free radicals when heated, meat should be cooked at a low temperature. Never eat burned or charbroiled meat.

Although the medical community has sheepishly lightened up about eggs, people still hold many misconceptions. The truth is that eggs provide us with omega-3 fatty acids as well as cholesterol, which are both necessary for life and important factors in attaining our genetic gifts. For recipes that call for raw eggs, be sure to purchase "pasture-raised" eggs. "Cage-free" does not always mean that the chickens roamed free pecking at grass, insects, larvae, and earthworms. If you are in doubt, call the supplier and ask. Pasture-raised organic meats and fowl can be purchased at health-food stores or online. On eatwild.com you can find sources for grass-fed meat from all over the country. Pasture-raised, organic eggs can be purchased at health-food stores and farmers' markets. Organically raised nitrate-free ham and bacon is available at health-food stores from farmers who allow their hogs to run, root, and roam.

North of Santa Barbara is cattle country, where small herds scatter across the hillsides. During the seven years I lived on a ranch there, I often stopped to talk to cows that congregated near the roadside mailboxes munching grass, weeds, scrub, wildflowers, and brambles. They're sweet, timidly curious, with soulful, long-lashed eyes. Spring welcomes new calves that, left to their own devices, comically suckle their mothers until they are ridiculously too huge. I never passed these cows without pondering the plight of factory animals.

Human beings have an innate drive to survive, and a primary aspect of survival is eating food. It has only been during the last 150 years that people in the developed world have been completely removed from the hunting, raising, and slaughtering of animals. The stresses and strains of survival have taken on entirely new and modern challenges. We no longer have to think about or want the added strain of thinking about how we will obtain our food.

Many animal lovers like myself struggle with the issue of eating meat. The brilliant animal scientist Temple Grandin, Ph.D.— who has designed half of the livestock-handling facilities in the United States—writes in her book *Animals in Translation: Using the Mysteries of Autism to Decode Animal Behavior*, "If I had my druthers humans would have evolved to be plant eaters, so we wouldn't have to kill other animals for food. But we didn't, and I don't see the human race converting to vegetarianism anytime soon. I've tried to eat vegetarian myself, and I haven't been able to manage it physically . . . the fact that humans evolved as both plant and meat eaters means that the vast majority of human beings are going to continue to eat both. Humans are animals too, and we do what our animal natures tell us to do."

In Charles Frazier's Civil War novel *Cold Mountain*, a wounded soldier, Inman, travels perilously back home and along the way is helped and hindered by others, including a goat woman who takes him in and feeds him. Frazier writes, "A little spotted brown-and-white goat came to her and she stroked it and scratched below its neck until it folded its legs and lay down. The old woman scratched it close under its jaw and stroked its ears. Inman thought it a peaceful scene. He watched as she continued to scratch with her left hand and reach with her right into an apron pocket. With one motion she pulled out a short-bladed knife and cut deep into the artery below the jawline and shoved the white basin underneath to catch the leap of bright blood. The animal jerked once, then lay trembling as she continued to scratch the fur and fondle the ears. The basin filled slowly. The goat and the woman stared intently off toward the distance as if waiting for a signal."

Most animal-loving meat eaters would like to know that the animals they are eating were raised and slaughtered as humanely as this little goat. Realistically, however, there is a huge difference between feeding two people and 300 million people. The sheer volume of meat necessary to feed our nation has resulted in corrupt, sloppy, inhumane practices in the meat industry first uncovered by Upton Sinclair. While Dr. Grandin has devoted her career to improving the lives and deaths of the animals we eat, one person cannot shoulder this responsibility alone.

In the film *The Last of the Mohicans*, Hawkeye is an Anglo-Saxon frontiersman who had been orphaned as a baby and adopted by the Mohican Chingachgook. The film opens with Chingachgook, his blood son, Uncas, and Hawkeye running silently through a heavily canopied forest, hunting an elk. When the elk is felled by the .59 caliber round of Hawkeye's five-foot rifle, the three men kneel at the beast. In Mohican, Chingachgook speaks to the elk, "We're sorry to kill you, Brother. Forgive us. I do honor to your courage and speed, your strength."

This moving scene depicted the reverential attitude that some cultures historically held for the animals that provided them sustenance. Although many animals lovers choose to eat meat, we do have choices as to the way animals we consume are raised and killed. Today there is virtually no reason—other than protecting the shareholder profits of mega animal agribusinesses—that we cannot restore this same reverence for the animals that give us sustenance. We must care, as a nation, and we must revise the treatment of animals, or we will continue to experience the furious retribution of nature: obesity, cancer, heart disease, autoimmune conditions, infectious disease—even variant Creutzfeldt-Jakob disease, the human variant of bovine spongiform encephalopathy (BSE), which is the bovine brain-wasting disease more commonly known as "mad cow disease."

Since saving money is paramount to factory-animal agribusinesses, downer cattle (cows too sick or injured to stand up) were, until 1997, slaughtered and fed to humans. When public outrage stopped that practice, these sick animals were slaughtered and ground up and fed to other factory animals (this practice was also supposedly stopped). Today a cow can still eat dried restaurant plate waste that could contain beef as well as newspaper poultry litter (chicken poop) that may also contain remnants of the cattle "meal" fed to chickens. And a cow can still eat a hog that has eaten a cow and so on. Furthermore, calves are still fed "milk replacers" made from cow blood. These practices compel herbivores—creatures that eat grass and shrubs—to be cannibals. With horrifying irony, we are now experiencing the furious backlash of nature, as feeding cattle to cattle is the generally accepted theory as to how cows can become infected with BSE.

Stanley Prusiner, M.D., a neurologist, won the 1997 Nobel Prize in medicine for discovering prions, which are the malformed proteins believed to cause BSE. When infected, prions accumulate in the brain, riddling it with holes. The human variant of BSE, called variant Creutzfeldt-Jakob disease (vCJD), has been linked to consuming BSE-contaminated animal products. To date it's believed that 170 people have died from vCJD, suffering unspeakable pain as their brains liquefied.

Although BSE prions are supposedly harbored only in nervous-system tissue, such as blood, eyeballs, and brain and spinal cord tissue, these tissues have routinely entered our food supply via sloppy slaughtering practices. In 2002 the USDA issued a survey showing that approximately 35 percent of high-risk meat products (hot dogs, hamburgers, pizza toppings, and taco fillings) tested positive for central nervous system tissue. And although central nervous system tissue has recently been banned for sale for human consumption, slaughtering practices pretty much guarantee that all factory meat eaters have consumed products contaminated with this tissue.[186]

Although BSE prions were previously thought to be harbored in nervous-system tissue, Dr. Prusiner said, "We don't know where and how prions move through the [cow's] body before they show up in its brain."[187] So, in addition to the possibility of meat products containing BSE prions, we have to wonder about factory milk, too. Since research has demonstrated that BSE prions migrate to infected organs, and infection of the udders is common in factory dairy cows, BSE prions could be harbored in the infected secretory tissue of these cows and could be passed to milk.

In the United States 35 million cattle are slaughtered each year. The USDA's current BSE surveillance program samples approximately 40,000 animals per year. [188]

Since 1986, when BSE was first diagnosed in Great Britain, there have been more than 180,000 cases of BSE worldwide. Since then, BSE has been confirmed in Austria, Belgium, the Czech Republic, Denmark, Finland, France, Germany, Greece, Ireland, Israel, Italy, Japan, Luxembourg, Liechtenstein, the Netherlands, Northern Ireland, Poland, Portugal, Slovakia, Slovenia, Spain, and Switzerland. BSE was confirmed in Canada in May

2003.[189] In December 2003, in Washington State, the first suspected case of BSE in the United States was detected in a downer cow. In June 2005, a second case of BSE was confirmed in a downer cow in the United States. It took seven months for the USDA to disclose this fact.[190] In both instances Americans were fed the message that we needn't worry and should have every confidence in the safety of our beef.

In addition to BSE contamination, although factory animals are given numerous drugs to combat disease, they are virtually all sick and often diseased. Factory pigs suffer pneumonia, dysentery, trichinosis (parasitic infestation), and numerous other health problems, including at the time of slaughter.[191] Chickens develop cancer and other serious health problems.[192] So when we eat these animal products we eat diseased flesh or eggs.

In addition, since factory-animal products are exposed to feces, vomit, pus, and urine we're also exposed to lethal infectious organisms. According to CDC, each year food-borne diseases cause approximately 76 million illnesses, 325,000 hospitalizations, and 5,000 deaths in the United States Five pathogens account for more than 90 percent of these deaths: *Salmonella* (31 percent), *Listeria monocytogenes* (28 percent), *Toxoplasma gondii* (21 percent), Norwalk-like viruses (7 percent), *Campylobacter* (5 percent), and *E. coli* (3 percent). *Escherichia coli O157:H7* is the variant responsible for a diarrheal syndrome in which bloody discharges are so copious that death is often the result.[193]

Instead of addressing the root of this problem by closing down CAFOs and setting animals free to roam their natural habitats so that they don't become diseased and aren't wallowing in bodily fluids, the USDA has initiated a campaign to irradiate all meat as a way of controlling the spread of infectious diseases. Irradiation, also known as the more innocent sounding "cold pasteurization," exposes food to nuclear radiation to render sterile the pests, eggs, larvae, and bacteria that decompose food. But it does not serve actually to remove the pest, egg, and larvae carcasses from produce, nor does it cleanse the feces, urine, pus, vomit, and tumors from the meat of slaughterhouse animals. Nuclear radiation breaks up the molecular structure of the food, generating free radicals and in turn creating weird science chemicals known as unique radiolytic products, which common sense—and science—tell us contribute to cancer and cause genetic and cellular damage. Irradiation also destroys the good bacteria and enzymes that are essential to life and rapidly disappearing from our food chain. As irradiation increases the number of free radicals in food it radically decreases antioxidant vitamins that scavenge free radicals from your body.

Although the FDA maintains that irradiation is nothing to be concerned about, numerous scientists worldwide disagree. The long-term effects of eating irradiated food are not known and have not been studied, but short-term studies link irradiated food to numerous health problems in lab animals, including premature death, fatal internal bleeding, cancer, stillbirths, mutations, organ malfunctions, and stunted growth.[194]

In recent years, TV news has offered up chilling new reports of avian and then swine flu, read over news footage depicting hideously abused domestic birds and hogs. Although scientists have yet to understand how these flus originated, just seeing footage of CAFOs that pack hogs together and shots of live birds caged by the thousands, manhandled and stuffed, live, into plastic bags to suffocate, common sense screams, *Well, no wonder*. Still, too many people believe that humans can behave this way with impunity and believe that we can rely on the factory-food industry to supply us with nourishing food.

Bill Maher cracked up his audience in an HBO stand-up special when he said, "We feed cows too sick to stand to people too fat to walk. And then you wonder why these diseases spring up. Mad cow and AIDS and Ebola. You know nature, it doesn't ask a lot. It really doesn't. Don't grind up the cattle and feed them back to each other . . . not big requests."[194a] This is an example of our affable camaraderie about our food supply. Many people laugh to cope, in part, because they don't believe they have alternatives. The alternative to factory-produced animal products are natural milk, meat, and eggs that come from well-treated animals, which are the same healthy historically consumed foods that produced the vibrant good health that Dr. Price documented throughout his research on indigenous peoples.

While natural milk is an excellent source of protein and saturated fat, as with saturated animal fat and polyunsaturated vegetable oils, there are controversy and misconceptions about milk. Since the USDA's "Got Milk?" milk moustache campaign, millions of Americans have increased their intake of milk. There's no other food that appears more comforting or healthy than a tall glass of frothy milk, even though studies dating from the early 1900s to the present demonstrate that factory milk is a contributing factor in the epidemic of allergies, asthma, precocious puberty, multiple sclerosis, and type 1 diabetes, as well as degenerative diseases.[195]

PART SIX

Milk: Deadly or the Perfect Food?

CHAPTER FOURTEEN

Factory Milk

On May 10, 1611, a straggly band of fortune hunters watched as Sir Thomas Dale, the newly appointed governor of Jamestown, Virginia, disembarked at Jamestown Harbor. Four years earlier, the ships *Susan Constant, Godspeed*, and *Discovery* had brought these spying men, whose hopes of finding riches and a northeast water route to India had been systematically dashed by Algonquian attacks, disease, and starvation. Several ships had since arrived carrying provisions and hundreds of replacement settlers; thus the ranks of the Jamestown colonists had swelled and shrunk. Now the men observed as the ship's crew labored to bring one hundred cows to shore. Dazed and weak from the four-month sea voyage, the cows ambled into the pastures, lured by tall native grasses. The arrival of milk cows spelled the beginning of prosperity in America's first permanent settlement.

Nine years later, in 1620, the Plymouth colonists arrived in Massachusetts. In the fall of 1621, the half who had survived the first year celebrated a feast of thanksgiving, eating maize, seafood, and game. "Survived" being the operative word. By 1623, an observer wrote that the colonists were in "very low condition, many were ragged in aparell, and some little beter than halfe naked."[196] If not for the arrival of three heifers and a bull in March 1624 on the merchant chip *Charity*, the remaining Pilgrims would have likely perished too.

Similar accounts of milk cows saving the lives of early Americans are documented in each and every colony in seventeenth-century America.

Since the early colonies, milk has been a healthy, life-sustaining part of the American diet.[197] Back in the 1940s, when Weston A. Price sent 20,000 food samples back to America for analysis, he also sent milk samples, which he characterized as "the most efficient single food known."[198]

Natural milk was consumed in the United States until the War of 1812 with England, when whiskey shipments from the British West Indies abruptly halted.[199] To address this problem, distilleries sprang up, extracting alcohol from grain to produce whiskey. Enterprising distillery owners, looking for a use for the chemically altered, acidic waste product known as "distillery slop," built dairies adjoining or in the basements of distilleries and fed the waste product to cows. Now the cities had their whiskey and their "slop" or "swill" milk.

Distillery dairies were filthy hellholes, sullying the air with horrendous fumes. Eating steaming slop from a distillery is not the same thing to a cow as grazing in an open pasture, but cows are sweet, docile creatures that will ultimately eat anything put before them. Still cows—like humans kept in dungeons—succumbed to disease.

The unnatural swill feed lacked the life-sustaining nutrients necessary to maintain healthy metabolic processes and was foreign and toxic to bovine physiology. Thus the resulting milk lacked nutrients and was unfit for human consumption. Swill milk was doctored with starch, sugar, flour, chalk, and plaster of Paris. Milkers went about their duties with filthy hands and often came to work sick. As the swill milk business boomed, infant mortality rose, with babies dying of tuberculosis, diarrhea, typhoid, cholera, scarlet fever, and diphtheria.

In the 1860s, Louis Pasteur discovered that heating milk killed off pathogenic microorganisms that led to many infectious diseases (and launched the germ theory of disease). There were two courses of action the food industry could have taken to halt the spread of infectious diseases through swill milk: They could have cleaned up the filth in the dairy industry and initiated the production of pasture-fed, clean, nutrient-rich milk in the countryside to feed city dwellers. Instead, the industry continued to produce filthy milk from diseased, abused cows and then scald the germs out of the milk.

Naturopathic physician Ron Schmid, author of *The Untold Story of Milk: Green Pastures, Contented Cows and Raw Dairy Foods*, told me, "Given the sorry state of milk supplies in the early twentieth century, pasteurization prevented a lot of sickness and death. On the other hand, we didn't need to treat good, clean, healthy milk the same way we treated tainted, unsanitary, nutrient dead milk."[200]

What was not known in Pasteur's time is that the heat of pasteurization kills vitamins C, E, A, D_3, and B complex, diminishes calcium and other minerals and makes them harder to absorb, and reduces the digestibility and lessens the nutritional value of protein. Most important, the heat of pasteurization destroys the enzymes in milk. The temperature at which substances feel too hot to touch—about 118 degrees Fahrenheit—is adequate to kill enzymes.

The ridding of enzymes from our food supply has been a major contributing factor to the downfall of Americans' health. Enzymes are essential to life because they are biochemical catalysts of cellular function both inside and outside of the cell. Without enzymes no biochemical activity would take place. Vitamins, minerals, and hormones cannot perform in the body without enzymes. The five thousand identified enzymes are divided into three categories: Metabolic enzymes enable all bodily processes and functions, including maintaining immune function. Digestive enzymes are manufactured in the pancreas to break down food. Enzymes in food jumpstart digestive processes when you eat.

Born in 1898, researcher Edward Howell devoted his life to researching and promoting nutritional approaches to chronic illness. In his book *Food Enzymes for Health and Longevity* (1939), he explained that eating foods that contain enzymes reduces the need for the pancreas to produce its own digestive enzymes. If your pancreas is overtaxed during your lifetime because you are not providing your body with an adequate supply of enzymes in food, its function will decline. The length of your life depends on how fast your pancreatic enzyme-producing capacity is used up. If you place constant demand on your pancreas to produce enzymes to digest and process incoming dead food, you will die sooner than if you eat enzyme-rich food. That's why food enzymes are one key to staving off degenerative disease, slowing accelerated aging, and promoting longevity.[201]

According to Dr. Schmid, although the belief took hold that we could pasteurize unhealthy milk and make it both safe to drink and healthy, the fact is that healthfulness of milk is determined by two factors: (1) The cow's diet and living conditions determine whether or not the cow is healthy, and (2) the health of the cow determines the nutritive quality of the milk.

The modern cow's diet and living conditions are not much better than a swill cow's of one hundred years ago. Modern dairy cows don't graze contentedly in pastures on farms like the precious cows I met on Dr. Schmid's farm. Today cows are housed in CAFOs, where they live out their short lives tethered in stalls shoulder to shoulder in pens, standing in manure.

Modern milk cows' production is maximized by selective breeding—the process of breeding for particular genetic traits—which has created cows with freakishly active pituitary glands that overproduce growth hormones that stimulate milk production. Selectively bred cows are highly stressed milk-producing machines that require massive amounts of species-inappropriate feed to fuel their aberrant metabolisms, as well as massive amounts of drugs to address the health problems caused both by the feed and by the stressful environment. Milk production is further increased by 10 to 20 percent by injecting cows with recombinant Bovine Growth Hormone (rBGH).

Confinement cows are fed soybean and grain feed, which are unnatural foods for ruminants (cud-chewing animals) that have four stomachs, designed to digest fibrous grasses, plants, and shrubs. Soybeans and grains lack the life-sustaining nutrients necessary to maintain healthy bovine metabolic processes. Grain-fed cows can become afflicted with a painful condition called sub-acute acidosis, requiring constant, low-level doses of antibiotics.[202] (And now we have ethanol plants springing up next to dairy farms where the corn mash by-product is being fed to dairy cows—exactly like the swill cows of old.)

Soybeans and grains are grown with herbicides and pesticides or are genetically modified to resist pests and are grown with chemical fertilizers, which are toxic to bovine physiology and also migrate to a cow's milk. Aflatoxins are cancer-causing chemicals found in moldy grain and are secreted in the milk of grain-eating cows.[203]

Grains also cause mastitis (infection of the udders). Normal milk contains low levels of white blood cells that are shed from the secretory tissue during milking. A somatic cell count (SCC) determines whether milk contains a normal white blood cell count or a high count, signaling mastitis. A SCC level of 300,000 indicates mastitis, yet federal regulations allow the sale of milk with SCC levels of 750,000, which in simple terms means there's a lot of pus in your milk.[204] Government regulators ruled that this is fine as this milk will be pasteurized, so you won't be drinking live pus but dead pus.

Because cows suffer health problems as a result of their stressful confinement and species-inappropriate diet, sixty-odd drugs are federally approved for use on dairy cows, including penicillin G. Antimicrobial sulfonamides are suspected human carcinogens that taint milk. Anti-worming agents also migrate to milk and are associated with bone marrow diseases and neurological disorders. Numerous nonapproved drugs are also used illegally.[205]

After this adulterated brew is milked, pasteurization kills some of bad bacteria in the milk and refrigeration keeps the remaining bacteria from growing but does not eradicate any of the contaminants; neither does ultra pasteurization, although it eliminates the need for refrigeration prior to opening the container, because it sterilizes milk.

The homogenization process breaks up butterfat globules into tiny particles, which keeps the milk "stirred up," so that the cream doesn't rise to the top, ostensibly making it more attractive to consumers. In recent years, a hypothesis has emerged suggesting that the sliced-up fatty particles can abrade arterial walls, which results in attracting a protective coating of plaque. But the jury is still out on whether homogenized milk contributes to coronary artery disease.[206] Still, homogenization is for the convenience of the manufacturer. "When unhomogenized milk is transported in a tanker truck," Dr. Schmid said, "the cream rises to the top as it churns. The result is butter and buttermilk."

Modern milk suppliers are well aware of the fact that the heat of pasteurization kills vitamins and enzymes and changes the chemical composition of calcium and other minerals. Like swill milk that in the past was prettied up with chalk and other substances, today's milk is fortified with calcium and synthetic vitamins. As previously stated, Enig and Fallon point out that vitamin D_2 was yanked from our milk supply as it causes hardening of the arteries and softening of the bones.[207]

Milk suppliers can never duplicate nature's perfect ratio of nutrients and create a nutritious food by adding synthetic nutrients into weeks-old, pasteurized, denatured milk that contains high levels of contaminants and is the commingled product of thousands of cows. Like swill milk, factory milk lacks nutrients because it's produced by abused cows in mostly unsanitary conditions. Said Dr. Schmid. "The best we can expect from commercial milk is that it might support people until they begin to wear out and die at age fifty or sixty and they can go for ten or twenty years into the medical industry." [208]

Twenty years ago the episode of *Nip/Tuck* in which Julia McNamara (Joely Richardson) discovers a bloodstain in her eight-year-old daughter Annie's (Kelsey Bateman) panties and realizes it's premenstrual spotting would have been far-fetched. In this episode, to soften the blow of telling her the facts of life, Julia and a friend throw Annie a "Princess Menses" party attended by a gaggle of little girls dressed in flowing white dresses and tiaras. "She's barely out of pajamas with feet," says plastic surgeon McNamara (Dylan Walsh) to his partner, Christian Troy (Julian McMahon), "How did this happen?"[209]

Millions of parents are asking that same question. The age of menarche has fallen from approximately 15 or 16 in 1850 to between 12 and 13 in 1990, and the age of puberty for boys has declined from around 16 to 13 or 14.[210] And today by age seven, 10.4 percent of white, 23.4 percent of black, and 14.9 percent of Hispanic girls have enough breast development to be considered at the onset of puberty. By age eight, 18.3 percent of white, 42.9 percent of black, and 30.9 percent of Hispanic girls are considered to have started puberty.[211] One percent of American girls now show signs of puberty before the age of three.[212] Nine-year-old boys are experiencing penis and testicular maturation and pubic-hair growth. It's only considered precocious puberty when a girl begins puberty earlier than seven, and a boy earlier than nine.[213]

Clearly there are many factors contributing to the rise of precocious puberty, one of which is thought to be chronic exposure to xenoestrogens, substances that have been found to mimic the actions of the hormone estrogen. Xenoestrogens are endocrine disruptors.

Female hormones, estrogens, are present in both sexes, but in larger amounts for women. Estrogens influence puberty, menstruation, and pregnancy in women, and they regulate the growth of bones, skin, and vital organs and tissues in both men and women.

Xenoestrogens are generated from a number of sources, including heating food in plastic, consuming fruits and vegetables grown with pesticides, herbicides, and chemical fertilizers, and consuming meat and dairy products from cows that were fed feed that contains pesticide, herbicide, and chemical-fertilizer residues. Chlorine and hormone residues in meats and dairy products can also have estrogenic effects. Factory dairy cows are fed soybeans, which are high in phytoestrogens (also estrogen mimickers). Estrogen mimickers xenoestrogens and phytoestrogens bind to estrogen receptors and have essentially the same effect as natural estrogen, setting up the potential to wreck havoc on reproductive anatomy and physiology and disrupting endocrine function.

Today the link between the rise of precocious puberty and the combined influences of increased body fat and prolonged high xenoestrogen exposure has been the topic of much study. Enhanced body fat implies reproductive readiness and signals the onset of puberty in both girls and boys.[214] For girls, more body fat ensures that there is enough stored energy to support pregnancy and lactation. So it may be that excess body fat and exposure to estrogenic substances operate in concert to hasten puberty.[215]

Xenoestrogens, which are much stronger than estrogens made by the body, have been prevalent in the environment only in modern times and are thought to be a contributing factor to fertility problems, genital malformation, reduced male birth rates, precocious puberty, miscarriage, behavior problems, brain abnormalities, impaired immune function, various cancers, and cardiovascular disease. Endometriosis is an estrogen-dependant disease first defined in 1920; there were only 20 reports about it in the worldwide literature by 1921. Today this painful reproductive and immunological disease affects more than 7 million women and teens in North America alone, with nearly 80 million more worldwide.[216]

In 1990, Danish pediatric endocrinologist Niels E. Skakkebaek set up a department at the National University Hospital in Copenhagen to study the phenomenon of male infertility and children's growth disorders.[217] Skakkebaek gained notoriety in the 1970s for his brilliant studies of testicular cancer, a formerly rare disease in which there has been an astonishing rise in the last fifty years. In his pediatric practice, Skakkebaek was seeing numerous boys with genital malformations and others with undescended testicles, a condition with links to sterility and a higher rate of testicular cancer. Skakkebaek and his colleagues found that even supposedly healthy men had surprising low-quality sperm.

Since 1938, sperm counts of men in twenty-one countries have plunged by an average of 50 percent, and testicular cancer has tripled. Skakkebaek suspects that the culprit is men's exposure (as fetuses and newborns) to estrogen-like chemicals found in their mother's blood and breastmilk.

Skakkebaek concluded that the most likely villains are chemicals in the environment, which masquerade as the female hormone, estrogen. These chemicals, which can have a temporary effect on adults, can cause permanent damage in boys whose sexual organs are not yet fully developed.

Since 1990, nearly fifteen million new cancer cases have been diagnosed, with a new cancer diagnosed every thirty seconds. Breast, prostate, and colon cancers have risen the most dramatically in the past twenty years. One out of eight American women will develop breast cancer, and one out of nine men will develop prostate cancer. One in twenty (men and women) will develop colon cancer. Could there also be a link between the rise of these cancers and the introduction twenty years ago of rBGH into our milk supply?

In 1980, this cheap variant of natural bovine growth hormone was created by Genentech, Inc., by inserting *E. coli* bacteria into the cow gene that creates bovine growth hormone. In 1981, Genentech sold the rights to recombinant Bovine Growth Hormone (rBGH) to Monsanto. In 1985, when Monsanto needed to conduct large-scale veterinarian trials on rBGH, the FDA approved of this study and also approved the sale of rBGH beef and milk from Monsanto's research herds and dairies to the public without disclosing the fact that the milk was obtained from rBGH-treated cows. The FDA based its approval on extremely short-term (28- to 90-day) experiments in which rats were fed rBGH. Monsanto claimed the rats suffered no apparent ill effects, so it was OK for humans to ingest rBGH milk. They neglected to mention details like thyroid cysts and changes to rats' prostate glands.[218]

FDA scientists who recognized the problems with the FDA approval process of Monsanto's trials were deemed potential whistleblowers, were treated with hostility and threats, and were even fired.[219] Although a handful of FDA scientists resorted to anonymously protesting to Congress, the sale of rBGH meat and milk from Monsanto's research farms and ranches was ultimately green-lighted. So American families were hapless guinea pigs, consuming rBGH meat and milk.[220]

One problem that couldn't be glossed over was the severe increased mastitis (infection of the udders), which required treatment with high levels of antibiotics. To address this problem, Margaret Miller, Ph.D., at the FDA, pushed through a dramatic increase in the allowable levels of antibiotics in milk. Dairy farmers were then free to crank up antibiotic treatments of their rBGH cows, and the heavily antibiotic laced rBGH milk was then sold to an unsuspecting public. [221]

Antibiotics don't distinguish between harmful and healthy bacteria. So consuming antibiotics for long periods of time can severely disrupt the balance of your healthy intestinal bacteria, causing gastrointestinal and immune function problems as well as yeast overgrowth. Chronic antibiotic intake from milk and meat products can also result in the harmful bacteria in your body becoming resistant to the effects of prescription antibiotics.

Back in 1989, cancer expert Dr. Epstein (introduced on page 63), who is the author of the investigative journalist-oriented *Got (Genetically Engineered) Milk? The Monsanto BGH/BST Milk Wars Handbook*, was alerted to the use of rBGH by dairy farmers who came to him inquiring about consumer risks. Dr. Epstein began to analyze the scientific literature and to write about the dangers of rBGH. Although Monsanto has done everything in its power to keep the truth about rBGH from the public, Epstein has fought to reveal the truth. From time to time, he's had help from unexpected sources. "Over the last thirty years, people in agencies and industries have sent me confidential documents," he told me. "Sometimes they give me their names. Sometimes they don't." [222]

The first box containing extensive "company confidential" Monsanto files arrived anonymously, shortly after Epstein began his research into rBGH. The files detailed the extensive adverse health effects in cows treated with rBGH, including a high incidence of reproductive failure; cows injected with rBGH had much higher rates of infection and suffered from infertility, extreme weight loss, heat intolerance and lactational burnout, gastric ulcers, arthritis, and kidney and heart abnormalities. The files also documented the high level of rBGH in milk.

Although Dr. Epstein forwarded copies of these files to Congress, an investigation was launched, and Monsanto and the FDA were charged with conspiring to manipulate critical health data, it was no more irritating than a buzzing gnat in the nostrils of Monsanto and the FDA. Ultimately cows continued to be treated with rBGH, and that milk was sold to the public.

By 1990, overwhelming scientific evidence demonstrated the health hazards of rBGH to both humans and cows. Incredibly, the FDA claimed "milk and meat from [rBGH] treated cows are safe and wholesome for human consumption."[223] What is true is that the injection of rBGH increases levels of a potent hormone called insulinlike growth factor one (IGF-1), which is then passed to the cows' milk. Although natural cow's milk contains natural growth hormone—as does human breast milk—Dr. Epstein writes that rBGH milk is "supercharged with high levels of abnormally potent IGF-1, up to ten times the levels in natural milk and over ten times more potent." Worse is that when rBGH milk is pasteurized, IGF-1 increases by up to 70 percent.

When humans drink IGF-1 milk, the hormone is absorbed through the gastrointestinal tract (and infants' gastrointestinal tracts are much more permeable than adults). Because IGF-1 causes cells to divide and because IGF-1 also behaves like insulin—another growth factor—when it is absorbed into the bloodstream, it can exert rapid cell growth on colon, breast, and prostate cells. IGF-1 also blocks the programmed self-destruction of cancer cells and enhances their growth and invasiveness. Numerous studies have demonstrated that unnatural levels of IGF1 dramatically increase your risk of developing breast, prostate, lung, colon, and gastrointestinal cancers.[224]

Nevertheless, in February 1994, the FDA granted approval for general use of rBGH and pushed through regulatory labeling guidelines, composed by Dr. Margaret Miller and Deputy FDA Commissioner Michael Taylor. The guidelines effectively banned the labeling of rBGH milk as "containing rBGH" or even "rBGH free" so that consumers would not be alerted to the fact that they were consuming rBGH milk—or even given the choice.[225]

These public servants were not focused with single-minded passion on your health or the welfare of your children. Miller, for example, was the laboratory supervisor at Monsanto and left the biotech firm to be deputy director of human food safety at the FDA where she was still publishing papers for Monsanto when she wrote the bovine growth hormone guidelines. Taylor was the former chief counsel for the International Food Biotechnology Counsel and Monsanto. Taylor's FDA guidelines were used by his former law firm to sue dairies that dared to label their dairy products "rBGHfree."[226] After the fact, Michael Friedman, M.D., who was deputy commissioner of the FDA from 1995 to 1999, went on to a position as the head of clinical research at Monsanto Co.'s G.D. Searle & Co. unit, which produces rBGH.[227]

Three concerned FDA scientists, Joseph Settepani, Alexander Apostolou, and Richard Burroughs, made numerous attempts to thwart the rBGH approval process but were stymied by internal intrigue, hostility, and threats. A month after the FDA approval of rBGH, they resorted to writing an anonymous letter to members of Congress. "We are afraid to speak openly about the situation because of retribution from our director, Dr. Robert Livingston," they write. "Dr. Livingston openly harasses anyone who states an opinion in opposition to his."[228]

Monsanto continued raking in the dough, and Americans unwittingly glugged rBGH milk. Meanwhile, by 1999, Canada had banned the use of rBGH. That same year, the Codex Alimentarius Commission—the U.N. food safety agency that represents 101 nations—unanimously ruled in favor of maintaining the 1992 European moratorium on Monsanto's rBGH milk.[229]

The American Medical Association (AMA) has dismissed rBGH critics as "fringe groups." The American Cancer Society (ACS) has trivialized the link between IGF-1 and cancer and come out in support of the use of rBGH.[230] And the FDA persists in their claims that rBGH milk is safe and wholesome. (The AMA is a partnership of physicians and professional associations dedicated to promoting the art and science of medicine and the betterment of public health, and the ACS is a national, voluntary cancer organization founded to eliminate cancer.)

Dr. Epstein added that the ACS has in the neighborhood of 340

"Excalibur industry donors" that each donate more than $100,000 per year. "Key amongst them are the techno chemical industries and agribusiness," Dr. Epstein told me. "The American Cancer Society is more interested in accumulating wealth than savings lives. Their CEOs have high salaries. They have a billion dollars of cash assets in reserves. They have major internal conflicts of interests. The National Cancer Institute and the American Cancer Society fail in their mandated responsibility to inform the public of avoidable risks of cancer." (The NCI is a government agency created for cancer research and education.)

Dr. Epstein is an outspoken critic of cancer organizations' focus on cancer drugs rather than prevention. "The National Cancer Institute's budget has increased from 200 million in 1971 to 4.6 billion today," he said. "Paralleling this increase is the increasing incidence of nonsmoking cancers. Very little money is spent on preventing cancer. The overwhelming emphasis of the National Cancer Institute is producing miracle drugs that possibly increase life expectancy by a month or two."

It appears that there are quite a few people (including companies that make chemotherapy drugs) are making an awful lot of money from Americans' consumption of rBGH milk.

Unlike factory milk, natural milk contains minimal contaminants. When I began researching this book, I had not had a glass of milk in going on ten years—something that has radically changed since I met Mark McAfee, owner of Organic Pastures in Fresno, California.

CHAPTER FIFTEEN

Raw, Living Milk to the Rescue

MARK MCAFEE GIVES THE impression of being someone you could trust with your life.[231] A certified paramedic for 16 years in Fresno, having run more than 14,000 service calls, McAfee said, "It was a constant adrenaline rush dealing with tragic, life-changing events of strangers." As paramedic of the year in 1994, Mark was at the top of his game. "I said to myself, I've saved many lives, and delivered many babies—I want to leave it there and do something else for the rest of my life." Mark had grown up on a farm. "In 1970, McAfee Quality Dairy was a small place, and I was the first slave. I learned to feed calves, milk cows, and work my butt off. Dairy farming was in my blood." In 1996 Mark and his wife, Blaine, decided to take over the family's 600-acre dairy farm and manage it organically. "I took my ability to be a student and learned organic production and the clinical health benefits raw milk can bring people, which are tremendous."

Perhaps the most stunning of all raw milk's attributes is the fact that unlike pasteurized milk, raw milk contains enzymes, without which life cannot be sustained. If you read *Ethan Frome* (1911), by Edith Wharton, the drama of star-crossed lovers Ethan and Mattie, you'll remember that the pivotal moment revolved around a pickle dish. When Ethan's wife, Zeena, found her prized pickle dish broken, she immediately suspects their affair. Zeena owned a pickle dish because the historical human diet contained fermented and otherwise enzymatic rich foods such as pickles, sour kraut, live beer, whole, raw milk, and ice cream (made without heat), as well as raw cream, yogurt, cheese, cottage cheese, and kefir. Enzyme and probiotics (healthy live organisms) in "sour" and clabbered (curdled) milk were consumed as digestives. Sour milk is made by allowing milk to ferment (curdle) at a warm temperature. This occurs when "good" bacterial flora such as *lactobacillus acidophilus* are present.

You don't have to consume clabbered milk (which might be a stretch for our palates these days), as simply drinking raw milk provides a biodiversity of good living bacteria that recolonize your gut with friendly bacteria (which heals the GI tract and builds immunity). However, pasteurization kills the good bacterial flora and leaves nothing but the unfriendly lactophilic germs. If pasteurized milk isn't constantly refrigerated, lactophilic germs quickly multiply, which produces acids that cause milk to putrefy. That's why you gag sour (rotten) milk into the sink after swigging out of the milk carton.

For an optimal healing approach, an enzyme-rich food should be incorporated with every meal. The easiest, of course, is a glass of natural milk. Raw milk contains much more than enzymes. Whole, raw, living milk contains butterfat filled with vitamins A and D_3, which are necessary for the assimilation of calcium and protein. Butterfat is also the richest known source of conjugated linoleic acid (CLA), which, as stated earlier, reduces cancer and atherosclerosis risk, increases metabolic rate and burns fat.[232] Raw milk and its by-products are also great alternatives for vegetarians as raw milk provides complete proteins. (See page 19 for amino acids/ complete protein.)

Mark said, "Raw milk is a medical super-food with no side effects or two pages of contraindications that include death. With rare lactose intolerance, a healing food for asthma, a healing food for IBS, Crohn's, ulcers, and ear infections, it's no small wonder why moms prefer it to visits to the pediatrician for yet another immune-system-destructive round of antibiotics. The more progressive doctors now prescribe raw milk to rebuild the immune system and avoid illness to begin with."

Mark's dairy, Organic Pastures, produces and retails certified organic raw milk and dairy products. They own 400 cows of which they milk 250, using a Grade-A approved, 60,000-pound mobile milk barn—the only one of its kind in North America. The mobile barn is moved from pasture to pasture weekly, making it possible to milk 100 cows an hour, eliminating the necessity for manure lagoons (disease-breeding pits where manure is pumped) or herding the cows into damp, concrete-floored barns for milking.

The milk is chilled to 36 degrees Fahrenheit within 30 seconds of milking. Prior to bottling, the raw milk is tested to assure it exceeds the standards of the California Department of Food and Agriculture (CDFA). (The CDFA is a state agency that works to ensure the safety and quality of food.) "The law stated that milk after pasteurization must have less than 15,000 bacteria per milliliter," Mark said, "Organic Pastures raw milk averages about 1,500 bacteria per milliliter. In all the years of intensive testing by the CDFA, Organic Pastures' milk has never once tested positive for *Salmonella*, *Listeria monocytogenes*, or *E. coli O157:H7*."

And the cows have names: Buddy, Rachel, Mousey, Mabel, Teresa. To get healthy, clean milk, Mark said, "You have to care for cows like family. My wife sings to them and walks around and talks to them. The health of milk has everything to do with the way the cow is treated. You have to follow Mother Nature's blueprint. A cow would never chose to stand on concrete or next to hundreds of other cows in a big manure pile. She'll go find a luscious pasture to mingle with a small group of cows and find something green to eat." Organic Pastures keep their herds fairly small and always have the cows in a lush green environment. Cows are grazed progressively, meaning that when a pasture gets depleted, cows are moved to fresh pastures, which are irrigated year-round.

Organic Pastures doesn't own, purchase, or breed selectively bred cows. A selectively bred cow couldn't survive in a pasture-grazing dairy, McAfee said. "Because selectively bred cows need a specialized high protein, high concentrated diet or they will waste away and die." A selectively bred cow produces up to 25 gallons of milk per day. A strictly grass-fed dairy cow produces up to 3 gallons of milk per day. "It's about striking a balance with the organic matter cows would normally eat and added nutrition to slightly increase milk supply."

Supplementation ups milk production to 4 to 6 gallons per day. To get that slight increase in milk production, Organic Pastures cows are fed 5 pounds of organic corn, and up to 25 pounds of organic alfalfa per day are added to their 30 to 40 pounds or so of pasture grass. In winter, cows are fed 40 pounds of organic hay.

Unlike pasteurized (sterilized) commercial milk, which is a pus-filled, commingled brew of thousands of selectively bred cows' milk, containing rBGH (hormones), antibiotics, drugs, GMO, and fertilizer residues, raw milk is produced by small herds of happy cows that are pasture grazed on species-appropriate food and milked with sanitary milking machines that transport the milk in sanitary stainless-steel tanks and refrigerated trucks. Clean raw milk not only contains nature's nutrients, it thwarts pathogenic bacterial growth, what Mark calls "bad bugs." When cows are pasture-grazed in clean environments bacterial problems do not arise, do not arise as often, or are often self-corrected. In one study, calves that had tested positively for *E. coli O157:H7* were divided into two groups. One group was sequestered in a barn, and the other group was set free to graze in a pasture. During a six-month testing period, the pasture calves showed no signs of *O157:H7*. Meanwhile, every barn calf tested positive.[233]

Despite all the evidence that demonstrates the health benefits of raw milk, the government has unilaterally rejected it. The FDA's website states, "[R]aw milk can harbor dangerous microorganisms that can pose serious health risks to you and your family. According to the Centers for Disease Control and Prevention, more than 800 people in the United States have gotten sick from drinking raw milk or eating cheese made from raw milk since 1998. Raw milk is milk from cows, sheep, or goats that has not been pasteurized to kill harmful bacteria. This raw, unpasteurized milk can carry dangerous bacteria such as *Salmonella, E. coli,* and *Listeria,* which are responsible for causing numerous food-borne illnesses. These harmful bacteria can seriously affect the health of anyone who drinks raw milk, or eats foods made from raw milk. However, the bacteria in raw milk can be especially dangerous to pregnant women, children, the elderly, and people with weakened immune systems."[234]

The same concern does not seem to be extended toward factory meat and the potential for contamination in factory meat, which has resulted in hundreds of thousands of hospitalizations and thousands of deaths. Eric Schlosser, author of *Fast Food Nation,* has written extensively about the centralization and industrialization of our food-supply system, which has increased food-borne illnesses. His research has demonstrated how fast-food chains and agribusinesses have thwarted effective government regulation, and how federal agencies that are supposed to regulate these companies have fallen under their control.[235]

Mark was well aware of the FDA and California Department of Food and Agriculture's (CDFA) negative position on raw milk. "Organic Pastures Dairy Company started out as an innocent concept in my heart where cows would truly be happy and the pastures would truly be green. In California that's exactly what the 'Got Milk' campaign artificially created in the minds of the consumer. The ugly truth is that CAFOs create stinky manure lagoons with 10,000 cows in cramped stalls being force-fed grain and injected with growth hormones and antibiotics, so they can be milked three of four times per day."

Mark's vision of the happy cow ultimately alienated him and his dairy from other California dairies and processors who didn't share his vision, pushing him near the precipice of a cliff, alone. "I didn't know when I conceived of organic pastures with cows actually grazing on them that I would ever be the foremost producer of raw milk perhaps in the world. My plan was to simply be organic and treat the cows with the regard they deserve."

From 1999 to 2007, all was well with Organic Pastures. The McAfees, their cows, the business, and consumers were flourishing in the new world of raw, living milk that Mark and Blaine had created.

Enter Stephen Beam, Ph.D., chief of dairy food safety at the CDFA, who sits on the Science and Research committee at the National Conference on Interstate Milk Shipments (NCIMS) and the FDA's Pasteurized Milk Ordinance. (The NCIMS is a nonprofit organization whose goal is to "assure the safest possible milk supply for all people.") Mark said, "Beam is as anti-raw milk as you can get."

In early 2007, Dr. Beam, [CA] assemblywoman Nicole Parra and Eric Stein, deputy secretary for legislation and policy, met secretly to create a "new standard" for California raw milk. This standard required raw milk for human consumption to contain "less than 10 coliform" per milliliter. The "less than 10 coliform" standard was originally developed in the 1930s as a way of determining whether milk had been pasteurized or was still in a raw state. Coliform wasn't "good" or "bad," as coliforms merely contain bacterial colonies that make lactase, a digestive enzyme. As lactase breaks down lactose (milk sugars), consumers—especially those with lactose intolerance—wanted some coliforms in their raw milk. Mark said, "Coliforms at low levels actually inhibit E. coli and other bad bugs."

The new "less than 10 coliform" standard deemed AB 1735 was buried deep in otherwise unremarkable CDFA policy legislation that was to be put before Governor Schwarzenegger. No hearings were held, no announcements made, and no dairy people consulted, so that raw dairy producers had no opportunity to discuss or debate it. Schwarzenegger signed the bill. And it was only then that Mark even heard about it.

California was ground zero for raw milk, as the life of Organic Pastures would affect raw milk sales in the rest of the country. The new standard would be enforced beginning January 1, 2008.

The fight was on. Organic Pastures led the charge by immediately sounding the alarm with 5,000 emails sent out to consumers. An emergency meeting was requested with Dr. Beam. The Sacramento meeting was attended by the who's who of the CDFA. Beam announced that the less than 10 coliform standard was made to "harmonize with the FDA raw milk policy." Mark replied, "There is no FDA raw milk standard. It doesn't exist." The meeting dissolved into a yelling match and was called short.

Nicole Parra was paying attention, though, and looked into the matter. She found that there was indeed no such FDA policy on raw milk. She changed sides then and tried to have the bill rescinded but was thwarted by the powerful Western United Dairymen processors. Still, Mark wasn't alone anymore. Along with Parra, Walter Robb, the co-president of Whole Foods, joined his efforts, as did former Veterans Administrator, pathologist Ted Beals, M.D., Australian biologist Ron Hull, Ph.D., 1,400 consumers, sundry scientists, and Sally Fallon, the president and founder of the Weston A. Price Foundation. Perhaps the most pivotal was Christine Chesson, a concerned mom with a master's degree from Columbia in mathematics, political connections, and money. Christine had three kids who drank Organic Pasture's raw milk. "For the first time in all their young lives the kids were healthy all winter long with no need for drugs or antibiotics," Mark said.

The first call Christine made was to her college friend from UCLA [CA] Senator Dean Florez. Florez toured Organic Pastures in early 2008, learned the facts about raw milk production, and quickly called hearings to discuss the future of raw milk in California. The hearings were attended by all of the supporters, but boycotted by the FDA and CDFA. Prior to the hearings, Mark had worked with Dr. Hull and Dr. Beals to create a new, enhanced Gold Standard Food Safety program for California milk producers for the Hazard Analysis Critical Control Points (HACCP) program (a food safety program in use across America that was originally developed by NASA.) "The goal of HACCP is to reduce or eliminate biological, chemical, or physical contaminants in food supply," Mark told me. "The problem with pure HACCP is that it ignores the value of living foods such as the biodiversity of good bacteria and active enzymes, and kills them all by irradiation or heat, which is called 'Kill Step.' Our RAMP program uses the same protocol to measure risks and document them and thereby reducing them dramatically but yet does not use Kill Steps."

The hearings resulted in legislation called SB 201 that would empower the CDFA to start a new program called Raw Milk Program (RAMP) for the HACCP. RAMP would include aggressive pathogen testing and other food-safety-focused objectives for California raw milk production instead of measuring coliforms, which are not pathogens and don't cause illness. These new standards would further enhance raw-milk safety for the California markets and consumers. RAMP would be the gold standard for raw-milk production in California—a standard that the rest of the world would likely follow.

The hearings were, according to Mark, "a landslide victory for raw milk and a huge embarrassment for the FDA, CDFA, and the Big Dairy processors, who could not offer up any reasons why kids get sick on pasteurized milk but get well when they drink raw milk. After hearings, calls to the Assembly and senators poured in. Mark recalls the day that he "got a call at my office begging me to call off the faxes and phone calls coming in not just from California, but Italy, France, England, Australia, and Canada. The world was fighting for California raw milk."

The legislation resulting from the hearings provided the general outline for the Food Safety program for the production of raw milk. SB 201 passed both houses of the state legislature but was vetoed by Schwarzenegger. It was a devastating blow to Mark, to consumers, and to all raw milk farmers whose farms and ideals were resting on Mark's victory in Sacramento. Ultimately, Organic Pastures rallied by putting their energies into figuring out how to pass the low bacteria count standard. Less than 10 coliforms is hard to pull off, Mark told me, especially when milk is tested on finished product not from the bulk tank. Milk that comes out of a healthy cow has coliforms fewer than ten. When raw milk is exposed to air and surfaces (even sanitary ones), the level of coliforms rise quickly. Agitation or pumping increases coliforms. "In raw milk coliforms are beneficial and inhibit bad bugs from growing," Mark said. "Coliforms kill pathogens." Organic Pastures eventually passed by taking away steps from the cow to the bottle and by developing new cleaning systems. "We spend fortunes on cleaning. But bad bugs don't come from milk lines, they come from unhealthy cows. Less than ten coliforms doesn't measure those kinds of bacteria."

Of his battle, Mark said, "We oppose the FDA when they say that only a drug can cure or improve an illness with their 'pill for every ill' policy system, which protects companies' profits. We work hard every day to teach how foods heal and foods prevent disease, which the FDA can't say about the drugs they support that kill hundreds of thousands of people every year. We fight alongside our consumers every day. And in the dying words of Weston A. Price, 'you teach, you teach, you teach.'"

Natural milk, meat, and eggs that come from well-treated animals are healthy, historically consumed foods that produce the vibrant good health that Dr. Price documented throughout his research on indigenous peoples. On a balanced diet of real, organically produced food, including natural animal products, Americans could quell our unnatural hunger and achieve our genetic gifts, and thus become as tall, attractive, cheerful, robust, sexy, and fertile and as relatively free from mental, dental, and degenerative diseases as our genetics predispose us to be. But we have been actually discouraged from eating natural foods. The vendetta against raw milk is one example. And Mark—a true American hero of the real-food movement—and his fight to provide real food to consumers, is a microcosm of what is happening in the fight between factory-food producers and real-food farmers and ranchers.

A huge part of this battle is the fact that corporate agribusiness has gobbled up all federal farm subsidies so that small farmers and ranchers have been driven out of business and off their lands, making natural food either very hard to find or more expensive than factory food. As a result, we have been indirectly encouraged to consume the diseased and drug- and hormone-infused animal products that are produced in CAFOs by these mega-corporations.

While the government endeavors to prevent us from drinking natural milk, there are health professionals who discourage the consumption of milk in general. The standard argument is that humans are the only species to drink milk past infancy and the only species to drink the milk of other species. I have never seen back-up research for those statements. Yet as I've said, I've seen 1,000-pound steers nursing from their mothers and cats and dogs lapping saucers of cow and goat milk. And we've all gotten the cute animal emails with photos of wild baby animals rescued by humans and nursed by their family cats and dogs.

Another argument is that animal milk was not a food of hunter-gatherers and thus is too "new" for modern humans to have adapted to. S.C. Gwynne writes about the hunter gatherer Comanches in *Empire of the Summer Moon: Quanah Parker and the Rise and Fall of the Comanches, the Most Powerful Indian Tribe in American History*, "Buffalo was the food the Comanches loved more than any other . . . If a slain female was giving milk, Comanches would cut into the udder bag and drink the milk mixed with warm blood. One of the greatest delicacies was the warm curdled milk from the stomach of a suckling calf." We also know that elsewhere in the world and much earlier in history, once easy-picking food supplies began to dwindle and hunter-gatherers began to dabble in domesticating plants and animals for food, animals that produced milk were of immediate interest. According to Jared Diamond in *Guns, Germs, and Steel: The Fates of Human Societies*, a domesticated animal is defined as one whose breeding and food supply are controlled by humans. Writes Diamond, "Milked mammals include the cow, sheep, goat, horse, reindeer, water buffalo, yak, and Arabian and Bactrian camels. Those mammals thereby yield several times more calories over their lifetime than if they were just slaughtered and consumed as meat."[236]

If you can't obtain raw milk, there are many organic milk suppliers who operate humane dairies and pasture-graze their cows, although all organic milk is pasteurized and many are ultra pasteurized (sterilized of enzymes as well as bad and good bacteria). Keep in mind that just because milk is "organic" doesn't mean their cows were treated humanely or fed species-appropriate food. Horizon is a very good example. Once a stellar example of an organic dairy, Horizon was bought out by Dean Foods, the largest supplier of milk in the country. Although the cartoon cows look happy on the carton, the truth is that the living cows are kept in feedlots and likely don't see a blade of grass. Just as with the food-industry-speak that has brought us factory food under the guise of "natural," the same twisted semantics are now bringing us pseudo "organic" milk. If you are ever in doubt about a food supplier, the Internet is a great resource, as there are people out there who are more than happy to tell you if a food provider is misrepresenting healthy claims or hiding something—like not letting their cows lie down in grass or eat their natural diet of grass, weeds, and shrubs.

You can find out if your state allows the sale of raw milk on realmilk. com and locate dairies on eatwild.com. In states that have outlawed raw milk sales, it's possible to purchase a share in a cow from which you are legally allowed to share in its milk production. However, just because someone has a backyard cow doesn't mean that they are properly versed in handling raw milk. I asked Mark for some guidelines. "There are a few things to look for if a family is going to source their milk locally. I suggest looking at the standards found at rawusa.org. Raw milk can be very safe if given a modicum of Mother Nature's care mixed with a little testing technology." If you are interested in defending the right of farmers, like Mark, to exist and want to buy their products, you can join the Farm-to-Consumer Legal Defense Fund, farmtoconsumer.org.

In the game of thimblerig—also known as the shell game—a swindler uses sleight of hand to shuffle an object between three cups. The player must then guess the location of the object. But the game is always rigged to defraud. Since the year 1900, an unhealthy symbiotic relationship has developed between our medical establishment, our government, the food, diet and pharmaceutical industries, and us, their fat, sick customers. We have been encouraged to consume the profit-rich products made with laboratory-concocted ingredients—processed, refined white sugar, refined grains, high-fructose corn syrup, MSG, aspartame, industrially processed soy, and processed polyunsaturated fats—as well as factory-animal products. Like shell game players, Americans believe the promises of good health, beauty, and satisfaction issued about these substances. But since these products both lack the life-sustaining nutrients necessary to maintain healthy metabolic processes and are mostly foreign and toxic to human physiology, we end up sick and fat.

PART SEVEN

Dieting Always Fails

CHAPTER SIXTEEN

The Malnutrition of Low-Calorie Dieting

IN GREEK MYTHOLOGY, SISYPHUS was a heartless king of Corinth condemned for eternity to roll a boulder up a hill only to have it roll back down just before he reached the top. Sisyphus' plight is analogous to dieting. Because every time you diet, you fail and must diet again. The main problem with diet books, programs, systems, products, and factory-made diet foods is that the focus is on losing weight through starvation (dieting). But no matter how hard you try to reach a weight-loss goal by starvation, you will end up failing. Although the weight-loss-by-starvation failure rate is high—we've rolled that same boulder up the hill many times—like Sisyphus, we get up and do it again . . . even though 95 percent of diets fail[237] and the vast majority of dieters understand that low-calorie dieting doesn't produce results. The truth is that dieting is a modern aberration that perpetuates malnutrition.

Current conventional wisdom points at the volume of food people consume as the reason people are overweight and sick. If only we had better portion control. In 1960, a serving of McDonald's fries contained 200 calories; in the early 2000s, a super-sized portion contained 610 calories. Then Morgan Spurlock's 2004 Sundance Film Festival award-winning documentary *Super Size Me*, which brought worldwide attention to the deleterious effects of eating an exclusive diet of McDonald's, shamed McDonald's into phasing out their super-size products. Has it made a difference in our collective weight? Not really. Today diet experts urge people to eat less fast food, fewer fries, and smaller portions of factory foods. Even Dr. Phil said in his book *The Ultimate Weight Solution*, "Another way to decrease your exposure to foods you buy for your kids is to purchase these foods in smaller packages. Rather than get a jumbo sack of chips that you're likely to scarf down in one sitting, why not buy smaller, single-serving sizes? With this approach, you've got automatic portion control." [238]

Are we really to believe that Americans could reduce body fat and maintain a healthy weight by simply, as Dr. Phil suggests, eating smaller bags of chips?

Low-calorie dieting has been around the longest, and it makes sense intuitively. Most physicians firmly believe in the calorie in/calorie out theory. We are told that you must restrict 3,600 calories, or 515 calories per day to lose one pound per week. Despite recent low fat and low carb tangents, Americans will always return to counting calories. That's why *The South Beach Diet*, which is billed as a low carb diet but is really a low calorie diet, has sold 22 million copies to date.

One hundred years ago, a hardworking man ate 6,000 to 6,500 calories and a hardworking woman ate 4,000 to 4,500 calories per day. Today an average woman needs 2,000 to 2,500 calories and an average man needs 2,500 to 2,800 calories. On the first day of the South Beach Diet, by my calculation, you're allowed 1,167 calories, which is 800 to 1,333 calories less per day than an average woman needs, and 1,333 to 1,163 less calories than the average man needs for optimal metabolic function. Still, you may be convinced that a low-calorie diet is the way to weight loss, because you have heard people say, "I lost thirty pounds on the South Beach Diet!" But losing weight is not the end of the story. It's what happens next that you need to consider.

There are five reasons why a low-calorie diet is counterproductive to weight management. The first reason is that human beings in the twenty-first century have the same physiology as our Paleolithic ancestors. In pre-historic times food was not always plentiful. People gorged when they had food, then went without eating when food was scarce. Prehistoric human physiology evolved an "insulin-directed" fat-storage system enabling them to survive to this "feast and famine" lifestyle. The hormone insulin, which is secreted from the pancreas when food is eaten, directs nutrients into the cells. In times of famine, prehistoric humans' pancreases adjusted, so the next time they gorged during a plentiful season, their insulin secretions were higher and more food could be stored as fat.

Twenty-first-century humans have this exact same fat-storage system. That means if you deprive your body of food it will perceive this deprivation as a time of famine and will adjust your insulin output so that, when you break your diet, more insulin will be secreted and more of what you eat will be stored as fat.

The second reason low-calorie dieting fails is that starvation signals your thyroid to slow down in an effort to save energy and keep you alive, leaving you with a new metabolic set point for calorie consumption. In German concentration camps during World War II, prisoners were fed subsistence diets ranging from 600 to 1,700 calories per day (1,700 calories applied to circumstances, such as hard labor, when it was useful to keep people alive). In Vietnamese POW camps, prisoners were fed between 300 and 1,000 calories per day. Many survived by eating rats and insects. Concentration camp survivors and POWs were emaciated when the camps were liberated at the end of the wars, but survivors subsequently suffered a greater tendency toward obesity due to down-regulated thyroid function. Likewise, babies born to malnourished mothers during the Biafra famine in Nigeria forty years ago are now struggling with obesity.[239]

This is how down regulation of the thyroid occurs: When you eat a low calorie diet, the meager fuel is quickly used up. Your brain needs an ongoing drip of sugar or you will lapse into a coma and die, and so it demands that you eat again. Your body keeps a ready supply of glycogen (sugar) stored in your liver and muscles to use to satisfy your brain and draw upon for fuel. But these glycogen stores are quickly used up. (Because glycogen is stored with water in a 1:3 ratio, when you burn off your glycogen stores you can see a drop in your weight of up to 10 pounds in one week.) When your glycogen stores are gone, your liver struggles to regulate the blood-sugar supply to your brain.

And so your adrenal glands work overtime to secrete the stress hormone cortisol, which breaks down bones and muscles to get the sugar (fuel) and amino acids (proteins for repair and rebuilding) that your body needs. By the time you break your low-calorie diet, you have two more problems: less lean body mass and a lower metabolic set point. Since the more muscle mass you have, the higher your metabolic rate and the less muscle mass the lower your metabolic rate, you now have a lowered metabolic rate. In addition, as a protective measure to prevent catastrophic muscle and bone mass destruction, your thyroid has down-regulated to slow down energy needs. That means every time you low-calorie diet, your body becomes a more effective fat-storing machine. By simply resuming a normal diet, you will put on more weight than you lost.

Today many Americans eat a subsistence diet of less than 1,500 calories a day—even when they are not actually dieting. When they have that small bag of chips, it all goes to their butts, bellies, and thighs. Those who follow the South Beach Diet after a period of time will have an up-regulated insulin response and a down-regulated thyroid, and less muscle mass, which contributes to a lower metabolic set point. Losing weight on a low-calorie diet is great if you want to eat that way for the rest of your life.

The third reason low-calorie diets fail is because starvation can provoke a binge response. Without adequate food, your neurotransmitters can't replenish. To get through the day, dieters often resort to using stimulants (coffee, diet drinks, tobacco products, alcohol, and OTC and prescription diet pills, as well as recreational drugs). Using stimulants may give your brain enough of a boost to resist powerful messages to eat. But ultimately you'll have to eat again, and then you may likely binge. People who have suffered from starvation (from war-time food shortages, as prisoners of war, from being marooned or shipwrecked) or those who have imposed starvation on themselves (anorexics and volunteers in semi-starvation experiments) suffer from uncontrollable urges to binge and have a greater tendency toward obesity. [240]

The most definitive study on starvation was conducted in the mid-1940s for the War Department at the Laboratory of Physiological Hygiene at the University of Minnesota. The study was intended to help starvation victims in war-torn Europe—but will likely never be repeated as today nothing this life threatening could be imposed on even willing volunteers. Forty twenty- to thirty-three-year-old men ate 1,570 calories a day for six months to lose 2.5 pounds a week, or 25 percent of their body weight. When the three-month nutritional rehabilitation began, the men's resting metabolic rates had declined by 40 percent, and their pulses and body temperatures had dropped, indicating hypothyroidism (down-regulated thyroids). They demonstrated all the symptoms of malnutrition, such as feeling cold, tired, hungry, having difficulty concentrating, insomnia, thinning hair, dry, thin skin, gastrointestinal problems, and no interest in sex. Even when given unrestricted amounts of food, researchers noted what they termed "semi-starvation neurosis": The volunteers were agitated and nervous, withdrawn, impatient, and self-critical, with distorted body images and extremely aberrant eating behaviors, such as voracious appetites followed by large and rapid food intake; they exhibited lack of control and distress over amounts eaten; they complained of hunger despite huge meals; they believed that eating "triggered" hunger; they suffered from cravings and obsession with food, as well as secrecy and defensiveness over food; they had a new preoccupation with body shape and weight; they scavenged or ate from garbage containers; they stole, hid, and hoarded food and manipulated others for food; they made bizarre mixtures of food; they ate unpalatable and inappropriate food (raw meat, scraps); they used excessive spicing and flavoring; they exhibited poor table manners (licking knives and bottle lids, collecting crumbs, gnawing at bones); they preferred to eat in isolation; they induced vomiting or ate until they vomited; they suffered self-loathing; they took drastic measures to resist binges; they relapsed into binge eating despite attempts to rehabilitate them. In addition, they became morose and obsessive; a few mutilated themselves, one man cutting off three fingers.[241]

On a healthy diet within nine months, the majority of the volunteers regained normal eating and emotional patterns, and their previous weight and thyroid function. What this experiment demonstrated is that the experience of starvation compels us to binge in an attempt to provide our brains with fuel and our bodies with a fresh supply of nutrients necessary to restore hormone balance and heal from malnutrition. It also demonstrates that on a diet of real, whole food, cravings, binging, and all the aberrant behaviors of unnatural hunger can be stopped.

The fourth reason low-calorie diets ultimately fail is that, although the United States is the richest country in the world, the majority of our citizens are suffering from malnutrition, even if they are obese. Our factory-food diet is viewed as a period of starvation to our bodies. Some people even attempt to diet on fast food. In addition to starving on a low-cal diet of fast food, you would also be consuming trans fats, chemical solvents, industrially processed soy, commercial milk, MSG, aspartame, refined white flour and numerous other toxic substances. In addition to hare-brained fast-food diets, there are diet factory foods such as the Special K challenge, a starvation diet that promises you will lose six pounds in two weeks by eating two bowls of their product every day (and now we have South Beach Diet cereal). Weight Watcher's, Jenny Craig, and Nutrisystem make industrialized meals that are devoid of enzymes and are otherwise nutritionally dead. These are but a few examples of the fake diet foods you can eat to perpetuate malnutrition.

A persistent state of malnutrition from eating factory food keeps Americans bingeing, obsessing, and ever seeking satiety. If you begin a low-calorie diet while in a malnourished state, you're beginning the diet with a preconditioned low metabolism, hormone imbalances, and other health issues. There's no way your body is letting go of your fat stores if your life is in danger. The reason is that we are hardwired for survival. This inherent programming to survive is the fifth reason dieting fails. Our bodies are programmed to hold onto fat cells in case we need that fat to survive in an emergency famine in the future.

In an interview on *Inside the Actors Studio*, Russell Crowe told James Lipton how bulking up 44 pounds to play the real-life tobacco industry whistleblower Jeffrey Wigand, Ph.D., for the movie *The Insider* ruined his metabolism for life. "I must have been clearing 235, 240, or something like that at the time. I'm only, like I said, five-eleven and a half and a bit, so that looks gigantic on me. But the one thing is my metabolism has never been the same since I did that film. Now I always have this incredible uphill battle."[242]

Crowe, who fattened up on cheeseburgers and beer, experienced an accelerated version of what many factory food-eating Americans are going through today. Getting fat on factory food bulks up fat cells, and your body does not like to let go of fat once it's onboard. Fat cells have just recently been recognized by the scientific community as something other than inert blobs. Fat cells are now recognized to behave like endocrine organs that secrete hormones. We're bombarded with xenoestrogenic toxins every day in factory food (including factory produce and animal products), chemical exposures, and city water.

Xenoestrogens aren't just causing the problems listed on page 151, they're also causing people to gain fat. Researchers think that these endocrine-disrupting chemicals—which are also referred to as obesogens— mimic estrogen and mis-program stem cells to become fat cells, and alter the function of genes. Obesogens are thought to inappropriately alter lipid (fat) homeostasis (all the metabolic processes that depend on fats and strive for equanimity in the body). Obesogens increase fat storage, change metabolic set points, disrupt energy balance, or modify the regulation of appetite and satiety to promote fat accumulation and obesity. The pesticides, chemicals, rBGH dairy, soy, and other toxins in factory food can deliver the estrogen mimickers xenoestrogens and phytoestrogens— obesogens—into your system and keep you fat.[243]

In addition to xenohormones mutating into obesogens, simply having toxins from factory food infiltrating your system may contribute to fat retention. When your body is confronted with a steady influx of toxins, those (mostly fat soluble) toxins have to be stored away somewhere, as your body cannot have toxins floating around in your bloodstream. So your body must retain fat cells as storage repositories. To convince your body that it's OK to let go of fat cells, you have to provide reassurance that there will be no more incoming poison. The more of a purist you are about eating organic, real food, the better your chances of losing fat.

Remember the people mentioned earlier who have suffered from starvation or those who have subjected themselves to starvation? They were found to have a surprisingly high amount of body fat, even if they were emaciated.[244] In other words, people who have starved down to skeletons still have fat cells. This is because body fat is your last defense against death and your body does not want to give up any fat if it feels threatened that you might die.

I don't fault people for being obese, and I don't fault obese people for resorting to extreme measures, such as gastric bypass surgery. I fault the FDA for allowing purveyors of factory food the freedom to inundate our food supply with grossly unhealthy, fattening, addicting substances that have created a population of neurotransmitter-imbalanced, unnaturally hungry people and then for allowing the diet industry to perpetuate obesity. When a person becomes morbidly obese there is often no turning back, and they have to have some recourse or their lives are virtually over, and so some resort to gastric bypass surgery.

Obesity is a complicated problem. Fifty years ago, Adelle Davis wrote, "To say that obesity is caused merely by consuming too many calories is like saying that the only cause of the American Revolution was the Boston Tea Party."[245] But it makes sense that factory food is the primary reason for obesity as this is the first time in history that humans have experienced this level of obesity. Often people become fat and even obese by eating the same number of calories of factory food as thin individuals who eat real food. Sweets, soft drinks, and alcoholic beverages make up almost 25 percent of all calories eaten by Americans, 5 percent is comprised of salty snacks and fruit-flavored beverages, and 10 percent is bread, rolls, and crackers. That means 40 percent of our intake is junk to our bodies.[246] What many Americans don't understand is that it's not the volume that is making us fat as much as it is what is actually being ingested.

I have a number of friends from foreign countries who gained weight when they came to the United States (or Canada) and ate factory food. Pedro from Brazil came to the United States as a fifteen-year old exchange student and gained 33 pounds in five months. When he returned to Brazil, he naturally lost the weight not by dieting, but by simply going back to eating the traditional Brazilian diet. Hadrien went to college in Canada, where he lived around the corner from a McDonald's. He returned to Paris 30 pounds heavier but lost it all and then some by simply eating the typical French diet. Fumiko from Japan came to the U.S. at age seventeen in to attend boarding school. She gained 20 pounds in ten months, but she too naturally lost the weight when she returned to Japan, not by dieting, but by eating the traditional real food Japanese diet. Today Fumiko is the dean of a woman's college in Tokyo. She told me, "One of my students who studied at our Boston campus gained 28 pounds in four months. The average weight gain among our girls who study in the U.S. is about nine pounds. But immediately after they return to Japan, they go back to their previous weight without dieting."

 Instead of ridding our culture of factory food and providing real food abundantly, affordably, and conveniently, our government has now agreed to allow "obesity" as a Medicare diagnosis, which paves the way for more people to turn to the surgeon's scalpel in a desperate attempt to "fix" their obesity. In his book *Complications: A Surgeon's Notes on an Imperfect Science*, Atul Gawande, a surgical resident and staff writer on medicine and science for *The New Yorker*, recounted a "successful" gastric bypass story in which he writes "[The patient] was concerned about the possible long-term effects of nutritional deficiencies (for which patients are instructed to take a daily multivitamin)."[247]

Gastric bypass leaves patients with stomachs the size of a walnut. More than one bite of food initially will cause them to become violently nauseous, and eating more will result in vomiting. Signing on for gastric bypass is voluntarily submitting to a procedure that will enforce starvation. In an attempt to supply the body with the nutrients it needs for 24/7/365 repair of cells, tissues, and bones and for replenishing hormones, neurotransmitters, and so on, the patient is advised to take a daily multivitamin.

In a perfect world, we could take the $25,000 to $30,000 that each gastric bypass surgery costs and instead sequester obese people in health facilities where they would get balanced meals of real, living food, any necessary hormone replacement, nutraceuticals (natural nutrients from plants that, when taken in specific doses, can have positive therapeutic effects), and other high-quality dietary supplements, exercise, emotional therapy, and lessons in shopping and preparing real food, so that after one year they would come out with balanced hormone levels and healed on the inside and out. Instead, we slice and dice their gastrointestinal tract and send them home to starve to death on less factory food than they would normally eat. One year later, they are emaciated down to an acceptable weight, but even more malnourished.

Anyone who is going to undergo gastric bypass would be wise to develop a relationship with a qualified clinical nutritionist who is capable of planning a nutrient-dense meal plan of real food, so that starvation can be achieved in the healthiest way possible, as bizarre as that sounds.

Your doctor may tell you that all of this is nonsense, as studies on mice, rats, monkeys, and even worms and protozoa (the smallest, single-cell animal) have proven that extreme low-calorie diets extend lifespan as much as 50 percent. In humans, nutrient-dense calorie-restrictive diets are believed to reduce the risk for cancer, diabetes, and atherosclerosis. Calorie restriction is said to reduce body weight, blood pressure, cholesterol, and glucose, factors that are all associated with good health and longer life. A number of hypotheses have been floated as to why calorie restriction provides greater life expectancy in studies, but so far no one knows for sure.[248]

However, problems associated with calorie restriction are feeling cold, dwelling on food, including engaging in obsessive behaviors, temporary loss of energy, decreased sex drive, and feeling socially isolated, and in women the resulting weight loss can affect fertility and increase the risk of developing osteopenia (bone loss), leading to osteoporosis as well as loss of muscle mass.[249] These are all symptoms of malnutrition.

There's a great scene in the movie *The Truth About Cats and Dogs* in which the thin, gorgeous Noelle (Uma Thurman) muses that she doesn't know what's inside of her since she never eats anything. Most people don't give much thought about what their bodies are made out of. Eating real food has several purposes. First, your brain needs a constant drip of sugar (fuel). Equally important, your body is constantly breaking down and building back up again, and it needs an ongoing supply of fats and proteins to build lean body mass on a cellular level, as well as essential amino acids, essential fatty acids, vitamins, minerals, and enzymes that are the chemical catalysts that fuel metabolic processes. People need to eat a variety of food in adequate quantity every single day to give their bodies all these necessary supplies.

If your goal is weight loss, like Sisyphus, who was condemned for eternity to roll a boulder up a hill only to have it roll back down just before he reached the top, this goal will be eternally out of reach. Let's say you are a 200-pound woman or a 250-pound man and you need to lose 80 and 60 pounds, respectively. You can go on the South Beach low-cal diet and lose 30 pounds in three months. By this time your face will be hanging down around your neck and you will still need to lose 50 and 30 pounds, respectively. But can you continue eating low-calorie for more months? Now that you have lowered your caloric intake to a famine level for a substantial period of time, your body now has a higher insulin response to incoming food, a down-regulated thyroid, a lowered metabolic set point, a biological inner drive for survival that is on red alert to hang onto fat cells, and a craving and bingeing response instigated by severe malnutrition. If you go off the diet, you will gain all of those pounds back and more.

If Americans would only turn to a balanced diet of real, living food, we could then achieve optimal health and body weight. Such a diet would balance our endocrine systems, heal malnutrition, ratchet up our metabolisms, calm unnatural hunger, and assure our bodies that we are not going to die so that it can let go of fat cells. In the first year, that 200-pound woman or 250-pound man may lose two pounds a week, but let's say they both only lose one pound a week. At the end of the year, they would weigh 148 and 198, respectively. And they would not have been suffering on a "diet." Furthermore, they will likely have exchanged 20 pounds of fat for muscle and may not even need to lose more.

Contrary to conventional medical wisdom, there is more to good health than losing weight. If you want to live into old age thinly and happily and die a peaceful death, you will not get there by starving your body. Low-calorie dieting is not the only starvation diet. The introduction of the lipid hypothesis 50 years ago ultimately led to the low fat diet, an extreme starvation diet.

CHAPTER SEVENTEEN

The Low Fat Diet Made Us Fat and Sick

THROUGH MY INFORMAL RESTAURANT and market research I've learned one very important fact about Americans: We don't like to chew. Check out the way people eat their cheeseburgers, fries, and Cokes. It's *bite, chew, chew, swallow. Bite, chew, swallow. Bite, chew, chew, swallow. Glug, glug, glug, glug.* While primitive humans spent many hours every day chewing raw meat, nuts, seeds, and roots, consuming 300 to 400 calories per hour, modern Americans bite, chew, chew, swallow, and glug entire meals in mere minutes. According to Daniel E. Lieberman, professor of biological anthropology at Harvard University, "The size of our faces has shrunk about 12 percent since the Ice Age when humans probably spent much more time chewing harder, tougher food to get the calories they needed for survival."[250]

As you recall, the lipid hypothesis centered around the beliefs that elevated blood-cholesterol levels were a risk factor for heart disease and that blood-cholesterol levels were elevated by eating cholesterol-laden foods and saturated fat. When this hypothesis was launched in the 1950s, the message to eat less saturated fat and cholesterol turned out to be a major boon to the food industry because this message threw a monkey wrench into our community consciousness about food and set the stage for the food industry to begin making billions of dollars. Americans didn't know what to eat if they couldn't eat what they had always eaten since the dawn of humankind. First we were told that historically eaten dietary fats were unhealthy and caused disease. Then we were told to eat a low fat, high carbohydrate diet consisting of grains, steamed veggies, and fruit.

If there was ever a population less suited to a fat-free veggie diet, it was the American public. How many modern bite-chew-swallow-glug folks do you think could down plates of steamed vegetables throughout the course of one day? Not many Americans choose the dry veggie diet as a lifestyle—a diet that has never been eaten by any people on the face of the earth in the history of humankind. (Even vegetarian swamis in India eat ghee, clarified butter, and it was butter that nutritional researcher Dr. Price found in all the healthy primitive diets he studied.)

As with all unnatural diets, there were immediate and more long-term problems associated with the dry veggie/grain diet. For starters, this diet does not provide enough fat to modulate the absorption of all that roughage, and people who tried this diet suffered from extreme gastrointestinal distress. A more serious problem with a dry veggie diet, besides the boredom, gastrointestinal distress, and all that chewing, was the fact that few people actually choose this diet of dreary, fat-free brown rice, dry steamed veggies, and salad with the dressing on the side. Instead, Americans went for the addictively tasty-carb factory foods. In fact, back when this diet was introduced, the recommended ADA breakfast for type 2 diabetics was cold cereal, milk, banana, and orange juice—all carbs. But as Americans ate more easily chewed carbs (sugar), the 1970s and 1980s saw an exponential rise in obesity and disease. To address this mysterious rise in obesity and disease, in 1992 USDA introduced food pyramid guidelines recommending Americans radically reduce fat and increase their consumption of carbs—foods like pasta and bread. The USDA advice to eat more pasta and bread was eagerly embraced by Americans and it led to binges on cereal, pizza, pretzels, bagels, and low fat cookies.

Here's where the long-term problems occurred. Since carbs are energy food and should be eaten in quantities that match a person's individual metabolic health and activity level, when you eat more energy than you are currently burning you'll gain weight. But Americans weren't given this message. They were virtually badgered into eating more carbs.

The most damaging result of our radical increase in the consumption of carbs was that Americans were now suffering with chronic high insulin levels. This is not a condition that creates immediate alarm. A person doesn't feel any different when insulin levels soar and remain elevated. But the damage occurs within, insidiously and inexorably. Chronic high insulin levels are implicated in every single degenerative disease, including type 2 diabetes (explained below), cancer (insulin is a growth factor for cells), and heart disease (high insulin levels encourage coronary artery plaquing).[251] In fact, studies on insulin and arterial plaque date back to the 1960s. Researchers actually infused insulin into the femoral arteries of dogs and arterial plaque occurred in every dog.[252] (High insulin levels are also caused by stress, dieting, caffeine, alcohol, tobacco, aspartame, steroids, sedentary lifestyle, recreational, and OTC and prescription drugs, but our focus here is sugar.)

Here's how it works: Hormones are the chemical communicators between cells. For the body to function well, they must be kept at normal levels, as hormones depend on each other to do their jobs. Because all the systems of the body are interconnected, one hormonal imbalance causes another. A key hormone to keep balanced is insulin, which is secreted by the pancreas. Insulin's major function is to regulate blood sugar levels, thereby protecting the brain and other vital organs from receiving too much sugar, which damages cells. When you eat carbs they turn immediately into sugar in your system, and when too much sugar is in your blood stream, insulin binds to insulin receptors on your cells so that they will open up and accept that extra sugar.

Years of eating too many carbs mean that your cells will be clogged with sugar. When they're filled to capacity and can't fit another sugar molecule, cells reduce the number of insulin receptors so there are fewer receptors for insulin to activate. This is insulin resistance. If you live long enough, you'll likely develop at least some degree of insulin resistance, which is a condition of aging. What's not normal is that elementary school children are now developing insulin resistance. The recent fashion trend of low-rise jeans (prehistorically known as hip huggers) has revealed a population of young American women with fat tummies. Today, because girls are raised on sugar, they're insulin resistant, with expanding middles, by the time they reach adolescence. The reason for this weight gain around the midsection is that when cells refuse to accept sugar, extra sugar in the bloodstream is diverted into fat production, and fat accumulates around the waist first.

When cells become insulin resistant, alarm bells go off in your body. Your pancreas will secrete even more insulin in an attempt to overcome this resistance. So now you have too much insulin in your bloodstream, which is called hyperinsulinemia. Your cells are being bombarded with insulin, which is like a frantic knocking, pleading to allow the excess sugar to enter. But stuffed as they are to capacity with sugar, your cells react by further reducing insulin receptors, which is increased insulin resistance.

If you continue putting too much sugar into your system until your cells have closed down all insulin receptors, the sugar has nowhere to go and remains in your bloodstream. You now have high blood sugar levels *and* high insulin levels, i.e., type 2 diabetes, an ugly progressive disease that causes blindness, kidney disease, nerve disease (leading to amputations), heart disease, stroke, and premature death.[253] One in ten Americans has type 2 diabetes, and it's the seventh leading cause of death in the U.S.[254] By the year 2050 the CDC predicts one in three Americans will have type 2 diabetes. We now have a generation of adults who are very likely to outlive their children, and in fact, experts predict that we will see teenage deaths of heart disease on a regular basis within the next decade.[255]

Aside from those who binge to overweight or obesity on carbs and consequentially suffer from chronic high insulin diseases, there are also thin people who eat very little, but everything they eat is carbohydrate. A person who has a teeny weenie piece of crumb cake with coffee in the morning (the no-calories-if-nibbling-while-standing-up mentality), a few bites of quiche in a white flour crust and a chocolate bon bon for lunch, and one egg roll, two Dim Sum, green tea ice cream and a fortune cookie, washed down with white wine for dinner, is a walking insulin factory. If you are able to control your portions but those portions are mostly sugar, you are cruising the danger zone as far as chronic high insulin levels are concerned and an insulin-related disease might lurk in your future.

Contrary to the absolute science that high sugar consumption leads to insulin resistance, back in 1992 the USDA's prioritizing of foods (urging more carbs) was wholeheartedly endorsed by doctors. So on top of all the carcinogenic, heart-disease-causing oils that people were consuming, they dumped in loads of simple carbs into their systems. It was logical. If you can't eat eggs, meat, butter, cheese, or cream, then you have to fill your diet with something else.

Despite all evidence to the contrary, the conventional wisdom of the day was "it's the fat, not the sugar" that makes you fat. The low fat craze morphed into the fat-free craze, which encouraged food manufacturers to remove all fat from their products and replace it with sugar. With the public becoming more confused about what to eat and what not to eat, along with the rampant rise of unnatural hunger and the resultant binge eating, factory-food makers understood that the market was ripe to hawk any product they could dream up. Americans went along as food makers issued their siren call with the introduction of thousands of factory-food products into our marketplace—products tagged with food-industry-speak pronouncements of good health, beauty, and satisfaction. The problem was that these products contained substances that were foreign and mostly toxic to human physiology—and, of course, all that sugar.

Then came the blame game. As we grew fatter and type 2 diabetes, heart disease, and cancer were skyrocketing, the medical establishment came to the conclusion that we were not compliant enough. They hammered harder on the "no saturated fats and cholesterol" message, encouraged us to eat more carbohydrates (sugar) and frantically advised us to lose weight. But Americans could not hear any warnings about their out-of-control eating because they were crazed on carbs. The medical community beat the drum harder about our weight. But how do you break through to people you've turned into carb-addicted, binge-eaters to get them to stop at one bowl of Kellogg's "heartsmart" Special K, when they have already eaten an entire box of SnackWell's low fat cookies?

Then there are actually people who can maintain—through superhuman willpower—a starvation diet of hot water with lemon peel and oatmeal with berries for breakfast, dry salad for lunch, and one cup of pasta with marinara sauce for dinner, accompanied by one half cup of steamed broccoli and a small salad with a twist of lemon. These are typically the women Tom Wolfe described in his novel *Bonfire of the Vanities* as "social X rays . . . They keep themselves so thin, they look like X-ray pictures . . . You can see lamplight through their bones . . ." Those who heroically restrained themselves from binging were disappointed to realize the low fat diet did not produce beautiful bodies. That's because low fat diets are typically devoid of the cholesterol necessary to make hormones and proteins that are the building materials necessary to rebuild or create new cells that compose skin, muscles, organs, nails, hair, brain cells, and bones. Without incoming supplies, the body is forced to cannibalize its own bones and muscles to obtain the proteins necessary to keep up the rebuilding processes. (Carbs are fuel; they don't supply building materials for your body to rebuild or replace cells.) If you happen to have the defiant willpower necessary to fight the biological drive to eat the food necessary for survival, you will see outward and inward manifestations of malnutrition sooner or later. In addition to developing a tubbier midsection, you may notice more cellulite taking over, along with saggy skin, thinning hair (the "male pattern balding" syndrome in women), brittleness and dryness, more wrinkles, dry eyes, ridged and shredding nails, as well as heartburn, insomnia, cravings and bingeing, infertility, type 2 diabetes, and coronary artery plaque.

A contributing factor to the wasted-away-with-a-fat-midsection look is that a diet low in protein results in diminished glucagon production, which is your body's fat-burning hormone. When you eat, two hormones, glucagon and insulin, are released from your pancreas. When you eat a balanced diet of real food these hormones are balanced. Glucagon is responsible for releasing fats from your cells to be used as fuel and building blocks within your body. Glucagon is released when you eat protein. Insulin is the fat- and nutrient-storing hormone that is released when you eat carbs. The ratio between these two hormones determines whether food will be used as building materials or fuel or stored as fat. If you eat only carbs, your insulin-to-glucagon ratio will be too high and those carbs will likely be stored as fat.

Human beings are made out of dynamic tissues that are constantly undergoing change and being replaced. This breaking-down process is essential for clearing out the old cells and cellular material (enzymes, hormones, neurotransmitters) to make room for new. The regeneration process is made possible by the fact that we eat the very same biochemicals that our bodies are inherently composed of: proteins and fats.

Of the low fat diet, Drs. Michael and Mary Dan Eades write in *The Protein Power Lifeplan*, "Clearly the low fat diet hasn't been the panacea that many had hoped for; in fact, it has turned out to be a dismal failure, a fact admitted publicly in 1996 by most of the world's experts in nutritional research." At the Second International Symposium on Dietary Fats and Oil Consumption in Health and Disease in April 1996, Drs. Eades listened to nutritional researchers from numerous countries talk about the effects of fat in the human diet. They were not talking about the low fat diet preventing heart disease but exactly the opposite. The major consensus was that the low fat diet is a failure.[256]

In *The Cholesterol Myth: Exposing the Fallacy That Saturated Fat and Cholesterol Cause Heart Disease*, Uffe Ravnskov, M.D., Ph.D., analyzed 300 scientific references to disprove the nine main myths of the lipid hypothesis that had generated the low fat diet, which are: (1) High fat foods cause heart disease; (2) high cholesterol causes heart disease; (3) high fat foods raise blood cholesterol; (4) cholesterol blocks arteries; (5) animal studies prove the diet-heart theory; (6) lowering your cholesterol will lengthen your life; (7) polyunsaturated oils are good for you; (8) the anti-cholesterol campaign is based on good science; and (9) all scientists support the diet-heart theory.[257] Dr. Ravnskov, the author of more than eighty papers and letters critical of the cholesterol hypothesis, told me, "An almost endless number of scientific studies have shown that animal fat and high cholesterol are not causing heart disease. Unfortunately, these studies are ignored by the proponents of the cholesterol campaign."[258]

Science writer Gary Taubes's *New York Times Magazine* article "What if It's All Been a Big Fat Lie?" hit the newsstands on July 7, 2002, sending shock waves through Americans' collective consciousness by questioning the validity of the low fat diet. In December 10, 2003, when asked in an interview what made him go after the topic of the low fat diet, Taubes, an award-winning journalist who often focuses on exposing poor and deficient science, replied, "I'd been reporting on salt and blood pressure, which is a huge controversy, and some of the people involved in that were involved in the advice to tell Americans to eat low fat diets, and they were terrible scientists. These were some of the worst scientists I'd ever come across in my 20-odd year career of writing about controversial science."[259]

The mother of all hormones is cholesterol. Cholesterol is needed to make vitamin D from sunshine, and without vitamin D the body can't utilize calcium. Brain function depends on cholesterol. Cholesterol creates a healthy immune system, decreases the risk of cancer, and decelerates aging. The low fat, low cholesterol diet made us fat, depressed, impotent, and sick. As the low fat diet took hold, drug industry profits soared with the sales of impotence drugs, antidepressants, osteoporosis drugs, chemotherapy drugs, and so on. Bafflingly, the low fat diet continued to garner support from the American Heart Association, the Centers for Disease Control, the United States Department of Agriculture, the National Cancer Institute, the American Medical Association, the American Diabetes Association, and so on.

Less than one year after this study, a $415-million, eight-year study published in the February 2006 issue of the *Journal of the American Medical Association* found that the subjects who ate a low fat diet had exactly the same rates of colon cancer, breast cancer, heart attacks and strokes as the subjects who ate whatever they felt like eating. It was deemed the "Rolls Royce" of studies and the "final word" on the low fat diet. In response, David A. Freedman, a statistician at the University of California who writes on the design and analysis of clinical trials said, "We, in the scientific community, often give strong advice based on flimsy evidence."[260]

In the decade prior to this "final word," and despite the medical community's wholehearted embrace of the low fat diet, many Americans rebelled and decided to look elsewhere for weight-loss solutions.

When cardiologist Robert Atkins published his first book, *Dr. Atkins' Diet Revolution,* in 1972, he was attacked by the AMA, which labeled his diet approach "potentially dangerous." This resulted in Congress summoning him to Washington to defend his diet. Thirty-one years and 15 million books later, "Atkins" was synonymous with low carb dieting.

CHAPTER EIGHTEEN

Low Carbohydrate Dieting Was a Bust

IN SHOWTIME'S COMEDY SERIES *Weeds*, newly widowed suburban mom Nancy Botwin (Mary Louise Parker) turns to dealing pot to help pay the bills. When she stops in to stock up at her suppliers' home, the conversation turns to cornbread. "I miss carbs," Nancy says. A young woman filling Baggies chimes in. ""My friend Heylia tried no carbs. She ate bacon and eggs for a whole month. I'm talkin' like five dozen eggs and a whole pig a day. She lost eleven pounds. That shit work."[261]

It seems like the no carb thing is brand-new, but actually this approach has been around for a long time. The very first low carb diet was made popular in 1825 by French attorney Jean Anthelme Brillat-Savarin in his book *The Physiology of Taste*. In 1863 a London undertaker, William Banting, published *Letter on Corpulence* after losing 50 pounds on a low carb diet. One hundred years later, when I was thirteen, I read about a diet that the military had been using. It was the first time I became aware of a low carb, high protein diet. I was mystified by the instructions to chow down on bacon, beef, and peanut butter but to absolutely avoid fruit and sweets. That was also the first time I ever heard the word "gluten." Glutens are plant proteins occurring in cereal grains, chiefly corn and wheat—in other words, what we commonly think of as starch. It was also the first time I heard the word "ketosis," meaning a state of starvation in which your insulin levels fall low enough to burn body fat for energy.

In 1963, a young, porky cardiologist ran across an article in the

Journal of the American Medical Association on low carb dieting (which may have been the same source for the military diet that I read). That cardiologist, Dr. Atkins, went on the program himself, lost weight, and subsequently wrote several bestselling books on low carb dieting. Forty years later, his approach hit the big time, and "low carb" and "no carb" became catchphrases.

Studies have shown that the low carb diet is initially more effective than a low fat diet, but that low carb dieters experience rebound weight gain within one year.[262] Our physiology dictates that a diet in which carbs are individually modulated is the only way to reduce body fat without sacrificing your health. But people are not approaching nutrition in an individualized way. People are recklessly eating radically imbalanced, close to zero carb, one-size-fits-all diets that do not provide adequate, well-rounded nutrition. For instance, the Atkins induction phase allows only two to three cups of vegetables every day and minuscule amounts of fruit and dairy. Many low carb dieters decide to take extreme steps and eliminate all carbs, including veggies, fruits, and dairy. Healthy metabolic processes are dependent on adequate macronutrients (proteins, fats, and carbohydrates). But the energy supplied by these macronutrients to fuel healthy metabolic processes is released by micronutrients (vitamins, minerals, and enzymes present in plant foods, fruits, and dairy products). This is a perfect example of why you are not going to get the full benefit of any one food without eating it in balance with other foods.

Atkins recommends that people move on to the maintenance diet, which is slightly more balanced. However, Atkins reminds his readers, "Induction not only jump-starts your weight loss, it is also a convenient refuge to which you can retreat whenever you need to get off a weight-loss plateau or to get back on the program after a lapse. So if you're fallen off your Lifetime Maintenance program for whatever reason, you can return to Induction . . ."[263] So that means people are going back to a diet of subnutritional value time and time again.

Unless great care is taken to eat grass-fed, pasture-raised animal products, Atkins followers consume excess amounts of factory-animal products from diseased animals that are permeated with carcinogens. All this without the benefit of the antioxidants found in fruits and vegetables.

And not to forget that zero carb dieters are often not versed in how to choose healthy fats and how to avoid poison fats. And so these dieters often munch on highly toxic fats such as deep-fat-fried pork rinds and the like.

To make matters worse, most people supplement this diet with factory low carb diet products. Before his death Dr. Atkins sold majority shares of Atkins Nutritionals, Inc., to the tune of $500 million.[264] In hot pursuit were Atkins wannabees, who unleashed a torrent of low carb substances onto the market. In January 2004, representatives from 450 food companies, including Kraft, ConAgra, and Wal-Mart, gathered for two days to brainstorm how they could take advantage of the predicted $25-billion low carb market.[265] While because of the unpalatability of low carb foods, Atkins Nutritionals, Inc., filed for bankruptcy in the summer of 2005, factory low carb products remain on our shelves.

Carbs are reduced in factory-food products by pumping up the volume with soy protein and substituting sugar with sorbitol, maltitol, and lacitol, which are sugar alcohols that are promoted as having little or no impact on blood-sugar levels and insulin secretion. (Some clinical nutritionists question this claim.) Sugar alcohols are molecules, like the weird science fake-fat olestra molecule, that are too big to be digested and that, like olestra, can cause gastrointestinal problems. Chemists are now hard at work trying to solve this problem by creating more science-fiction sugars—like Splenda—in labs.

Splenda (sucralose), a chemically derived, chlorinated molecule, is 600 to 1,000 times sweeter than sugar, with no added calories. It was FDA-approved for use in food and beverage products in 1998. Splenda has been heavily promoted in some of the most gorgeously produced and directed TV ads airing today, which would have us believe that Splenda will transform our dreary lives into a veritable fairyland of giddily surreal

Technicolor. The makers of Splenda assure us that their sweetener is "Made From Sugar, So It Tastes Like Sugar." But the sugar industry has also been all over that claim in the courts, claiming false advertising, asserting that it is more like chlorine than sugar.

Just like aspartame, sucralose does not promote weight loss—and in fact, it can stimulate the appetite. All artificial sweeteners sabotage weight-loss efforts because when your taste buds register a sweet taste, your body's natural ability to gauge food intake is flummoxed. This results in overindulging in sweet foods and beverages.[266] And so your risk of obesity goes up 41 percent if you drink diet soda.[267]

Testing of sucralose has demonstrated that it causes shrinkage of the thymus gland, which is crucial to your immune system, as well as enlargement of the liver and kidneys.[268] Although makers of sucralose claim it's not absorbed into the body, scientists report that 20 to 30 percent is absorbed and that it accumulates in organs and causes DNA damage in gastrointestinal organs.[269]

If you have chosen to ingest this chlorinated sugar, which happens to carry the same risks of regular old chlorine exposure (such as cancer, immune function malfunction, birth defects) you have to ask yourself, is it worth the risk? Serious illness changes your life forever.

"Net carbs," "net impact carbs," or "effective carbs" are arrived at by ignoring the fake sugar and subtracting the grams of fiber from the total carb count. If a product has 30 grams of carb and 16 grams of fiber, its net carbs would be 14. Factory-food producers have foisted this low net carbs concept on a pubic eager for gluttony with impunity. The net carb concept only serves your body well when you eat real foods that contain fiber. For example, you can have a piece of stone ground, whole grain bread that contains 24 grams of carb and essentially cut that number in half. That is why you can eat plates of nonstarchy vegetables and count them as zero carbs.

Since none of us slimmed down on SnackWells low fat cookies it is not likely that we will slim down on SnackWells Carb Well Fudge Covered Grahams either because any type of dieting is starvation to human physiology, which is designed to operate on a balanced, varied diet of real whole foods that provides enough quantity so that all the vital nutrients are onboard every single day. When you combine starvation with diet factory-food, you're not going to produce a good-quality human being. Going on any kind of "healthy diet" that includes factory-food products is like saying you're quitting smoking while you have a smoldering cigarette dangling from your lips.

Reclaiming your genetic gifts is possible if you stop dieting, stop eating factory food, and start give your body the necessary building blocks of nutrition. If you are unhealthy, you can radically improve every aspect of your health, including balancing your hormones and brain neurotransmitters, in a cell-by-cell process by eating real food.

CHAPTER NINETEEN

The Basics of a Real-Food Diet

WHEN I REFER TO a historic real, living food diet, I'm not talking about "health food." If you're old enough, you might recall the TV commercial for Post Grape-Nuts in which Euell Gibbons asked, "Ever eat a pine tree? Many parts are eatable," which was famously spoofed as, "Ever eat a picnic bench? Many parts are eatable." A common misconception is that eating "health food" is comparable to eating a pine tree or picnic bench. Another misconception is that health food is esoteric stuff found in health-food stores. In the episode of *Nip/Tuck* referenced earlier, one of Julia McNamara's friends informs her, "Health food is the new plastic surgery." Julia resolves to transform her family's eating habits and serves them Chinese mushrooms and seaweed for dinner. The kids storm off to their rooms, slamming doors.

If you go into any store advertising real, whole food you'll see there is more than mushrooms and seaweed. But you'll also see that the health-food industry is peddling similar products as supermarkets. The differences are that efforts are made to provide organic products or products that claim to be organic, to eliminate additives, to add a lot of soy substances, and to make health-food claims on the packaging.

From ages fifteen to twenty-two, I lived in Japan, India, Sri Lanka, Spain, and Switzerland. Right after I returned to the United States, I remember attending a birthday party, taking a bite of Duncan Hines cake, and saying, "This cake makes my mouth burn." Once you've eaten real food as I did all those years, factory food tastes science-fictiony, leaves an icky taste in your mouth, and we won't even go there with what it does to your G.I. tract. You just have to give up factory food for a while to allow your taste buds to reboot, and you'll see what I mean.

Maybe you haven't eaten real food all your life, but you can still provide your body with the materials it needs to repair so that it can shrink down to your ideal body weight. A balanced diet of real, living food won't result in a skin-and-bones fashion model look. The only women I've known who achieved that look were either bulimic or were some of the actresses and models I worked with in the film industry who lived on cigarettes, candy bars, and amphetamines combined with several hours of extreme exercise per day. Eating a balanced diet of real food will, over time, produce a muscular, attractive body as your body changes on a cellular level. Your ideal body weight means that you have arrived at a metabolic set point, and you can stay there by eating three balanced meals every day.

A balanced diet means eating proteins, fats, nonstarchy vegetables, and carbs together, three meals a day.

By providing your body with adequate fats and proteins, your body will be able to break down and rebuild lean body mass (muscle and bone). An amplified example of the internal breaking down and building up phenomenon that continually occurs within our bodies was demonstrated by Hilary Swank when she trained four hours a day for two months to prepare for her Academy Award–winning role as female boxing champ Maggie Fitzgerald in the 2004 film *Million Dollar Baby*. Swank put on 15 pounds of muscle prior to shooting. Because extreme training causes muscles to break down and build up in an accelerated fashion, more protein is needed for the rebuilding process. The actress (who needed to sleep nine hours every night) actually awoke in the middle of every night to down an extra protein drink to provide her body with enough supplies to keep up the accelerated rebuilding process. This is not to say that American women should "bulk up." But only that a beautiful body can be achieved by ignoring the number on the scale and focusing more on what you look like in the mirror.

Americans direly need to eat as many raw and cooked organic non-starchy vegetables as humanly possible every day to obtain the micronutrients necessary to utilize proteins and fats. Remember the bite-chew-glug people who can down a thousand calories and hundreds of carbs in a burger, fries, and sodas in a few bites, chews, and swallows? Americans need to learn to chew. Studies prove that a fiber-rich diet is a crucial factor in weight management. Indigestible fiber was the main component in the hunter-gatherer diet. Hard to chew and digest raw meat, nuts, seeds, roots, and other plant materials kept primitive humans' digestive systems working overtime. (Lathering veggies in butter helps immensely with the chewing and will facilitate the assimilation of fat-soluble vitamins. And eating meat, fish, and poultry along with veggies creates an appetizing meal.) Current research points to tissue inflammation as a cause of chronic diseases, including cardiovascular disease. Both vegetables and fruits have anti-inflammatory properties.

Examples of nonstarchy vegetables are amaranth leaves, arugula, asparagus, bamboo shoots, bean sprouts, beet greens, bell peppers, broccoli, brussels sprouts, cabbage, raw carrots, cauliflower, celery, chicory greens, chives, collard greens, cucumber, dandelion greens, eggplant, endive, fennel, garlic, ginger root, green beans, hearts of palm, jicama, jalapeño peppers, kale, kohlrabi, mushrooms, mustard greens, onions, parsley, radicchio, radishes, shallots, snap beans, snow peas, spinach, summer squash, Swiss chard, turnip greens, and watercress.

Fear of carbs has become as extreme in our culture as fear of fat. In *The Devil Wears Prada*, Emily (Emily Blunt), fashion-slave gopher to *Runway* magazine editor-in-chief Miranda Priestly (Meryl Streep), is mystified by the fact that "the fat smart girl" Andy Sachs (Anne Hathaway) has scooped her to accompany Priestly to Fashion Week in Paris, lamenting, "You eat carbs!"

But carbs are not all bad. Carbs are necessary to feel happy and to not feel unnaturally hungry, as the release of the feel-good neurotransmitter serotonin is stimulated by eating carbs. We need carbs as part of a balanced diet, yet balance is the key. Keeping meals balanced means that you'll have balanced insulin levels throughout the day—and you'll eliminate the risk of developing diseases associated with chronic high insulin levels. Therefore, to your balanced meals of protein, fats, and nonstarchy vegetables, add a sensible portion of real, whole, living carbs.

Basic physiology dictates that weight management is determined (in part) by how much energy you put into your system versus how much energy you expend. Any carb, whether it's an apple or a candy bar, turns into energy (sugar) in your body, which is used as fuel. Since carbs are fuel, if you're unhealthy and fat and are lying in bed reading the paper, you obviously need far less fuel than someone in the third stage of an Iron Man competition. But if you're that same fat, sedentary, unhealthy person who is working harder than normal, you need to take in more fuel. It's common sense. If you are overweight and sedentary, you need proteins, fats, and nonstarchy vegetables to fuel ongoing metabolic processes and for internal repair, but you need very little energy food. If you are active, you need a moderate amount of carbs. If you are an extreme athlete you need more energy. (See *Healthy, Sexy, Happy* for a complete breakdown of set points and carbs.)

Examples of healthy real (as opposed to factory-refined) carbs are fruit, grains, legumes, nuts, seeds, sugars such as honey and molasses, milk, kefir, and yogurt, as well as starchy vegetables, such as acorn squash, artichokes, beets, butternut squash, cooked or juiced carrots, corn, green peas, leeks, lima beans, okra, parsnips, potatoes, rutabagas, sweet potatoes or yams, and turnips. (See *Healthy, Sexy, Happy* for a complete list.)

Like caffeine, refined white sugar, cocaine and heroin, salt is a white crystalline compound and, second to sugar, is the most seductive ingredient in factory food. Salt is used to increase the heft by binding moisture; this is a cheap way to increase profits for manufacturers. Salt is also used to make consumers thirsty and, like MSG, to make otherwise unpalatable fake fare taste good.

Still, salt is essential to life. Human blood plasma and lymphatic fluids closely resemble the electrical balance and chemical composition of ocean water. Salt and water comprise the inorganic or mineral elements of your body and play specific roles in the functions of cells. Salt helps carry nutrients into cells and pump waste materials out. Salt helps regulate blood pressure and fluid volume, keeps the pressure balance normal in the lining of blood vessels, and is necessary for absorption and digestion of food, to name just a few of the important functions dependent on salt.

Seventy percent of supermarket salt is stripped of minerals through chemical processing, which is then sold to the chemical industry for other purposes. The stripped salt is adulterated with anti-caking agents—often aluminum compounds that pose serious health risks. The FDA had synthetic iodine put into our processed salt supply some generations back to prevent goiter (enlarged thyroid), which leads to childhood mental retardation and dwarfism. Dextrose (sugar) is added to stabilize the volatile iodine, which dyes the salt purple. To make it nice and pretty, the salt is bleached white. The resultant salt pours freely out of your saltshaker but should really only be used to melt the ice on your driveway.

Natural sea salt crystals are hand-harvested worldwide from shallow, evaporated tide pools. These salt crystals contain more than 80 minerals and trace elements, including iodine. There are varied flavors in sea salt—you just have to experiment to find the ones that suit certain cuisines. A natural diet seasoned with sea salt is not likely be an overkill of sodium.

In addition to sea salt, non-GMO and nonirradiated spices lend delicious flair and a distinctive edge to flavors, as well as provide antioxidants to your diet.

In the United States, for numerous reasons—our frantic lifestyles, the cheapness of factory food, and our belief that real food is deadly—we've lost the art of food. I believe that anyone, at any age, can change his or her diet and that those changes will have positive impacts on the person's health and happiness. Even if you were raised exclusively on factory food—as I was—you can still do a complete about face. My mother went grocery shopping once a month at the Navy commissary, so you can imagine the shelf life of the food items I grew up on. Thankfully, the desire to rekindle the art of food is immerging in our collective consciousness. And in the wealthiest society on earth, Americans really owe it to ourselves to make eating a delightful experience—every day, not just on special occasions.

In our artless food culture, people grab a bagel with cream cheese for breakfast with several cups of aspartame-dosed coffee. Lunch is a Jack-in-the-Box Bacon Cheeseburger with onion rings and a large Diet Coke. Dinner is DiGiorno pizza, an iceberg salad with Kraft Light Done Right! Ranch Dressing washed down with Bud Lite.

Once you gain an understanding and appreciation for the art of food, your day might start with an organic spinach omelet made from pasture-raised eggs with deep orange yolks, a bowl of sweet organic strawberries, and a glass of creamy whole raw or organic milk. Coffee would be organically grown or Swiss-water-processed decaffeinated, with raw or organic cream (although quitting coffee is optimal). Lunch could be a fragrant mixed-greens salad tossed with olive oil and rich balsamic vinegar topped with strips of naturally raised ham and quartered ripe heirloom tomatoes brought alive with a sprinkling of aromatic sea salt, followed by juicy organic watermelon chunks and cherries. Dinner might be a succulent, naturally raised lemon- and rosemary-roasted chicken or slices of naturally raised roast beef, steamed organic asparagus spiked with herbs de Provence and drizzled with melted organic butter, crisp russet potato quarters roasted with coconut oil and seasoned with sweet paprika, sea salt, and freshly ground black pepper, and a wonderfully bitter watercress salad that requires just a hint of pungent olive oil. Raw cheese and tart organic apples would be dessert. These are not hard meals to put together; preparing delicious, gourmet meals need not be labor intensive.

Simple two-step guidelines for achieving good health and your ideal body composition are: (1) Stop eating anything made of or containing refined white sugar, refined corn, refined grain, refined soy, refined oils, or chemicals; and (2) instead, eat organically produced meat, fish, poultry, dairy, vegetables, fruits, grains, legumes, seeds, and nuts that could (in theory) be picked, gathered, milked, hunted, or fished, and that have not undergone any science-fiction processing.

After World War II the food industry introduced snacking, with snack foods. Now that large portions have been identified as the reason people are fat, factory-food makers reacted to the public outcry over supersizing by making 100-calorie "snack" packs—which are the same price as the previous full-sized versions—and in three years reaped $300 million. The factory snacks packs, in addition to being laced with high-fructose corn syrup, colored dyes, preservatives, and so on, are also generally made up primarily of genetically modified, highly processed wheat flour (i.e., refined carb).

But snacking has now been replaced by the more benign-sounding "six meals a day" campaign to ostensibly balance our blood sugar to keep us from binging. I find this extremely interesting, as it's just another way to keep people thinking about and eating food all day long. Many of the proponents of the six small meals a day method are makers or supporters of energy bars, meal replacements, and so on. Most people (except those with severe blood sugar imbalances) do not need to snack regularly. The American diet always comprised three meals a day until the food industry inundated our environment with factory snack products. Historically, people didn't snack. Rather they ate meals and came to the table hungry. Eating a meal, going hungry, eating a meal, and going hungry is a microcosm of human experience prior to 1900. People ate and went hungry, ate and went hungry. This pattern gives our systems a chance to assimilate food from the previous meal before more food enters and for all the hormones to complete their processes. (This is different than gorging and starving, which is the prehistoric feast-and-famine phenomenon that resulted in higher fat storage after each binge.) That said, there are times when we cannot get to the next meal soon enough. But that doesn't mean we should eat a Snickers or even a Balance Bar.

An optimal meal or snack should contain (in this order) protein, fat, and a small amount of carbohydrate. With a little thought, you can dream up all kinds of interesting snacks, like peanut butter with apple quarters, raw cheese, a handful of walnuts and a couple of dried figs, a leftover chicken breast with a cut-up bell pepper, tuna fish salad with grapes and cucumber slices, hummus with carrot sticks, or deviled eggs. By opening your horizons while shopping, you'll discover delicious foods to snack on.

America is a nation of night eaters who complain about not feeling hungry in the morning. But everyone needs to eat a good breakfast. Eating a protein-based breakfast of real food sets your inner thermostat for the rest of the day and bestows your body with the building materials for the ongoing metabolic repair and building processes.

On the contrary, skipping breakfast or eating sugar tells your body it's famine time and your inner thermostat must ratchet down. Sumo wrestlers gain their massive girth by skipping breakfast, training on an empty stomach, eating lunch, taking a four-hour nap, eating dinner, and going to bed—and they apparently don't even eat that much. Not feeling hungry in the morning is an obstacle that can only be overcome by forcing yourself to eat a big protein-based, balanced breakfast as soon as you get up.

One hundred and fifty years of eating science-fiction food products followed by the further malnutrition of low calorie, low fat, and low carb dieting has created a society that is obese, disease ridden, and on a trajectory toward ugly death. So now that we're fat and sick, we're sold on miracles in a bottle, snake-oil supplements, and drugs.

PART EIGHT

Miracles in a Bottle, Snake-Oil Supplements, and Drugs

CHAPTER TWENTY

That @*#!& Stress Is Making Us Fat!

IN THE EARLY 2000S Americans were introduced—through a series of endless and mindnumbly obnoxious commercials—to the concept of taking a pill to lose 30 pounds virtually overnight. The ads for CortiSlim claimed that persistently elevated levels of the adrenal stress hormone cortisol were the underlying cause of weight gain and that CortiSlim controlled cortisol levels, balanced blood-glucose levels, reduced cravings, and increased metabolism, thereby burning the fat around "your tummy, thighs, and stomach." We were invited to join the "CortiSlim lifestyle," to reshape our future with the "resolution solution," to "get your hopes up, get excited," and to "be part of television history."

CortiSlim TV ads ran so repetitively that I could not hit the mute button fast enough. "I'm Dr. Greg Cynaumon, and no offense to casual dieters, but if you only want to lose five to ten pounds, then CortiSlim is not for you. CortiSlim is the weight-loss capsule created by my associate, Dr. Talbott, for people who are disgusted with diets and quickly want to lose fifteen pounds or more." This particular TV ad ended with Cynaumon holding up a bottle of CortiSlim and smirking. Clearly, he knew that millions of Americans were sprawled out on couches in front of TVs with fists buried to the wrists in bowls of caramel corn. And he knew that thousands of those people would decide then and there to try that CortiSlim stuff, because Greg Cynaumon's a doctor, and so sincere. Cynaumon was right. Countless people logged onto the Internet or called the 800 number and ordered one-month supplies of CortiSlim for $49.95. What a relief to know that second-day mail was going to bring a magic bullet that was going to solve all of their weight problems.

The CortiSlim claim that stress-induced cortisol production leads to midsection fat accumulation is true. When you're stressed out, your adrenal glands secrete adrenaline in response to dramatic, acute stress (like getting into a car wreck) and cortisol in response to everyday stress (like working too late). (Your adrenals secrete numerous other hormones, but our focus is these two.) One primary objective of these hormones is to supply your brain and body with the sugar (fuel) necessary to deal with this stress. Adrenaline releases glycogen (sugar) that's stored in your liver and muscles for emergency use. And cortisol actually breaks down your lean muscle mass to convert it into more sugar. Now that you've got a dump of sugar into your bloodstream, your pancreas secretes insulin, which stores any unused sugar away into cells. After years of pounding stress, your cells will be stuffed to capacity. As you read earlier, when cells can't accept one more sugar molecule, they then reduce the number of insulin receptors so there are fewer receptors for insulin to activate. This is insulin resistance. One hallmark of insulin resistance is weight gain around the middle, because, though it may strike us as an unfair mistake of nature, fat stored as a result of insulin resistance is hoarded around the waist first.

Our autonomic or unconscious nervous system, which regulates metabolic processes, is divided into the sympathetic and the parasympathetic nervous systems. During the day we're predominantly in the sympathetic state. It's appropriate to be in a sympathetic state during the day, because our bodies need the operational metabolic processes that take place during this time.

The parasympathetic mode, which occurs predominantly at night, counteracts the sympathetic mode by turning on the repair processes such as making new cells, membranes, tissues, enzymes, hormones, and neurotransmitters (thus nighttime sleep is appropriately referred to as "beauty sleep"). In times past, humans didn't necessarily sleep uninterrupted all night long, because of problems such as threats to safety, vermin, smelly chamber pots, crowded conditions, hunger, and other irritants.[270] In the last hundred years, however, for the first time in history a major population has been swathed in creature comforts and provided the opportunity and luxury of sleeping soundly all night. When it gets dark, hypothetically, our systems could change rhythm from daytime work (sympathetic) to night-time rest (parasympathetic), the natural repair and rejuvenation phase. But this is not the reality. Instead, we're enslaved to technologies provided by electricity and to pressing demands. Our circadian rhythms are shattered by overwork and jet travel. We overuse stimulants and indulge in other adrenal assaults that keep our bodies in a constant state of sympathetic dominance. So while we have the allowances to sleep, these other factors have resulted in epidemic insomnia. And all this pounding stress is taking a toll. One of the major signs that we're not allowing our bodies to spend enough time in the parasympathetic mode are the spare tires we're lugging.

The solution to reducing the accumulation of stress-induced midsection body fat is to lower our cortisol and insulin levels, which will reverse insulin resistance (i.e., empty fat cells). This can only be accomplished by overhauling our lifestyles, not by popping a pill. One of the pluses of achieving overall health is that your body will shrink down to its natural body weight. Maximum health is accomplished by stopping eating factory-food, eating a balanced diet of real food, reducing stress, cutting down on or quitting all stimulants (sugar, caffeine, tobacco, etc.), drinking only moderately (giving up alcohol until you lose the fat), quitting recreational drugs or any unnecessary OTC and prescription drugs, avoiding toxic exposure and drinking plenty of water to flush poisons from your system, indulging in mind-clearing playtime, and going to bed as early as possible to get eight hours of rest, as well as taking hormone replacement if you need it.

By 2004 a nationwide class-action suit was settled for $4.5 million against the makers of CortiSlim, charging them with making invalid and unsubstantiated weight-loss claims, but it hasn't stopped copycats from marketing versions in health-food stores and magazine ads.

In early 2004, two class action suits were also filed against the makers of another weight-loss supplement, TrimSpa, alleging violations of California and New York's false and misleading advertising business practice laws. On February 9, 2004, the late Anna Nicole Smith, the product's spokesperson, appeared on *Larry King Live* in what could only be viewed as the paradoxical spokespitch of the century. And you could view the syntax-fracturing, 69-pound-lighter Smith in magazine advertisements and on the TrimSpa website cavorting with a creepy gigolo-ish guy under the tag line "Be Envied." But should we envy anyone who took TrimSpa?

TrimSpa contains a South American herb, *Hoodia gordonii*, which has been used as an appetite suppressant. We now understand that starvation always results in a higher insulin response to incoming food, a lowered metabolic set point, a craving and bingeing response that is a normal biological response to malnutrition, and an inner drive that is on red alert to hang onto fat cells as insurance, so that you will not die of famine. When you get sick of starving and go back to eating, you will blimp out.

But that is not the only problem with products like this.

TrimSpa originally contained the natural stimulant ephedra, which is extracted from the Chinese herb ma huang. Ephedra was restricted by the FDA after being linked to more than 150 deaths related to cardiac arrest.

So-called "natural" stimulants, such as green tea, ma huang, and guarana, cannot be used with impunity just because they are natural. Ma huang is a very good example of the diet industry's abuse of a useful therapeutic Chinese herb. Henry Han, O.M.D., my coauthor on *Ancient Herbs, Modern Medicine*, told me, "My teacher, Song Tian Bing taught us, 'Ma huang has energy like a wild untamed horse, so you never want to relinquish control. Don't ever forget when you use ma huang that you saddle it so that you have the reins.'"

Stimulants keep your body in a state of sympathetic dominance by mimicking and magnifying the actions of adrenaline, which revs cellular functions. You think faster. Your heart beats faster. But the human body isn't meant to be in a state of sympathetic overdrive. Stimulant users will eventually begin to feel agitated. Although most people do not enjoy the pounding heart and jittery nerves, they get hooked on stimulants by the initial good feelings and keep going back for more. People in later stages of burnout reach for stimulants in a vain attempt to recreate that initial boost of energy and momentary lift in mood. (The stimulant rush is caused by the same outpouring of insulin and the resultant dump of feel-good neurotransmitters in your brain that you get from eating sugar, which we reviewed on page 20.)

After the FDA ruling against the use of ephedra, TrimSpa was reformulated. A daily dose of TrimSpa now packs 1,050 milligrams of caffeine.

In America we have a skewed definition of "drug users." Since the passage of the Harrison Act in December 1914 that banned nonmedical use of cocaine (which previously provided Coca Cola with its "medicinal benefits"), our judicial system has come down hard on reprobate users of illegal drugs. Thousands of dopers rot in prisons at taxpayers' expense. After 9/11, John Ashcroft instigated marijuana raids on "drug users" who incidentally happened to be dying from AIDS and cancer. You may not think of yourself as a drug user. Like a friend of mine said, "I've never tried drugs." Really? Well, try going without your coffee tomorrow, then let me know if you want to issue a revised statement.

People are unaware of how much caffeine they ingest daily since caffeine is the only drug that's widely added to the food supply and manufacturers can add caffeine to any food or beverage without disclosing the dosage. The majority of Americans are frothing at the mouth from dehydration and we seek to slake this thirst by drinking dehydrating caffeinated drinks like Starbucks Breakfast Blend, which packs 327 milligrams of caffeine, Diet Coke at 47 milligrams of caffeine per can, and other newly introduced caffeinated drinks like Shock, which boasts "Sleep is overrated" and contains 200 milligrams of caffeine.

When you jump-start your heart with caffeine, the odorless, slightly bitter alkaloid substance is rapidly absorbed in the digestive tract and diffuses into nearly all of your tissues. Using caffeine keeps your body in a heightened state of sympathetic dominance with your adrenals overproducing stress hormones so that your body cannot rest. Like all drugs, caffeine provokes the desire to consume more and more as your addiction drags on.

Ultimately your adrenals will become fatigued and that is why many people who used to be able to "diet" by drinking coffee eventually find themselves fatigued, unable to get the same jolt from more and more coffee, and worse, now they are overweight and riddled with chronic conditions. Caffeine does so many bad things that space here does not allow your basic A-to-Z list. Suffice it to say, caffeine use is linked to heart disease, cancer, ulcers, heartburn/GERD, and urinary and prostate problems in men; accelerated aging, infertility, fetal loss, and spontaneous abortion in women; and to fetal growth retardation, anxiety, sleeplessness, addiction, and withdrawal symptoms in children, among other problems.[271]

I understand that my stance on caffeine may alienate some readers. Maybe you can keep your coffee intake to one eight-ounce cup a day. But if caffeine is controlling you and destroying your health, and you want to cut down or quit, it's important to note that that quitting cold turkey halts the demand on your adrenals too suddenly and you'll experience withdrawal symptoms that can include headache, fatigue, lethargy, muscle pain, and an overall nasty mood.[272] It's best to wean slowly. Decaffeinated coffee still contains significant amounts of caffeine, and all but Swiss water-processed decaffeinated coffee is decaffeinated with methylene chloride, a carcinogen, which you then ingest with your decreased caffeine.[273]

(The best drink of course is purified water. The human body is 75 percent water. Optimal is one half of your body weight in ounces.)

All stimulants stress your body and lead to adrenal disaster both by causing the release of adrenaline and by mimicking and exaggerating the actions of adrenaline. This eventually results in depleting your adrenal reserve, which will lead to anxiety, mood roller coaster, and insomnia. In addition to damaging your adrenals, using stimulants also taxes and depletes your body's balancing and calming neurotransmitters, which creates the potential for panic attacks—something that is not very pretty, if pretty is what you're after. However, if you would rather be dead than fat, you can always buy Emagrece Sim, better known as the Brazilian Diet Pill, online; it contains the extremely dangerous cocktail of Fenproporex (a stimulant that is converted in the body to amphetamine), Librium (a sedating hypnotic drug to counteract the jitters), and Prozac (to make you feel better about ruining your health).

Many Americans are willing to saddle up a wild horse and relinquish the reins when it comes to using stimulants to lose weight. Never was George Bernard Shaw so correct in saying, "Youth is wasted on the young" as when it comes to young people resorting to extreme diet measures in an attempt to lose or maintain extremely low body weight. Because such measures—taking natural stimulants, guzzling coffee and diet drinks, and taking "metabolism enhancers," fat burners, appetite suppressants, carb blockers, fat blockers, smoking cigarettes, vomiting, taking laxatives, or using steroids, human growth hormone, and thyroid replacement outside of the care of a physician—erodes the beauty or good looks with which a person is born.

The diet industry focuses solely on thinness. But there are many thin people walking around who are disasters on the inside, whose bodies do not have adequate building materials to replenish existing cellular structures or make new ones. Without the necessary building blocks of nutrition, bones weaken, endocrine systems falter, brain neurotransmitters become off-kilter, and ultimately, organ function begins to flag. Outward manifestations of internal disaster can be seen in dull and thinning hair, brittle nails, dry skin, wrinkles and skin disorders, and an overall lackluster appearance—all of which the beauty industry capitalizes on with a myriad of preparations to apply to the outside.

Americans idealize youth and beauty, but the fact is that many if not most Americans are on an accelerated aging path. Imagine the forces of nature young American men and women would be if they stopped eating all factory food, never used stimulants or other diet products, and ate balanced diets of real, living food. Right now, there are not many forces of nature walking around. Instead, and ironically, the drive to be beautiful in this country has caused people to inflict disaster upon themselves. It begins with young girls tossing back diet pills with their diet drinks and if they can keep up with the extreme dieting measures necessary to remain bone-thin, it ends with chronically ill, middle-aged, emaciated, hormone-depleted insomniacs sucking up coffee and cigarettes (or, if they are "health-minded," hot water with lemon peel) to dampen their hunger pains so they don't have to eat. Then there are the "failures"—the majority of people who indulge in chronic dieting using diet aids—those who are overweight/obese due to the factors we talked about earlier.

Stimulants are not the only scams in a bottle. Another current diet pill favorite is acai berry, a Brazilian berry sold in concentrated form that is said to have such startling colon-cleansing and detoxifying effects that it causes your body to shed a pound of fat a day. Common sense tells us if this were true that it would be the subject of numerous double-blind, placebo-controlled studies reported above the fold of the *New York Times, Wall Street Journal*, the *Economist*, the *Huffington Post*, and so on. Another diet is the HCG diet featuring a hormone that is made by the placenta during pregnancy and that is required to mobilize nutrition for the fetus (men also make a small amount of HCG). This hormone is either taken sublingually (under the tongue) or injected, along with a 500 calories per day diet. We've already looked at low calorie dieting, and as far as hormones go, the entire goal of eating a balanced diet of real, living food is to balance your hormones. Taking a hormone that you don't need doesn't lend to that plan since all hormones work in an interconnected fashion, and one imbalance creates another until there is a slippery slope of hormonal imbalances.

Then there are the diet supplements that fall into the category of "let's just make up science as we go along." The Shape Up! supplements that went along with the HFCS candy bars discussed on page 27 provide an example of exploitation of fat people. These supplements were supposedly formulated for two body types: Apple bodies notoriously carry fat as paunches, while pear bodies pack fat around the hips, butt, and thighs.

One of the specially designed Shape Up! supplements supposedly helped Apples "metabolize carbohydrates," whatever that meant, and another purportedly promoted fat metabolism and increased the pear body's ability to burn calories. Adding the "Intensifier" was promoted to take weight management efforts to the next level. Taking either apple or pear versions along with the Intensifier cost consumers $120 per month.

The supplement labels claimed, "These products contain scientifically researched levels of ingredients that can help you change your behavior to take control of your weight." But there were no scientific studies to back up the claim that apple and pear bodies need different nutrients to lose body fat. Jules Hirsch, M.D., a nutrition and obesity researcher and professor emeritus at Rockefeller University, called the claims "gibberish." Another leading expert in nutrition policy referred to the supplements as "a recipe for making money."[274] It was a great marketing ploy until a Federal Trade Commission (FTC) investigation and a class-action suit brought on by dissatisfied customers compelled the company to stop marketing the products.[275] (The Federal Trade Commission is an independent agency of the government that provides consumer protection from harmful business practices.)

It doesn't look like anyone is going to be called to the carpet any time soon, at least not by the FDA, until after the fact. With Americans spending $40 billion per year on diet products, the makers of miracles in a bottle rake in so much money that they can't be stopped by consumer class-action lawsuits, warning letters from the FDA, or legal action by the FTC. With the astronomical success of CortiSlim, the sales of diet pills have reached a feverish pitch on TV, targeting everyone from testosteronized teenage boys to matronphobic menopausal women by trotting out remarkable before and after testimonials, attractively no-nonsense Ivy League doctor-spokespitchers, and incredible free offers for products that can be summed up as X-TREMEBS4U. And if you're so inert that you can't even get off the couch to walk your dog, you can now give him/her Slentrol, the FDA-approved diet pill for dogs approved in early 2007.

Diet pills are not the only pills that are being foisted on the American public eager to see magical weight-loss results, as one diet pill's marketing campaign claimed, "by doing nothing" but "taking a pill." Because fat is not our only problem.

CHAPTER TWENTY-ONE

Snake-Oil Supplements

AMERICANS LIVE ON science-fiction food and are sugar-, caffeine-, ciga-
rette-, and alcohol-dependant. We buy the latest and greatest mattresses
hoping against hope that we'll get a good night's sleep. Instead of eating
vitamin-B-rich real foods that foster healthy, shiny, thick hair growth,
men turn to Avacor, which, according to the ads, grows hair like a Chia
pet. We gobble cocktails of OTC medications and prescription drugs to
treat our obesity, hemorrhoids, heartburn, gas, constipation, diarrhea,
sinus infections, asthma, allergies, migraines, chronic inflammation,
arthritis and allover body pain, zero sex drive, chronic colds and flu,
exhaustion, anxiety, depression, low self-esteem, and so on.

Because Americans eat a diet that lacks life-sustaining nutrients, and
many of the ingredients in this diet are foreign and toxic to human physiology, and because we exacerbate this nutrient drain by dieting and popping diet pills, we're falling apart from the inside out. All you have to do is
turn on the TV to understand that Americans do not look or feel as well
as they could. Now we have an awareness of supplements, and with our
pill-popping mentality a lot of people think they can take supplements the
same way that they take drugs—that they can continue unhealthy eating
and lifestyle behaviors and fix any problems that arise as a result by taking
supplements.

In 1994, the U.S. Congress passed the Dietary Supplement Health
and Education Act, which classified botanical and herbal supplements as

food. For that reason, manufacturers of dietary supplements don't have to demonstrate that their products are safe, nor are they required to report adverse affects to the FDA. They do not even have to demonstrate that their products are effective. They can insinuate on labeling that their product improves or supports or gives balance to or any number of quasi-claims as long as they don't say "cures."

That said, and all evidence to the contrary, the FDA does regulate the manufacturing of nutraceuticals and dietary supplements. They regulate what ingredients can be included or not included, the potency, the accuracy of labeling, and the standards for manufacturing. The FDA also monitors compliance to some degree by stopping by manufacturers periodically.[276] This regulation falls down because there is a dire lack of funding, organization, and education within the FDA regarding nutraceuticals and dietary supplements. And furthermore, the FDA is highly regulated by corporate lobbyists.

Because a natural substance cannot be patented, pharmaceutical companies have no incentive to research the benefits of vitamins, minerals, and herbs. If a company were to spend millions of dollars researching natural substances and find that certain natural supplements were superior to drugs, companies could not recoup their research costs in the spectacular fashion they have become accustomed to with drugs.

Still there are companies that choose to do their own research, and these companies are supplying top-grade supplements to the market. Since the FDA has done such a poor job in monitoring drugs and food additives, it would not serve consumers for the FDA to regulate supplement manufacturers. If this were to happen, multinational drug corporations—and con artists who have gotten rich off of bogus products—would likely inundate the market with inferior products, while the small top-quality supplement manufacturers would get bogged down in fees and regulatory expenses so that their quality supplements would become economically unobtainable by the average person. The best way to force inferior products and snake oil out of the marketplace is to not buy them.

Nutraceuticals and dietary supplements are important today as we have more toxins and stress and less nutritive soil than in times past. But contrary to the claims of the snake-oil salesmen, nutraceuticals and supplements can't perform alone to make you healthy and thin, sleep better, and improve your sex life. Nutraceuticals and supplements can only help you go the last fraction of the distance after you have addressed the most important factors of good health. We should get the bulk of our nutrition from real, living food. Supplements are supplemental. Too many people gobble handfuls of supplements arbitrarily without having a clue what they are taking. Worse, they are taking synthetic supplements. Ever notice how teeny tiny those vitamin pills are? The synthetic nutrients are compacted into hard little bullets that are cheap for manufacturers to make and easy for lazy consumers to swallow. The nutrients in those hard little pebbles are virtually inaccessible to the absorptive surfaces of your digestive system. Quality supplements are loosely packed, bio-available tablets and capsules.

Cheap supplements are made with synthetic versions of nutrients and are bulked up with toxic fillers and additives. Quality supplements are made with pure nutrients without fillers and additives. Dietary supplement makers that produce hypoallergenic, high-quality supplements are more expensive than health-food-store brands and considerably more expensive than supermarket, drugstore, and Big Box brands. However, you get a bigger bang for your buck if you take fewer supplements made by a company that is dedicated to improving the quality of Americans' health than you do by popping pills made by corporations that are interested solely in shareholder profits.

By consulting a qualified health practitioner to determine what is right for you, you maximize the effectiveness of your protocol (you see and feel results), do not end up wasting money on junk supplements, and do not put money into the coffers of junk-supplement businesses.

Miracles in a bottle and useless supplements are not the only pills that Americans are reaching for today. Since the time of Louis Pasteur, when medicine turned away from nutrition as standard care and embraced drugs as the primary modality in the practice of medicine, Americans have become convinced that drugs are the answer to *curing* illness. However, more recently, a new trend in medicine has arisen: using drugs to prevent disease.

CHAPTER TWENTY-TWO

Drug Pushers

IN THE LAST TWO decades pharmaceutical companies have begun advertising on TV. The phenomenon started slowly but has grown to a truly alarming frequency as more and more people in America have become ill or are at risk for disease, and as drug companies recognize an opportunity to compete for our business. Drug ads typically focus our attention on our *hopes*, for which they sell us *quality of life*, and our *terror*, for which they sell us *hope*. We know what cancer centers to go to should we be diagnosed with cancer and what drugs to take to prepare for chemotherapy. We've learned that our cholesterol comes from food and from Grandma Rose and all about the cholesterol-lowering drugs, which pharmaceutical companies are making $492 billion per year selling and will soon have doctors prescribing to children. To treat our type 2 diabetes we are reassured by ads, like the ones with B.B. King and Patty Labelle grinning happily even though they have a life-threatening illness. It's comforting to know that our insulin and/or glucose-modulating medications can be delivered right to our doors by that nice man, Wilfred Brimley.

My stance is not anti-drug. It's anti too many drugs. Some drugs have their place and can be beneficial when used judiciously. The purpose of this book, and in particular this chapter, is to point out that the food industry has ruined our health, and that the medical community has embraced drugs to treat (and now prevent) disease. There are many drugs that don't need to be taken and, in fact, are either exacerbating our health problems or creating new ones, or the condition they are supposedly addressing could be easily corrected by eliminating all factory foods from our diets and eating real, living food and by using alternative or natural healing or preventative approaches. Unlike real, living food as a therapy for healing, when it comes to taking drugs, you always get a two-fer. First you get the benefit of the drug, though not always. Allen Roses, M.D., geneticist for the world's largest pharmaceutical corporation, GlaxoSmithKline, said that 90 percent of drugs work for only 30 to 50 percent of people.[277] A new study confirms that not only are 85 percent of drugs useless, but the toxic side effects and/or misuse of prescription drugs make these drugs a significant cause of death in the United States.[278]

Even if you do get the purported benefit, all drugs have side effects, sometimes multiple and potentially life-threatening. Unfortunately, many Americans are bewildered about so called alternative approaches outside of conventional medicine. Bioidentical hormone replacement therapy (which we talked about briefly in chapter 8 and which is explained in greater detail in *Healthy, Sexy, Happy*) is an example of a controversial "natural" therapy that is confounding many women today. If you recall, drug companies don't study natural substances because they can't be patented and therefore can't produce the same returns on research investment that patented drugs do. Suzanne Somers is an outspoken advocate of bioidentical hormone replacement therapy (BHRT). However, in the winter of 2006, Somers was taken to task on *Larry King Live* by a panel of doctors for including a bioidentical hormone protocol from an unaccredited "independent researcher" in her book *Ageless*. The protocol in question is designed to cycle women through estrogen and progesterone levels that match the hormone levels of a twenty-five-year-old woman—in other words, high estrogen and high progesterone. Although I don't personally endorse this approach, rather than having a reasoned discussion about the pros and cons of the various approaches of BHRT, the panel was reduced to a catfight, leaving Somers unable to get a word in edgewise and making room for a consultant to pharmaceutical companies to step in and discredit bioidentical hormones. He referred to the panel as "a cult" and went on to claim that "the physicians [who prescribe BHRT] are selling promises, silver bullets, against aging with barely a nanoshred of evidence."[279]

David R. Allen, M.D. of the Longevity Medical Center in Los Angeles has spent thirty-five years researching holistic methods of treating his patients and is an advocate of bioidentical hormone replacement. He said of this *Larry King Live* show, "A hundred and thirty years ago when homeopathic medicine was introduced there were high dose advocates and low dose advocates. Rather than have a reasoned discussion of the benefits of homeopathic medicine, both camps were at each other's throats. Ultimately homeopathic medicine was dismissed by the conventional medical community."

Although the food, diet, and drug industries have fought hard to convince us that synthetic is as good—or better—than nature, when it comes to bioidentical hormone replacement millions of women disagree and millions more continue to be confused. Advocates run headfirst into the financial interests of mega pharmaceutical corporations. For now we still have the ability to make choices, although Wyeth (the maker of the equine-drug hormone called Premarin) has launched a legal, lobbying, and PR campaign to malign BHRT and influence Congress to ban BHRT (i.e., eliminate their competition).

Just as Mark McAfee of Organic Pastures was targeted to eliminate raw, living milk from our food supply, corporations can use their legal, financial, and political clout to eliminate competition in other types of foods, supplements, and hormones. Still, a growing population of real food eaters, like me, are looking at ways to heal using natural alternatives, like food, supplements, and hormones.

Brain-neurotransmitter imbalance is a prime example of a condition that could be corrected by stopping eating all factory food and eating real, living food, and by using alternative or natural healing or preventative approaches. As it stands, millions of American children suffering from ADD and ADHD are medicated to enable them to function in school and in society. Family schedules are disrupted by stressful, expensive shrink appointments.

If drug companies have learned one thing from the sale of ADD and ADHD drugs, it is that medicating children is extremely lucrative. Incredibly, the largest growing market for antidepressant drugs is the age group between infants and children five years old. [280] This is truly the most illustrative example of what I'm talking about in this book: As a baby gestates, instead of eating real food that provides the crucial amino acids, essential fatty acids, cholesterol, and other nutrients humans need for healthy brain development and neurotransmitter production, his/her mother eats sugar and chemicalized factory-food products. As a result, the baby enters the world with a lesser brain than he/she could have had, is then deprived of mother's milk, and instead, is fed antinutritious soy juice and is weaned on sugar and industrialized junk.

When the neurotransmitter-imbalanced baby starts showing understandable signs of going haywire, he's given antidepressant drugs. And the baby could possibly be among the 2 to 3 percent of children taking antidepressants who suffer from suicidal thoughts or behavior as a result of taking theses drugs. Tarek A. Hammad, an FDA analyst who conducted a review of selective serotonin reuptake inhibitors (SSRIs—drugs that inhibit the disposal of serotonin in the brain) and other antidepressants, said that this outcome "is beyond the suicidality as a result of the disease being treated."[281] In other words, it wasn't the depression that caused suicidal thoughts or behavoirs.

FDA employee and Vioxx whistleblower Dr. David Graham, introduced in chapter 7, said, "In early 2004, SSRI antidepressants and suicidal behavior was a big safety issue. The FDA suppressed a report written by a colleague of mine in drug safety and had prevented him from presenting this information in an advisory committee meeting. That information leaked to the media, embarrassing the FDA because it had been caught suppressing very important information—that most antidepressants don't work for treating children."[282]

It's merely a continued revenue stream when neurotransmitter-imbalanced children grow up to be neurotransmitter-imbalanced adults. Lonely men and women who self-medicate with binges on FDA-approved, caffeinated, high-fructose corn syrup sodas, baked goods, ice cream, and other factory products, then take FDA-approved SSRIs and other antidepressant medications in an attempt to dredge up a modicum of interest in life as well as a shred of self-control and self-esteem. (More than 164 million prescriptions were written in 2008 for antidepressants, totaling $9.6 billion in U.S. sales.)

The dopamine reuptake inhibitor Wellbutrin XL's big pitch is that it has a "low risk of sexual side effects." Ads feature hysterically happy people with the caveat: "There is a risk of seizure with Wellbutrin XL which increases with higher doses. Taking more than 450 mg/day increases the chance of serious side effects. Don't use it if you've had a seizure or eating disorder, or if you abruptly stop using alcohol or sedatives. Don't take with MAOIs, or medicines that contain bupropion. When used with a nicotine patch or alone, there is a risk of increased blood pressure, sometimes severe. To reduce risk of serious side effects, tell your doctor if you have liver or kidney problems. Other side effects may include weight loss, dry mouth, nausea, difficulty sleeping, dizziness, sore throat, constipation, or flatulence."

Yet the ads are convincing. A recent Cymbalta commercial asked, "Where does depression hurt? Everywhere. Who does depression hurt? Everyone!" and featured a piece of music that was so beautiful and compelling, it drove people online to try to find it.[283]

On June 24, 2005, Tom Cruise appeared on NBC's *Today Show* to promote his film *War of the Worlds*, but quickly segued into a passionate discourse against antidepressant drugs. It began when host Matt Lauer mentioned the fact that Cruise had criticized Brooke Shields on a TV interview with *Access Hollywood* for taking antidepressants to treat her suicidal postpartum depression. Cruise, a member of the Church of Scientology, described psychiatry as a pseudoscience and said that people should turn to exercise and supplements rather than taking drugs to treat psychiatric problems such as postpartum depression. "I'm saying that drugs aren't the answer," Cruise argued. "These drugs are very dangerous. They're mind-altering, antipsychotic drugs. And there are ways of doing it without that so that we don't end up in a brave new world."[284]

A week later, on July 1, 2005, the FDA issued a public health advisory regarding the link between increased risk of suicidal tendencies in adults taking antidepressants, but this got virtually no press.[285]

In the meantime, Cruise was eviscerated by much of the media. Mike Duffy from the *Hollywood Reporter* summed up the general consensus: "We're seeing Tom Cruise gone wild and it's not pretty." Other reporters suggested that his stance against antidepressants and psychiatry would alienate fans.[286] (The *New York Times* supported Cruise's behavior as a refreshing departure from publicist-controlled, scripted happy talk.)[287]

I honestly don't have a clue what Scientology is all about, but I do have to say that I agree with Tom Cruise in his stance against antidepressants and other psychotropic drugs. Why aren't more doctors interested in the food people were gestated on, raised on, and are currently eating? Hypothyroidism, adrenal fatigue, sex hormone imbalances, depleted vitamin D levels, low omega-3 intake, low amino acids, sugar and stimulant addictions, hypoglycemia, food allergies, heavy metal loads, vitamin and mineral deficiencies, a sedentary lifestyle, and many other factors can make people depressed.

Of course there are new mothers who suffer from life-threatening postpartum depression, the extreme example being Andrea Yates, whose postpartum depression ambushed her into a psychosis so dark that it compelled her to drown her five children. People with deep depression and especially psychosis can be spared a comparable tragedy by being offered a temporary lifeline of antidepressants. But for the millions of others who are not likely to experience a psychotic break due to their depression, there are options to taking drugs.

Logically one would think of starting by eliminating high-fructose corn syrup altogether from our diet. Yet, as Op-Ed columnist Nicholas D. Kristof writes, "Imagine if Al Qaeda had resolved to attack us not with conventional chemical weapons but by slipping large amounts of high-fructose corn syrup into our food supply. That would finally rouse us to action—but in fact it's pretty much what we're doing to ourselves."[288]

Another idea would be to use a "natural" remedy for depression. In the standard (albeit cruel) test of the efficacy of antidepressant drugs referred to as a "forced swim," rat subjects are tested to compare how long it takes for them to stop swimming (i.e., "give up") when given antidepressants as compared to rats that were not given antidepressants. Researchers at a Harvard-affiliated hospital found that rats respond to omega-3—as in cod liver oil—as an "antidepressant."[289]

Remember back in chapter 8 when we talked about the association between neurotransmitter imbalance and violence? A dietary experiment conducted in a maximum security institution for young offenders in Aylesbury, Britain, demonstrated that essential fatty acids can also calm violent tendencies. More than 200 inmates took part in a doubleblind, randomized, placebo-controlled study. Those given multivitamin, mineral, and fatty-acid supplements, as in cod liver oil, experienced a 25 percent drop in antisocial behavior and a 35 percent stay of violent incidents. Among the placebo group there was no change.[290]

And if we're going to talk about placebos, a recent study reviewed twenty-plus years of research on antidepressants, concluding that although antidepressants can lift depression in most patients, the benefits are hardly more significant than what patients experienced when they (unknowingly) took a placebo.[291]

Aside from a natural food diet, there are alternatives to drugs for many conditions: acupuncture, Chinese, Ayurvedic and other types of herbs, hypnotherapy, neurofeedback therapy (a type of biofeedback that retrains brain wave patterns), neural therapy (injections of novacaine at meridian sites to correct painful syndromes), bioidentical hormone replacement, heavy metal chelation, hyperbaric oxygen therapy, nutritional supplements, yoga, meditation, massage therapy, craniosacral therapy (a type of massage to move spinal fluids), osteopathy and chiropractic (both of which treat disorders of the musculoskeletal system), and many other modalities. But since insurance companies do not pay for noninvasive, safe, and effective healing and preventative approaches to keep people well, drugs and procedures after people get sick are the only choices available for most people.

Although some people felt that Bill Clinton deserved to be impeached from the office of the President of the United States because he lied about a dalliance in the Oval Office (and many parents were incensed that they had to explain to their children what "oral sex" meant), today there is no uproar about children learning that men who take impotence medications should seek medical attention if their erections last more than four hours.

Let's take a closer look at this issue because it truly represents the levels that drug companies will stoop to in order to get us to buy their drugs. In the last decade pharmaceutical companies have branded the human condition. The purpose of branding is to cultivate and maintain a loyal customer base. These days, without branding, it's virtually impossible to market a product. Branding begins with identification. The drug industry would like you to identify with disease. And so the drug industry, which is intent on convincing us that we are diseased and that the "cure" is their drugs, brands our sicknesses with acronyms. The list of conditions that have been abbreviated and woven into the daily fabric of our lives is endless. One "disease" that has become alarmingly familiar has been branded with the acronym ED, for Erectile Dysfunction.

The term "erectile dysfunction" is a frightening, insulting, degrading, and humiliating condemnation for any man. And the cloying way this "disease" is presented on TV commercials would make any man feel like a mouse. It would make any man willing to do whatever it took to restore his manhood. Even if it meant taking pills that could cause blindness and erections that last over four hours.

Way back in 1954, Adelle Davis wrote in *Let's Eat Right to Keep Fit*, "Studies of men in prison camps, of the conscientious objectors in the starvation experiments at the University of Minnesota, and of numerous clinical investigations show that libido decreases or disappears when the nutrition is inadequate."[292] And in his book *A Brief History of Everything*, philosopher Ken Wilbur writes, "It appears that testosterone basically has two, and only two, major drives: fuck it or kill it." Now both the connection between inadequate nutrition and libido and the relationship between sex hormones and male drives take us back to Francis Pottenger's cats that were fed nutrient-dead diets. If you recall, the females were she-devils, and the males meek and cringing. Could we find some similarities in men and women who eat nutrient-dead diets? Yet instead of focusing on providing adequate nutrition for endocrine glands to produce the sex hormones necessary for a healthy libido, men take Viagra, Cialis, and Levitra (giving new meaning to the adage "Love is blind").

One commercial for ED tells men that high blood pressure and type 2 diabetes are conditions that could result in ED. The commercial doesn't tell men that there are ways of dealing with high blood pressure and type 2 diabetes, like not eating that KFC bowl of industrialized mashed potatoes, chemicalized sweet corn, deep-fried factory chicken, classic glurk gravy, and factory cheese. The commercial doesn't say, "Hey, get some exercise, eat real food, stop taking so many drugs, and you'll feel like having sex." OK, if you are a man over fifty, you might have to take bioidentical testosterone or, if you're a woman, testosterone, estrogen, and progesterone, but that is due to a natural decline in sex hormones; it's not because you're "diseased."

Gastrointestinal problems are a multibillion-dollar source of revenue for the drug industry. These problems could mostly be resolved by stopping eating all factory food and eating only real food. Comedian Bill Maher said it best in his HBO stand-up special: "Congress [passed] this giant Medicare entitlement prescription drug bill . . . And it's going to cost literally trillions and trillions of dollars. And while they were debating this, nobody ever stood up and said, 'Excuse me, but why are we so sick? Why do even older people need this amount of drugs?' Could it be because we eat like Caligula? You know the top five of those prescription drugs that are so popular, they're all antacids, antibloating medicines, digestive aides, all things to put out the fire in our stomach from the poison that we call lunch. Folks, it's the food. I know that people hate to hear that. But when you look at those ads on the evening news at night, people farting and burping and bloating, it's all shit trying to get out of you. Take a hint . . . You're not going to die from secondhand smoke, or SARS, or monkey pox. It's the food. The call is coming from inside the house. The killer is not West Nile or avian flu or shark attacks. It's the buffalo wings. It's the aspartame and the NutraSweet, and the red dye number two and the high-fructose corn syrup and the MSG and the chlorine and whatever shit is in special sauce."[293]

Ads on the tube for gastrointestinal medications invariably feature people eating pizza, fast-food chili, and other glop that is made up of that very same special sauce Maher referred to.

Then there are those who get the call from inside the house but suffer from chronic all-systems lockdown, which they seek to break through by consuming all sorts of truly repugnant sounding OTCs such as X-LAX, Rite-Aid Col-Rite Stool Softener, and Metamucil. Constipation is not just a little inconvenience, but a sign that something serious is taking place within your body. GI health (which I cover extensively in *Healthy, Sexy, Happy*) is imperative to life because your gut is where nutrition enters your body. The medical community, however, aided and abetted by the drug industry, doesn't focus on gut health.

Tissue inflammation is the culprit behind the pain that causes people to seek out prescriptions for Cox-2 inhibitors. Cod liver oil contains omega-3 fatty acids, which are used to make hormones that control inflammation. In addition to taking cod liver oil, eating anti-inflammatory foods, such as cold-water fish and their oils (mackerel, salmon, sardines, and tuna), walnuts and organically fed, free-range eggs, seems like a less life-threatening approach than taking pills that have already been proven to cause damage to the heart and even death.

Would you be surprised to learn that, despite alarming statistics, osteoporosis is really a very rare condition? Embroidered statistics have been brought to us courtesy of drug companies who have redefined the testing of low bone mineral density. As it turns out, the measure of your bone mineral density (BMD) is only one of many factors that determine the risk of bone fragility. The reality is that everyone will naturally lose bone density as part of normal aging, and all bones, no matter how dense, will break if smacked hard enough. But the new standards in testing have made it nearly impossible for anyone over fifty to have a "normal" diagnosis.[294] Thus those of a certain age are scared silly about falling down, fracturing a hip, and dying a horrible death. Or they are panicked about developing a dowager's hump from spinal compression (vertebral fractures).

Using the new BMD statistics, commercials and print ads for FDA-approved osteoporosis drugs sell us on products that have a grab bag of side effects and contraindications—drugs like Actonel, which encourage women to "Act early with Actonel". The ad warns, "You should not take Actonel if you are allergic to any of the ingredients, if you have problems of the esophagus which delay emptying into the stomach, if you have low blood calcium (hypocalcemia), have kidneys that work poorly, or *cannot sit or stand for thirty minutes.* [Emphasis mine.] Stop taking Actonel and tell your doctor right away if you experience difficult or painful swallowing, chest pain, or severe or continuing heartburn, as these may be signs of serious upper digestive problems . . . Side effects may include stomach pain, upset stomach, or back, muscle, bone or joint pain, sometimes severe."

Fosamax is another such nasty drug that is linked to cancer of the esophagus and dramatically increases the risk of stomach ulcers when taken with the arthritis drug Naprosyn.[295] (Bear in mind that many osteoporosis patients also suffer from arthritis.) Fosamax has also been linked to osteonecrosis (bone death) of the jaw.[296]

Bones are living tissues that are constantly breaking down and rebuilding in order to maintain structural integrity. Bones are like tubes that are made of and filled with protein and hardened by calcium. It's the hardening of this protein that makes bone solid. The osteoclast cells break down and eliminate old bone, and then osteoblast cells lay down new bone matrix, which is made up of collagen. Collagen, a protein, is the structure of bone. After the bone matrix is laid down, hormones direct calcium to be laid down on top of the protein. This new bone matrix is thus calcified.

When Fosamax kills osteoclast cells, bones get denser temporarily, but in time, bones weaken because the natural process of breaking down and building up has been disrupted. Think of what it would be like to allow your fingernails to grow indefinitely and what they would ultimately look like. Disrupting normal bone metabolism means less bone formation and increased bone breakdown, which ultimately results in osteopenia (less bone) and then osteoporosis (fracture).[297]

It's disputed whether Fosamax has reduced hip fractures by even 1 percent. In other words, 90 women who were at risk for fracture would have to take Fosamax for three years to prevent one hip fracture among the group. The other 89 women would have taken the Fosamax in vain.[298] In October 2010, the FDA announced that they would require warning labels about risks of thigh fractures associated with drugs such as Fosamax and Boniva.[299]

Unlike a teaching skeleton that can hang pretty much indefinitely in a classroom, a fifty-year-old woman does not have the same skeleton that she had when she was thirty. Every single cell has been broken down and replaced numerous times. And does anyone really believe that her skeleton can be replaced with enriched cereal, Tums, calcium-fortified orange juice, Fosamax, Actonel, or my all-time favorite, the once-a-month "bone builder" Boniva? It's common sense that living tissue can only be replaced by eating the same biochemicals that make up bones.

In a perfect world, thinning of bones that results in osteoporosis (bone breakage) would be prevented by using BHRT, quitting smoking and other stimulants, and abstaining from factory food, and instead, eating real, living foods that provide adequate protein, fat, calcium, and other minerals, vitamins, and enzymes for optimal metabolic processes. Aside from eating real food, the next best thing you can do for your bones is to stress them through weight-bearing exercise. Think of your bones exactly as you think of your muscles. They are dynamic. They bruise when you hit them, for example. They break down, like muscle, and they build back up. If you don't stress them, just like muscles they will weaken. Exercising outside in the sun is optimal in order to obtain the vitamin D necessary to utilize calcium for bone growth.

There are many other examples of drugs that are making matters worse, but the most classic are the cholesterol-lowering drugs. Because of the lipid hypothesis, the subsequent low fat diet, and the accompanying science-fiction fats that caused the epidemic of heart disease, drug companies are now cleaning up by selling us these drugs.

We're not hearing messages on TV to stop eating chemical- and heat-treated polyunsaturated vegetable oils, partially hydrogenated polyunsaturated vegetable oils, refined white flour, refined white sugar, high-fructose corn syrup, MSG, aspartame, factory-produced animal products, and other science-fiction substances. No, we continue to get messages to eat heart-unhealthy oils, like canola and soy.

For more than fifty years we've had hammered into our heads the misconception that total cholesterol numbers are the number one indicator of our risk of a heart attack. The fear of cholesterol is so entrenched in our culture that it's likely here to stay. Almost without fail, when I meet someone who hasn't read my books but learns I write about health, I hear comments about his or her low cholesterol efforts.

Numerous studies have demonstrated that high cholesterol is not a risk factor for women, that women with high cholesterol live longer than women with low cholesterol, and that it's more dangerous for women to have low cholesterol than high. People who suffer from heart disease sometimes have elevated blood cholesterol numbers, but not everyone who has elevated blood cholesterol numbers develops heart disease. Everyone with heart disease does not have elevated blood cholesterol numbers. In fact, most people with heart disease do not have elevated blood cholesterol.[300]

Study after study has proven that your cholesterol number, regardless if it is high or not, is not an indication of risk or lack of risk for heart disease.[301] Dr. Enig told me, "Blood cholesterol levels between 200 and 240 mg/dl are normal. These levels have always been normal. In older women, serum cholesterol levels greatly above these numbers are also quite normal, and in fact they've been shown to be associated with longevity. Since 1984, however, in the United States and other parts of the western world, these normal numbers have been treated as if they were an indication of a disease in progress or a potential for disease in the future."[302]

Dr. Enig maintains that cholesterol in the blood is a good thing. "The official advice to lower serum cholesterol levels has brought about numerous supplements with the attached claim that consuming them will lower cholesterol. This further supports the myth of cholesterol as an undesirable component of body and diet. In fact, the body uses cholesterol to repair and to protect. When improvement to the health of the body brought about by good changes in lifestyle or diet results in a lowering of serum cholesterol, it can be counted as an example of the body no longer needing the extra circulating cholesterol. The repair has been accomplished."[303]

Cholesterol is a waxy compound that maintains the structure of every single cell in your body. In fact, every cell in your body makes its own cholesterol, and your liver manufactures it day and night for use throughout your body. Your body has a system of checks and balances so that it will always have enough cholesterol to keep up the ongoing repair and replenishing of your body on a cellular level.

Cholesterol and triglycerides, which are water insoluble, are packaged into water-soluble lipo-proteins so they can float through your watery bloodstream. Your total cholesterol is arrived at by adding together the three different cholesterol-carrying lipoproteins: high-density lipoproteins (HDLs), low-density lipoproteins (LDLs), and very low-density lipoproteins (VLDLs). HDLs, LDLs, and VLDLs are delivery vehicles that take cholesterol and triglycerides to and fro within your body via your bloodstream. They have been labeled good and bad, but each lipoprotein actually has a healthy purpose in your body.

HDLs are said to be "good" lipoproteins because they recycle cholesterol back to the liver. LDLs carry cholesterol from the liver to your cells for use as raw material. LDLs are labeled "bad" because they can get damaged in route and thereby waylaid, and they can end up depositing cholesterol in your artery walls. Damage occurs to LDL lipoproteins by oxidation caused by free radicals.

Another way LDLs get damaged is from excess blood sugar, which "caramelizes" LDL lipoproteins, similar to dunking an apple into a bubbling cauldron of caramel candy. In addition to coating LDLs, this candy coating also builds up on your cells and arteries. So by stopping eating factory food and eating only real food, you will protect your LDLs.

VLDLs carry triglycerides (fat) throughout your body for use as energy. Since HDL and VLDL levels are like kids on a teeter-totter, if your eating and lifestyle habits raise your HDLs you are going to see your VLDLs go down proportionately. The opposite is also true.

Since HDLs, LDLs, and VLDLs all perform different functions, adding them up to arrive at a total cholesterol number does not tell you anything one way or another. But this is just another example of the medical establishment getting stuck on something and having it so entrenched in our society that it is likely, and very unfortunately, here to stay.

The food, diet, and drug industries have made billions of dollars on cholesterol-lowering measures such as "heart healthy" food products, lab tests and so on. The drug industry would also like each and every adult (and now children) to take cholesterol-lowering drugs even though study after study has concluded that atherosclerosis increases in patients whose cholesterol is decreased by more than 60 mg/dl and that atherosclerosis worsens just as fast or faster when cholesterol levels go down as when cholesterol levels go up, that people with low cholesterol levels suffer from just as much atherosclerosis as people with high cholesterol levels, and that lowering cholesterol levels increases your risk of dying from violence or suicide.[304]

Statins deplete the body of the essential molecule coenzyme, CoQ_{10}. A lack of CoQ_{10} weakens the heart muscle and can lead to congestive heart failure, muscle weakness, neurological disorders, and even death. Even more alarming is that statin drugs suppress vital immune cells called helper T-cells, which help protect us against from cancer as well as fungal, bacterial, and viral infections. By taking statins you are lowering your immunity.[305]

If you don't eat enough cholesterol to sustain your body's need for cholesterol, your body sees this deprivation as a time of famine and activates the enzyme HMGCoA Reductase in your liver, which overproduces cholesterol out of the carbs you eat. Cholesterol-lowering drugs work by switching off this enzyme. Switching off HMG-CoA Reductase means that your body may not be getting the cholesterol it needs for important ongoing building and replenishing.

One study that compared high doses of Lipitor (made by Pfizer) with less potent Pravachol (made by Bristol-Myers Squibb, which sponsored the trial) showed that patients taking Lipitor were significantly less likely to have heart attacks or to require bypass surgery or angioplasty. Lipitor was shown to halt plaque growth; Pravachol was shown to only slow plaque growth.[306]

I asked Dr. Eades to weigh in: "The study showed only very modest benefit (0.6 percent reduction in occurrence rate of heart attack in five years) at an enormous cost. One hundred and sixty-five healthy people would, over a period of five years, have to spend $1.2 million purchasing Lipitor to extend the life of one person by five years. The money comes out of the pockets of consumers, insurers and taxpayers. Statins don't come without side effects, some of which are merely debilitating, some of which are lethal. Although the statin class of drugs do indeed lower cholesterol, a number of recent studies have begun to dispel the notion that elevated cholesterol is even a player in the development of heart disease. Moreover, if lowering cholesterol is the point, a recent study of modern hunter-gatherers shows that these groups naturally maintained LDL levels below the magic 100, without benefit of statins, simply by following a healthy meatbased diet, higher in protein, lower in carbohydrate, and replete with good fats. Our advice: Eat real foods, save the money you'd spend on statins, and don't risk the possibility of serious side effects." [307]

Factory-food makers are married to drug manufacturers in two important ways: First, factory foods make people sick, thus the need for drugs. And second, factory foods and drugs are both purchased by individuals who are convinced that what they are doing is healthy. In addition to eating "healthful" factory substances approved by the FDA, the AMA, and the AHA, we are now convinced that Americans are heart attacks waiting to happen, and to prevent a heart attack from occurring we must take cholesterol-lowering drugs. If the (global) $492 dollar per year cholesterol-lowering drugs we are taking are so effective, why are Americans still dying from heart disease?

Since cholesterol is necessary to make many hormones, the factory-food diet (including phytoestrogenic soy) has lowered testosterone in some men. Since cholesterol is necessary to convert sunshine to vitamin D, which is necessary to utilize calcium, this diet has eroded the bones of women. Since brain cells and neurotransmitters are made from cholesterol and protein, factory products have ravaged our brains. And drug companies have jumped in with drugs to fix these problems.

What is really sad is that people are now programmed into thinking that they can continue eating factory-food substances as long as they take drugs. Moreover, many people are deathly fearful of the real food diet that would save them from developing the maladies that are causing them to be prescribed drugs in the first place. These are the people who look askance at a rib-eye steak and real butter but fearlessly admit to being on a perilous cocktail of drugs including statins, antidepressants, and impotence drugs. Americans have become so acculturated to drugs that having a medicine cabinet full of drugs is normal.

Philip Roth's novel *Everyman* explores the remorse of a man whose philandering and hedonistic obsessions had left him bereft of meaning and companionship in his golden years. Along the way he suffers one cardiac event/surgery after the next. A background cast of characters are by turns decimated by drugs. One is laid low by chemotherapy, one has a stroke from taking a risky migraine drug, and another's back pain cannot be alleviated by pain pills so she downs enough to do herself in. Since drugs, drugs, drugs, and more drugs (and their side effects) are perfectly natural for us, drugs are thus a likely backdrop for "everyman's" story. Meanwhile, our anti-real food, socially acceptable pharmaceutical (but not recreational!) drug mentality, perpetuated by organizations like the American Heart Association—"the most respected source for health and nutrition"—is killing Americans.

It's important to note that stress can temporarily cause your cholesterol numbers to skyrocket—so if you are stressed out about having high cholesterol the day that you have your labs drawn, the number that comes back is likely not going to be an accurate account of what is really going on with your cholesterol. Nevertheless, it's not any one lipoprotein number or the total cholesterol number that should scare you. And the emphasis on your genetics is just another unnecessary detour. A genetic predisposition does not automatically mean that you are doomed. There is more and more evidence that heart disease is caused by a constellation of factors related to eating and lifestyle habits.

Deficiencies of B vitamins in the diet (folic acid, vitamin B_6, and vitamin B_{12}) raise the level of an amino acid called homocysteine in the bloodstream. When elevated, homocycteine has been found to cause arterial damage and plaque. You can reduce your risk by eating foods rich in vitamin B or by taking vitamin B supplements. Foods high in folic acid are brewer's yeast, oranges, green leafy vegetables, wheat germ, asparagus, broccoli, and nuts. Foods high in vitamin B_6 are whole grains, meats, fish, poultry, nuts, and brewer's yeast. And foods high in vitamin B_{12} are meat, fish, poultry, eggs, and dairy.

Prolonged high insulin levels, as we talked about earlier, encourage coronary artery plaquing. (High insulin levels are caused by sugar/refined carbs, stress, dieting, caffeine, alcohol, tobacco, aspartame, steroids, sedentary lifestyle, recreational, and OTC and prescription drugs.)

It's now understood that inflammation is a major risk factor for heart disease. Normal inflammation is part of the immune reaction that helps your body to heal from injury. When the immune system refuses to turn off, inflammation can result in a relatively small arterial plaque ballooning and blocking the passage to the heart, causing a heart attack (heart muscle death). Why are we so inflamed? Could the gallons of coffee and Diet Coke have something to do with it? The cocktail of OTCs and prescription drugs? Sitting with our laptops or watching TV and eating carbs and trans fats? An anti-inflammatory diet includes fish (small fish so you are not getting a bi-weekly dose of mercury), wheat germ and walnuts, healthy oils (reviewed on page 114); and any brightly colored vegetable or fruit.

Chapters 9 through 11 told you all about the relationship between chemical- and heat-processed polyunsaturated fats and heart disease (i.e., the relationship between trans fats and free radicals and heart disease). I would venture to say if these fats had never entered our food chain we would not be discussing heart disease today.

In the past several decades, Americans have turned their attention toward preventative measures and healing because our instincts are telling us that we are sick on a deep level. Although we may not be conscious of it, the repercussions of our individual ill health manifest in the collective ill health of our society as a whole. For example, if a child does not do well in school because he or she suffers from neurotransmitter imbalances it ultimately affects society as a whole for the span of that child's life.

Medicine discarded nutrition along with the focus on disease prevention. Instead, the focus has been on treating disease after it occurs, primarily with drugs, and unfortunately, more recently the focus has shifted to preventing disease with drugs. However, you can't hit one health issue with a sledgehammer and expect to feel and be well because all drugs have an impact on your body's homeostasis. Whenever the body perceives an abnormal state, its coordinated adaptive responses attempt to return it back to homeostasis, or the status quo.

When the baby boomers started aging, antiaging medicine began to emerge that focused on nondrug, preventative modalities such as balanced nutrition, stress reduction, bioidentical hormone replacement therapy, nutraceuticals/dietary supplements, and exercise. Antiaging medicine is generally viewed by mainstream medicine as a vanity-driven, fringy, wayward cousin to real medicine. But lo and behold, as a result of the advances in antiaging medicine, another branch of preventative medicine sprang up, spearheaded by clinical nutritionists who broke ranks from the traditional dietitian mentality of old—those dietitians who planned the Ensure-cornflakes-coffee hospital meals described earlier. Clinical nutritionists and a growing contingent of enlightened physicians are developing a new medical approach based on the philosophy that many health problems (including obesity) can be resolved or at least significantly helped by this same protocol.

This new frontier in medicine takes us back to Hippocrates, who focused on the effects of food, occupation, and environment in the development of disease. Today's new breed of enlightened health practitioners understands that seeking to balance the entire body is the key to optimal wellness. And the primary factor in overall balance is keeping or bringing hormone levels into balance.

People tend to think of menopausal women in connection with hormone imbalance. But as you now understand, many diseases such as type 2 diabetes, heart disease, and some cancers are the result of prolonged high-insulin levels caused by eating too much sugar, eating a low-fat diet, stress, dieting, drinking too much caffeine and alcohol, using tobacco, ingesting aspartame, using steroids, having a sedentary lifestyle, using recreational drugs, and taking too many OTC and prescription drugs. Stress, sugar, and stimulants have also resulted in cortisol imbalances (adrenal burnout). Overeating goitrogenic (thyroid inhibiting) foods like soy and chemical exposure have resulted in a rise in hypothyroidism. Millions of children who were raised on sugar, soy, and chemicals are medicated for depression and other neurological disorders, which are imbalances of brain neurotransmitters. Factory-food-eating men and women are going into early andropause and menopause. And twenty-something women—raised on factory food, diets, and drugs—have the estrogen levels of menopausal women.

When your body's various systems (endocrine, immune, neurological, and so on) are not operating at capacity, there are health consequences. If you're fat and unhealthy, it is guaranteed that your endocrine system is not operating as smoothly as it could and that you have some type of hormonal imbalance, whether it is insulin, sex hormones, melatonin, thyroid, cortisol, or other.

This doesn't mean that you should rush out and self-prescribe. Since all systems of the body are interconnected and hormones are the chemical messengers, it stands to reason that we would want to be hypercareful about the hormones we take. If you're fat and sick, your first course of action should be to attempt to rebalance your endocrine system by stopping eating all factory food and eating only real food. Then if you still suffer from symptoms of hormone imbalance—or if you're over the age of say, forty—you are likely to need BHRT.

Unfortunately, in the richest country ever, there are millions of poor people who couldn't dream of getting BHRT. The poor are left to self-prescribe, if they can afford it, with the "herbal hormones" we see on TV. The middle class can afford health care and so end up with doctors who think that Premarin is a hormone. It's only people with money in this country who can afford real, bioidentical HRT. If you're one of the lucky few, its important to find a qualified, enlightened practitioner who you feel in sync with and who can prescribe BHRT and monitor your results and symptoms.

The examples in this chapter of "preventative" drugs demonstrate how industry has clutched American consumers in the death grip of an unhealthy symbiotic relationship in which they are fattened up on factory-food and "treated" for subsequent obesity and disease with diets and drugs. And to keep us in this relationship, these industries play on our emotions.

PART NINE

Madison Avenue and Us

CHAPTER TWENTY-THREE

Playing Us, and Playing Along

IN 1968, AT AGE 18, I was swept into the mass exodus of the love generation overland from Europe through Turkey, Iran, Pakistan, and Afghanistan, to India and Ceylon (now Sri Lanka). In the jungle in Ceylon I met my lifelong friend Jitka Gunaratna, then a Czechoslovakian expatriate, fishing with a safety pin and a shred of coconut. It was less than a year after the infamous Prague Spring, and Jitka, who had been in Czechoslovakia during the Russian invasion, was still reeling from that horrible event. As we ate her fish, she cried when she reiterated the story to me.

Twenty-five years later, Jitka visited me in Santa Barbara, where I caught her in front of the TV watching a chemical company ad about caring for some bird. "You're not crying, are you?" I asked her.

"Well, I see this advertisement on CNN International and I find it so touching," she sniffed. "I always cry."

"Jitka," I said darkly, "aren't you the little Czech girl who also cried when Russian tanks rolled over your fellow citizens in the Wenceslas Square in Prague in 1968, and cried again when that Communist regime decimated your country?"

"Uh-huh," she admitted, smiling sheepishly as she wiped away a tear.

"*You*, of all people, should understand the meaning of *propaganda*."

"But it's so heartwarming," she insisted. "Those birds."

Propaganda works. In fact, a campaign of effective propaganda that plays on our emotions has ensnarled us in an unhealthy symbiotic relationship with the medical establishment, the government, and the food, diet, and drug industries.

Back in 1966, when professor Timothy Leary was launching himself as a psychedelic visionary, a media-savvy friend gave him some advice: "The key to your work is advertising. You're promoting a product. The new and improved accelerated brain. You must use the most current tactics for arousing consumer interest. Associate LSD with all the good things that the brain can produce—beauty, fun, philosophic wonder, religious revelation, increased intelligence, mystical romance. Word of mouth from satisfied consumers will help, but get your rock and roll friends to write jingles about the brain."[308]

This sounds vaguely familiar because if you look at the emotional tactics companies use to get us to eat, diet, and take drugs, it involves all of the above-mentioned strategies. For example, Americans are ga ga goo ga over celebrities. They're beautiful, fun, sexy, romantic. You could even say their images provoke philosophic wonder and religious revelation (to some). And so they are used prolifically to woo us into consuming products. But the reality is that professional athletes, movie stars, celebrities, and musicians don't know what's best for us just because they're on an athletic field or court, on TV, in a movie, or on a musical stage. Historically, actors, athletes, buffoons, fools, jesters, singers, musicians, jugglers, and other entertainers were societal outcasts, tolerated only to the extent that they could amuse and entertain. Today celebrities have enormous power that translates into lucrative spokes-pitching deals. Even though no celebrity would accept an endorsement contract to pitch gas-guzzling cars, urge us to blast our airconditioners in a heat wave, take longer showers, or leave lights blazing in our homes, there are still many celebrities—who are already earning obscene amounts of money in their professions—who sign contracts to woo us into eating factory food with promises of good health, beauty, fitness, satisfaction . . . and fun. One that jumps out was the deal J.K. Rowling made giving Coca-Cola the global marketing rights for the

Warner Brother's Harry Potter franchise, which has earned her millions of more dollars, even though she's already worth one billion dollars.

Aside from celebrities (human or cartoon), the food industry uses blatant seduction. For example, the Denny's breakfast ads that air on prime time TV, wooing us with powdered sugar French toast and oozing syrup so that we're psychologically primed to go to Denny's ASAP in the a.m.

Product manufacturers twist science and semantics to assure us that their products are healthy. The General Mills website, which is dedicated to "health," maintains that, "On average, U.S. shoppers place at least one General Mills product into their shopping cart each time they visit the grocery store." Some of these products are: Betty Crocker, Pillsbury, Fiber One, and Cheerios. General Mills' mission is "to nourish every one by making their lives healthier, easier and richer." They claim, "More frequent cereal eaters tend to have healthier body weights and lower Body Mass Index [BMI] measures. It's true of men. It's true of women. It's true of kids. And that includes people who eat presweetened cereals." So let's see. If 68 percent of the population is overweight or obese, and on average, shoppers place at least one General Mills product into their shopping cart each time they visit the grocery store, and these frequent cereal eaters have healthier body weights, then how does that compute? If you go deeper into the site, you'll find the kid cereals. "Big G cereals are delivering millions more servings of whole grain every day." They urge moms to "Give Your Kids More of What They Need To Be Their Best": Lucky Charms, Cinnamon Toast Crunch, Trix, and Cocoa Puffs."[309]

The mangling of science takes extreme forms such as the Glucerna candy bars and shakes that are pitched to a population of diabetics in danger of going blind and suffering amputations with such messages as, "Including Shakes, Bars, and Cereal in your meal plan is a smart way to help get the right kinds of carbs every day." Their website assures diabetics that "the Glucerna product advantage comes from the unique blends of slowly digested carbohydrates and key ingredients scientifically designed to help meet the needs of people with diabetes."[310]

Without exception, companies that claim their products are healthy back up their claims with voluminous scientific research. But either the claims, such as whole grains are healthy and slowly digestible carbs are necessary to salvage a diabetic's life, are, in fact, true but not applicable to highly refined, sugary cereal, shakes, and candy bars; or the claims, such as the anticancer and other health claims made by the soy industry, have been produced by studies paid for (directly or indirectly) by the industries that stand to profit.

The food industry, aided and protected by the government, does everything in its considerable power to convince consumers that industrialized products are natural food. And now that the organic movement is sweeping the nation, they are doing everything in their considerable power to take over that movement.

Beginning in the mid-1990s, Americans were already catching the scent of an ill wind blowing in our food industry. In an effort to protect themselves and their children, they joined the organic food movement, shopping in more expensive health-food stores and local farmers' markets. This increased demand increased supply, and more and more people were able to find organic food in their areas. Now the food industry's goal is to render the term "organic" as meaningless as the word "natural" has been since the recipe for granola got away from that hippie girl way back when.

Organic labeling for dairy products, for example, generally means that the product is free of antibiotic, herbicide, pesticide, growth hormone, chemical fertilizer, and genetically modified organism residues, and that animals have outdoor access to pastures and are fed 100 percent organic feed. But, as it turns out, "organic feed" does not necessarily mean that the animals are fed a species-appropriate diet or that they spend all their time, or even a majority of their time, or any time at all, in the pasture, even though the nutritional value of the milk crucially depends on these factors.

Horizon Organic Dairy (owned by Dean Foods, the largest milk supplier in the United States) controls between 57 and 85 percent of the organic retail market (varying in every state).[311] Their own labeling declares that their milk is ultra pasteurized (sterilized). Numerous watchdog agencies have reported that Horizon Organic has circumvented the organic regulations and that their cows are not pasture-grazed, but rather (according to the Center for Global Food Issues, a watchdog group that conducts research and analysis of agriculture and related environmental concerns) Horizon operates industrial organic dairy-processing centers called "dry lots, where thousands of Horizon cows never see a blade of grass."[312]

This example rocks the organic food movement's dreams of supporting small, local farmers and of treating animals humanely and the environment responsibly in the process of producing the highest-quality food for human beings. But Dean Foods is taking it a step further. The $12 billion company controls so much of the milk market that in January 2010 a federal antitrust suit was filed by the U.S. Department of Justice, in conjunction with Wisconsin, Illinois, and Michigan, that alleges that because of its voracious acquisitions, Dean has too much control over milk pricing and supply, a position that squashes market competition.[313] And as they say in commercials, but that's not all! Because Dean Foods has patiently cultivated its organic consumers, now the company is going to stealthily introduce a new, lower-priced product category called "natural dairy." This non-organic milk is intended to siphon off distracted consumers who really don't have the time or energy or money to think past what they already are assured of—that Horizon provides organic milk from happy, healthy, grass-grazing cows.[314]

Unless monitored by consumers, organic ideals and dreams could be obliterated as the multibillion-dollar, dominating corporations charge in with their wallets open, buying up small organic farms and ranches, and proceed to market established brands with lax standards about animal caretaking and human nutrition. The newly acquired operations, with the brilliant marketing strategies of companies like Dean Foods, will evolve into exactly the kind of monster commercial industries that organically minded consumers are trying to escape. Meanwhile, these pseudo-organic producers' innocent-looking packaging denies there might be something else going on.

The government helps commercial industries in their quest to lure us in with false information and glossing over truths. One prime example is the USDA's dairy "checkoff" program, which requires farmers and ranchers to pay for generic advertising aimed at boosting industry sales. One such program is the "Got Milk?" campaign.

Joseph and Brenda Cochran and their fourteen children own and operate a third-going-on-fourth-generation family farm in Westfield, Pennsylvania. The USDA collects a mandatory fee of 15 cents per hundred pounds of milk from dairy farmers like the Cochrans to pay for checkoff programs such as the popular "Got Milk?" campaign. But the Cochran family didn't want to continue contributing to a campaign that was not being straight with the public.

"The checkoff system treats all milk the same, and that's simply not the case," Joe told me. "People who graze cows have a different type of milk. Some dairies treat their cows with growth hormones. The milk that comes out of those cows is different from our milk. The advertising fund takes money from us and puts it into a generic fund that gives consumers a sense that there's really no difference. This type of advertising does not give the consumer enough information to make informed choices."

Although these milk suppliers did not endorse the government "Got Milk?" campaign, they were forced to take legal action to be released from contributing to it. Supported by the Center for Individual Freedom in Alexandria, Virginia, on April 2, 2002, the Cochrans filed suit against the government seeking to end the payments that were costing the family business up to $4,200 per year. The Cochrans' suit maintained that the First Amendment granted them the right to speak *and* the right to remain silent. After two long years of legal wrangling, on March 5, 2004, the court ruled, by unanimous decision, that the dairy checkoff program was unconstitutional under the First Amendment.[315]

This story illustrates the government's participation in a program that ignores the fact that there is a difference between milk produced by ill-treated, sick, unhappy cows in factories and pure, healthy, natural, organic milk produced by pasture grazing, happy cows that contain nature's nutrients.

The science-fiction fat olestra, sold under the brand name Olean, is a rather mind-boggling example of a substance that was allowed into our food supply by the FDA, with no regard to human health and welfare. Olestra is a synthesized from sucrose (sugar) bonded to fatty acids in a way that makes the molecules too large to be absorbed through the intestinal wall. It supposedly has the same taste and mouthfeel as fat, but since it passes through the GI tract undigested, it doesn't translate to calories. It also prevents the absorption of vitamin D, vitamin E, vitamin K, vitamin A, and carotenoids.

According to Olean's website, "it's what helps make great-tasting foods for today's health conscience lifestyles."[316] Health conscious eaters can find Olean in Lays, Tostitos, Doritos, and Ruffles chips and even buy a "proprietary blend" of Olean and vegetable oils so they can bake their own cookies at home.

Although Procter & Gamble originally admitted that there were some problems with the interference of vitamin absorption and that olestra caused anal leakage, a condition known as "steatorrhea," on January 24, 1996, the FDA approved olestra for use in chips, crackers, and tortilla chips with one caveat: Products had to carry a label that stated, "This product contains olestra. Olestra may cause abdominal cramping and loose stools. Olestra inhibits the absorption of some vitamins and other nutrients. Vitamins A, D, E, and K have been added."

Indeed, olestra snack products were off and running (as it were). A year later, more than one thousand reports of adverse reactions to olestra products were submitted to the FDA, and this appeared to represent only a small fraction of the people sickened by olestra-containing products.

When the FDA held advisory committee meetings to review the safety and labeling of olestra, Procter & Gamble argued that complaining consumers could not prove that it was olestra that was causing fecal incontinence, projectile vomiting, projectile bowel movements and diarrhea, cramping, bleeding, and yellow-orange oil in toilet bowls and in underwear—symptoms so severe in some consumers that they required hospitalization, surgery, and colonoscopies.[317]

By 2000 the FDA had received 20,000 negative reports about olestra.[318] Yet, in August 2003, the FDA ruled to no longer require companies that manufactured products containing olestra to put warning labels on their products as they had "conducted a scientific review of several post-market studies submitted by P&G, as well as adverse event reports submitted by P&G and the Center for Science in the Public Interest. The FDA concluded that the label statement was no longer warranted".[319] Olestra is banned in the United Kingdom and Canada.[320]

On March 15, 2004, Eric Peoples, a thirty-two-year-old former factory worker at the Gilster-Mary Lee Corporate microwave popcorn plant in Jasper, Missouri, was the first of thirty workers with lung disease to be awarded $20 million in compensatory personal injury damages. (As a tort attorney friend of mine once said, "I would never trade places with a million dollar winner.") The jury ruled against International Flavors and Fragrances, Inc., and its subsidiary Bush Boake Allen, Inc., the manufacturers of the chemical in the butter flavoring diacetyl, which is used in butter-flavored microwave popcorn. Diacetyl, currently being studied by the Environmental Protection Agency (EPA—a government agency founded to protect human health and the environment), is believed to cause lung damage when its vapors are inhaled. The jury didn't need to get the EPA report before they ruled against the chemical manufacturers. When the microwave popcorn verdict broke, media reports claimed that "health officials" insisted that making and eating microwave popcorn at home is perfectly safe.

In 2004, the House of Representatives approved legislation called the Personal Responsibility in Food Consumption Act, (also known as the

"Cheeseburger Bill"), which bars suing industrialized food restaurants for making people fat. In the same week, the government issued a report that obesity-related illnesses were soon to surpass tobacco-related illnesses as the number one preventable cause of death in the United States. The enduring sentiment was expressed by Representative F. James Sensenbrenner, Jr., (R-WI), chairman of the Judiciary Committee who charmingly remarked, "This bill says, 'Don't run off and file a lawsuit if you are fat.' It says, 'Look in the mirror because you're the one to blame.'"[321] The bill passed the House but stalled out in the Senate and has not been debated since.

Meanwhile, the food industry has the money and means to defend itself against any and all attacks. In the late 1980s London Greenpeace passed out leaflets entitled "What's Wrong with McDonald's? Everything They Don't Want You to Know," accusing McDonald's of exploiting food producers in developing countries, children and employees, destroying rain forests, producing unhealthy food, and torturing and murdering animals. McDonald's sued for libel. Two Greenpeacers, Helen Steel and Dave Morris, known as "The McLibel Two," were compelled by lack of funds to act as their own defense in what was the longest, most complex, most expensive civil trial in Britain's history. McDonald's spent $15 million pursuing two people whose combined incomes were $12,000 per year. Although Justice Rodger Bell found evidence to support some but not all of the leaflet's claims, he ultimately ruled against the defendants. Steel and Morris were ordered to pay £40,000 to McDonald's in libel damages (about $66,000 at that time). Ultimately, McDonald's dropped the claim and limped away, humiliated by the press, with the entire world alerted to the toxic nature of their industrialized food.[322]

This is but one example of how questioning industry standards can land you in an expensive, protracted lawsuit with a huge damages award and even criminal sanctions.

Listen carefully and you will recognize threats in print ads, TV commercials, and newscasts. Back in 1970, Fleicshmann's threatened American parents with the question, "Should an eight-year-old worry about cholesterol?"[323] Since that time there have been no end to the threats of impending heart disease that coerce Americans into eating an ever-expanding array of deadly factory food with the promise of "lowering your cholesterol." These threats can take on a saccharine tone, "You already know Honey Nut Cheerios is packed with an irresistible honey sweet taste, but did you also know the soluble fiber from whole grain oats in Honey Nut Cheerios makes it irresistible for your heart? As part of a heart-healthy eating plan, Honey Nut Cheerios can help lower your cholesterol. This is great news for you, your family, and your heart!"[324] (This one truly falls under the rubric of gag me with a spoon.)

The makers of Plavix, which is marketed to people who have already had a stroke or heart attack, claim that the drug "helps keep blood platelets from sticking together and forming clots." They take a boogieman approach in their ad that shows a man standing at the edge of the Grand Canyon, with the headline that reads, "You don't want another heart attack or another stroke to sneak up on you."[325]

The barrage of cholesterol-lowering drug ads tell us that the industry is making a killing on these drugs; otherwise, it could not afford the millions of dollars it takes to produce and air TV ads. The makers of Crestor originally used a lighthearted, endearing tone, with annoying narration that was actually delivered in pseudo Dr. Seuss verse; another featured an actor who is not-really-a-doctor-but-played-one-on-TV. "Crestor's not for everyone," the actor reassured doctorishly, "including people with liver disease and women who are nursing or may become pregnant. A simple blood test is needed to check for liver problems. Tell your doctor . . . if you experience muscle pain or weakness because they may be a sign of serious side effects." It's a revealing commentary that we are worn down to the point that we're so inured to the possibility of drug side effects that we'd consider for even a fleeting moment to take something that might cause severe liver damage.

It does really blow my mind that people willingly take drugs with bizarre side effects, like the those for Mirapex: "Patients taking certain medicines to treat Parkinson's disease or RLS, including Mirapex . . . have reported problems with gambling, compulsive eating, and increased sex drive"; and Requip: "Impulse control symptoms, including compulsive behaviors such as pathological gambling and hypersexuality, have been reported in patients treated with dopaminergic agents."

TV ads for Actonel, a prescription osteoporosis medication, threaten, "One out of every two women over 50 will have an osteoporosis-related fracture in her remaining lifetime."[326] The Purple Pill features "comical" TV spots with actors portraying acid reflux suffers trying to get to sleep. A man cranks up the head of his bed using a car jack to prevent nocturnal heartburn—and the cat slides off, yowling. "Desperate for nighttime heartburn relief? For many, Nexium helps relieve heartburn day and night."[327]

Today thirteen states—Alabama, Arizona, Florida, Georgia, Idaho, Louisiana, Mississippi, North Dakota, Ohio, Oklahoma, South Dakota, Texas, and Colorado—have passed "veggie libel" laws that have made illegal "the false disparagement of perishable food products," which makes it easier for factory-food producers to sue people for "libel" (remember the famous Oprah Winfrey suit brought by Texas cattlemen).

All of this emotional manipulation from the food, diet, and drug industries creates an effective fog machine to keep you distracted from what you're consuming. But we have to come to grips with our own culpability if we want things to change.

In the 1980s I was living in Los Angeles and would occasionally swing by Randy's Donuts on West Manchester Boulevard. Because of the familiar enormous donut on top of the donut shop, Randy's is often used by filmmakers in montages to establish that the scene is L.A. One morning both of the owners were at the pickup window. "I have a love/hate relationship with you," I said as I accepted my donut bag. "What do you mean?" asked one owner. "She loves me, and she hates you," quipped the other. I laughed. Of course, I meant the donuts.

Americans joke and laugh off the fact that our factory-food diet is damaging our health. Everyone else is eating it, so it must be OK. Ha. Ha.

In fact, it's socially acceptable to eat an unnatural, disease-causing diet. In fact, in his HBO comedy special, Bill Maher had his audience rolling in the aisle when he said, "In 1900, the average woman's shoe size was four. In 1980, it was seven. Now it's nine. We are evolving into a completely new species with webbed feet to support our massive girth."[328]

The media plays a huge role in our acceptance of factory food, diets, and drugs. Today all bad news is delivered by bubbly newscasters. Terribly wrong nutritional advice is presented by these same trustworthy messengers. Many nutritional experts, fearing being pegged as fringy, kooky, or downers, soften their messages to the point of practically siding with the food, diet, and drug industries.

We're the most highly evolved capitalistic, mercenary society to ever walk the face of the earth. So every detail, every molecule of copy on every factory-food package has been scrutinized, analyzed, test marketed, and reviewed to arrive at an image and message that is most likely to hook you into succumbing to your addiction. Madison Avenue refers to consumers as the lowest common denominator, and Madison Avenueites make it their business to know all the personas currently in vogue so they can best target our egos. If you want to be perceived as a cool, popular kid, sexy, brainy, a good parent, heman, caveman, manlyman, or master of the universe, there are products that will appeal to your sense of self.

Consumers are no longer targeted with quaint print ads and TV commercials. Susan Linn, Ed.D., associate director of the Media Center of Judge Baker Children's Center, instructor in psychiatry at Harvard Medical School, and author of *Consuming Kids: The Hostile Takeover Of Childhood*, said, "Comparing the marketing of today with the marketing of yesteryear is like comparing a BB gun to a smart bomb."[329] Companies use product licensing, promotions, and contests, co-branding (like Coca Cola Barbie), program-length commercials, advergraming (putting products into computer games) and kiosks, carts, and vending machines in schools. They infiltrate our minds subtly with product placements. Product placement plays perfectly into our sense of community when it comes to consuming factory food, diets, and drugs.

TV executives have one goal: to get companies to buy commercial time during their programming. Companies have one goal, and that is to get you to spend money on their products. It's part of the symbiotic relationship. David Chase, the creator of *The Sopranos* said, "The function of an hour drama is to reassure the American people that it's OK to go out and buy stuff. It's all about flattering the audience and making them feel as if all the authority figures have our best interests at heart."[330]

Celebrity doctors contribute to our cavalier mentality about what we consume with books, pills, diet systems, TV shows, products, infomercials, and so on that make us feel all chummy about our obesity problem. Many people have the impression that M.D.s and Ph.D.s have all the answers and that is why they make such perfect spokespeople for the diet industry. Because doctors wield a lot of influence, some doctors are looking for ways to capitalize on their credentials beyond practicing medicine. For example, Dr. Agatston, author of *The South Beach Diet,* has developed factory-food products for Kraft. Dean Ornish, M.D., founder of the Preventative Medicine Research Institute and author of five bestselling books on the low fat diet, including *Dr. Dean Ornish's Program for Reversing Heart Disease: The Only System Scientifically Proven to Reverse Heart Disease Without Drugs or Surgery*, is a paid consultant to the McDonald's Corporation, PepsiCo, and ConAgra Foods. Kenneth H. Cooper, M.D., the "father of aerobics" and author of numerous books on the merits of exercise, beginning with *Aerobics* (1968), profits by allowing his name to accompany "health tips" on packages of FritoLay's baked chips.[331] Then there are doctors who are in the diet business to make money and who don't care one bit about you or the quality of your life. As one bestselling diet doctor told me, "The more I charge, the more people want to see me."

Over the past few decades, celebrities have gained such elevated status in our society that what they say is gold. And it doesn't take much to achieve celebrity status these days. Even those glossy-lipped, thin, beautiful, diet soda drinking girls are perceived as celebrities in our society. If they got on TV they must be, like, actresses or something. One of the top publicists in the country told me, "You can't launch a book or product anymore without a celebrity endorsement. The morning TV shows won't even talk to you unless you have a celebrity attached to your project. It doesn't even have to be an actual star. It can be as insignificant as some celebrity's hairdresser or ex-personal assistant. But it has to be someone who the public perceives as having celebrity status. If you've got a celebrity, you can sell anything to the public." For many consumers, a celebrity or even a quasi-celebrity's word is even more credible than a doctor's.

The public has come to expect tantalizing real-people stories attached to any nonfiction enterprise. Case histories can take the form of "before and after" fat stories, they can illustrate how well such-and-such health or diet approach works, or they can infuse drama with tragic sagas of suffering. A well-known health book writer recently emailed me about her struggles to get a very important book into the public eye. "I met with producers from *20/20*, *Dateline*, National Public Radio, *Good Morning America*, *The View*, etc. in NYC and they told me flat out that they would be very interested in airing [my book], but only if I can get some of the parents [in the case histories] to go public, show their faces on TV, cry in public about their [tragedies]." In other words, the important message her book had to offer was not enough. Real-life pathos was necessary to sell it.

Indeed, many Americans are anesthetized to anything but the screaming of their own pain. Many Americans are numbly gorging on chemicalized factory food in a demoralized, deflated, and defeated state, and sheepishly laughing it all off. And when people are in this neurotransmitter-depleted state, companies can release their seductive siren call with promises of health, beauty, and satisfaction. All you have to do is eat, drink, or swallow their products—and go back for more.

Americans bear such enormous burdens that we've been compelled into our complacency as a coping mechanism. First we have the obvious problems we've discussed above, such as the ubiquitous mind-controlling messages we are continually fed that seduce us into indulging in the abundance of factory products in our food supply. Then, even when we want to eat real food, we cannot even locate a source for real food in all-poison-sandwiches-all-the-time situations such as when driving on the interstate, airplanes, or hospitals, or at entertainment venues such as zoos, theme parks, movie theaters, sports arenas, and so on. Compounding these problems, we also have virtually no one in places of power taking our side. Instead, we're told that what we're "personally responsible" for what we eat and what we feed our children. Never are we as justified to retreat into our complacent cocoon as when this personal responsibility argument is used on us.

The factory-food industry has taken this defensive "personal responsibility" stand against arguments that it is wrecking American's health. They argue that (1) the responsibility is on individuals for being overweight, (2) the factory-food industry is only responding to consumer demand by supplying us with factory food, and (3) free enterprise allows them carte blanche to market as they see fit—and any impingement would be an assault on their freedom.[332]

When the U.S. Surgeon General finally got around to acknowledging that cigarette smoking is bad for our health, cigarette advertising was banned from TV and cigarette smoking advertising directed toward children was ultimately banned, including, for example, the Camel cigarette cartoon character whose image was designed to target children. But today it's still perfectly OK, even cute, for Ronald McDonald to peddle poisonous, extremely fattening and addicting factory food to children (and precious when he visits them in hospitals). Then when children grow up with compulsive eating problems, we have weighty legislation, such as the "Cheeseburger Bill," which is supposedly for our own good as it will help these fattened-up-on-fast-food adults be more responsible.

I have no problem with people making money. I love stories about people who have taken a great idea and made a cool million or billion, as the case may be today. America was built on great and innovative ideas. People should make money on their ventures. But writers, celebrities, doctors, and anyone else who presents a health message to the American public through books, TV, newspapers, radio, or the Internet have the responsibility to be accurate, truthful, and, most of all, rabidly focused on improving the quality of Americans' lives. We can't continue to make excuses about our free market system when people are dying on the vine. If a writer, celebrity, doctor, or food supplier is not part of the solution, then he or she or it is part of the problem. And those who are part of the solution must be committed to ending the trickery and seduction that leads people to eat factory food and must not be contributors to the exploitation of those people once they get fat and sick.

I've never watched a Dr. Phil show or even seen him on TV, so I may be completely off base targeting him as a celebrity who used his power to sell fattening diet products to overweight people. Still, I believe in our urgent obesity crisis that celebrities need to step up to the plate and be responsible—just as Dr. Phil undoubtedly preaches on his therapy show. Dr. Phil has been unapologetic about his foray into the nutritional food and supplement market. In an interview, when asked about his Shape Up! products, he replied that he didn't consider endorsing these products to be a commercial venture because proceeds would go to a charitable foundation (though he didn't elaborate). "I think it's a good product," he said, "and I'm doing it for a really good reason and purpose, although if I was doing it for a commercial—as a brand extension of my own—I wouldn't apologize for that either."[333] I'm confused because I thought that if you have your grinning thumbs-up photograph plastered all over a product line that millions of people see and buy that that is a brand extension.

We'll never know if Dr. Phil would have gotten hip to the fact that he was eroding the credibility of his brand and alienating his faithful by endorsing his so-called "nutritional" bars, supplements, and other such products if his hand hadn't been forced by the FTC and by the class-action suit. He's since broken off with CSA Nutraceuticals and dissolved the shapeup.com website. It originally appeared that Dr. Phil was concerned about restoring the credibility of his brand so he could continue to exploit fat people with other weight-loss products designed to inspire affable camaraderie, including complete non sequiturs like (I am not kidding) "I Love Dr. Phil" T-shirts (up to size 3X), photo coffee mugs, and baseball caps. Now you can only buy books and cassettes on his site.

Once we've determined that these messengers probably do not have our best interests in mind, the next step is to fully examine and come to terms with our own culpability. One area in which Americans are not scoring very high marks is in the feeding of their children.

PART TEN

The Home Front

CHAPTER TWENTY-FOUR

Change Begins at Home

MOBY DICK'S ON CAPE Cod, Massachusetts, like many New England restaurants, serves up fried seafood, but they also have fresh lobster, coleslaw, grilled fish, and salads. On one beautiful summer afternoon at Moby Dick's, I sat across from a mother, father, and teenage son who appeared to weigh in at 200, 250, and 350 to 400 pounds, respectively. They ordered fried seafood, fries, milk shakes, and ice cream sundaes. This family also had an adorable ten-year-old boy who was about 150 pounds, a boy who was condemned by virtue of the family he was born into to become a binge eater, to possibly reach 400 pounds like his brother, and likely to die young from a heart attack or complications of type 2 diabetes.

In the year 1900, only 5 percent of Americans were obese. Obesity rates have remained constant for the last five years among men and constant for ten years for women and children. Nearly 34 percent of adults are obese, and 17 percent of children are obese.

Acceptance of fat has changed dramatically in the past three decades. In the 1978 film *Midnight Express*, the true story of American drug trafficker Billy Hayes who was imprisoned in Istanbul's infamously brutal Sagmalicar prison, the fat twin sons of the Turkish head guard Hamidou represent the juxtaposition of Hamidou's brutalization of Billy and his allegiance toward his own. Back in 1978, when the boys first come on-screen, the reaction to the sight of them was both shocking and sickening—first, that they were so fat, and second, knowing that the boys were safe and protected, eating baklava by the pound, as Billy starved, forsaken by his government and victimized by Hamidou. Today we see fat kids on-screen too, but they are cast merely to represent normal kids in movies and TV commercials.

Recently on a trip to South Beach, Florida, I got up at 5 a.m. to catch an early flight home. From the third-floor hotel window, I watched a full-on gang fight on the street below, with a policeman brandishing a gun, the arrival of several police cruisers, a chase, and a bust. I had never seen anything like that before in real life, and the violence was disturbing. But what struck me was that—although I hadn't previously equated "tubby" with "tough"—the homies were *fat*.

Another time in the Phoenix, Arizona, airport, while waiting for a flight, sitting across from a Burger King, I watched enormous people lumber in and out of that establishment. What impressed me about that experience was that some of the obese people were with other obese people, but many were alone.

Although being overweight today is the norm, it is not yet socially acceptable to be obese. In a study that asked college students who they would be the least inclined to marry, an embezzler, cocaine user, ex-mental patient, shoplifter, sexually promiscuous person, communist, blind person, atheist, marijuana user, or obese person, the students said they would rather marry (in this order) an embezzler, cocaine user, shoplifter, or blind person before they would marry an obese person.[334] Children who were shown pictures of children in a wheelchair, missing a limb, on crutches, facially disfigured, or obese said they were least likely to play with the fat child.[335] Obesity is the last acceptable area of discrimination, and obese adults are discriminated against in many areas of life, including every stage of employment cycle (selection, placement, compensation, promotion, discipline, and discharge). Overweight people are even stereotyped as emotionally impaired, socially handicapped, and possessing negative personality traits. They get paid less money.[336]

The fact is that children of overweight/obese parents are more likely to be overweight/obese.[337] And once a child is overweight, he or she is likely stay that way for the rest of his or her life.[338]

Although obesity often condemns people to less than happy lives, our society accepts that a child born into a family of binge eaters will likely become a binge eater as well, and we shrug. Oh, well. Sad, isn't it? And to make matters worse, our medical community has labeled this pattern "genetics." Most doctors and most people cling to the belief that genes make people obese. Genes—not behavior. Everyone in my family is overweight. My genes are working against me. Type 2 diabetes runs in my family. Oh I see, genes give people type 2 diabetes, not the fact that by the time the little boy from Cape Cod was ten years old, he had eaten twelve hundred pounds of sugar, give or take several hundred pounds. This is not even counting the hundreds of pounds of other carbohydrates, like cereal, toaster pastries, chips, French fries, candy, cookies, cake, pie, pastry, donuts, bread, pizza, pasta, waffles, pancakes, muffins, and cornbread that American families typically eat. If a family feeds their children huge quantities of sugar/carbohydrates/factory food over the prolonged period of their childhoods, that is not genetics—that is behavioral programming that creates the conditioned response we talked about way back in chapter 3.

It's becoming more common to hear heartrending stories of children and obesity in the news. Like the three-year-old British girl who weighed in at 83.6 pounds when she died of congestive heart failure and the thirteen-year-old California girl whose 680-pound, bedsore-ridden body was found nude on her mother's living room floor, instigating a five-day trial wherein the mother was acquitted of felony child abuse. In the summer of 2010, a couple was arrested after authorities found their two children obese and living in filthy conditions. The five-year-old daughter, who could barely walk, and who had matted hair, rotten teeth, and bug bites, weighed 158 pounds. The four-year-old girl, wearing a soiled diaper and drinking from a bottle, weighed 89 pounds. As of this writing, the couple is facing felony child cruelty charges.[339]

You may say, "Well, those children were abused." True, they were abused beyond just being fattened up way beyond a normal body weight for their ages. As much as it may be unpopular, shocking, and alienating to some readers, it's my position that causing children to become obese or sick as the result of feeding them factory-food products is child abuse, with or without the bug bites and diapers.

Along those lines, I also can't understand the bizarre concept of "kid food." On one of my research outings, I went shopping at Star Market in Boston. At the checkout, I stood in line behind an overweight, early-thirties father and his chubby two-year-old son. The man spent $200 on a head of iceberg lettuce and three plums. I'm exaggerating. He only spent $3 on a head of iceberg lettuce and three plums. The other $197 were spent on Austin Zoo Animal Crackers, Nabisco Barnum's Animal Crackers, ice cream, Kraft HandiSnacks, Elfin Magic Iced Apple Cinnamon Bars, Keebler Journey Peanut Butter with Fudge Chunks, Nestle Nesquik Chocolate-Flavored Milk Mix, and other cartoon-emblazoned kid food products. It was all I could do not to grab the man and plead, "Please buy some food for your son!"

In *The Ultimate Weight Solution*, when Dr. Phil urged his readers to "Begin today to reprogram your environment and set yourself up for success," he went on to say, "Okay, I suspect that right now you're thinking, 'Well, that sounds fine and good, but there are foods I need to keep around for my kids. They aren't fat. Why should they suffer?" Dr. Phil suggests designating a "specific cabinet" in your kitchen for kid food such as "pizza, brownies, potato chips, and all the rest."[340] This is supposed to protect you from temptation but allow your kids to eat factory products. In other words, a major role model and bestselling psychologist tells us that not feeding kids poisonous substances would cause them to "suffer." Have you ever noticed that these so-called kid foods are the most processed, chemicalized and sugar-laden foods on the market? Can you imagine feeding that stuff to your dog? I've heard many people say, "People food isn't good for dogs!" In other words people feed "kid food" to kids, but not to dogs. In conversations about nutrition, I've heard parents say, "Oh, we just go to McDonald's for a treat." With all due respect to parents, as I understand how time-consuming raising children is, if McDonalds is considered "a treat" in your family, you really need to carve out some time to learn how to cook.

You might be saying, "But my kids won't eat anything healthy. All they like is pizza." Let's say that pizza makers listed Drano as a pizza ingredient. Would you still feed them pizza? Of course not! Drano's poison! But many pizzas contain partially hydrogenated fat (trans fats). Sodium hydroxide (i.e., lye, an ingredient in Drano and Easy-Off) and phosphoric acid (a chemical used in bathroom cleaners) are both used to process vegetable oils before they are hydrogenated.[341]

I don't have children and am aware that the obstacles parents face today are formidable; however, I've yet to understand how parents can feed their children sugar and then sit in the dentist's waiting room strumming through magazines and listen to the whine of the dentist drill excavating cavities from their kids' teeth—and then (according to my dentist), greet their shell-shocked children with rewards of candy bars.

Consider this scenario that we've all witnessed in restaurants: A mother, father, and their four-year-old son sit down to eat, and the waitress comes to take their order. "Honey bunny," asks the mommy, "want the macaroni and cheese with chips?" To the waitress, "He'll have the macaroni dinner." The waitress writes it down.

"I don't want it!" the kid whines.

"What do you want then, precious? How 'bout the hot dog and fries?" To the waitress, "Change that to the hot dog." The waitress writes it down.

"Noooo," the kid whimpers, squirming in his seat.

"Hmm, well, don't the pancakes with chocolate chips sound yummy?" The kid nods.

"Make that the pancakes instead." The waitress writes it down.

"I want another Coke," the kid bellyaches.

To the waitress, cloyingly now because everyone's nerves are tautly stretched, "Could you please bring another Coke when you have a sec?"

"I want it now!" the kid screeches.

"Listen, mister, I'm going to take you outside if you don't lower your voice."

The order comes. The kid takes one look at the pancakes. "I don't want it!"

"What's the matter, honey, you don't like the nice pancakes?"

"I want French fries."

The father takes the boy's plate. "I'll eat it."

The mother pleads, "Could you please bring the hot dog dinner?"

So it goes. I'm sitting there thinking about my mother's (sorry, Mom) unappetizingly overcooked pot roast, mashed potatoes, and peas that I sat and ate at least once a week for my entire childhood, whether I liked it or not. I am not saying that kids should be forced to eat my mother's recipes, but only that someone needs to be in charge when it comes to selecting the foods that kids learn to like. In Japan kids eat the slimiest, strangest, most God-awful-looking stuff, with chopsticks no less. In India, toddlers eat eyeball-melting curries with their fingers. Millions of children all over the world happily dine on insects. I have seen children in France refuse an offer of dessert at the end of a meal. Tastes for food are established in childhood—some experts say as early as three years old. That explains why Indian babies can munch on chili peppers that would send us to the ER, why German children will eat liver, Finnish children will eat stinky dried fish, and French children will eat green vegetables like candy.

Here in the United States kids eat pretty much nothing but "kid food," and many get fat. The logical response is to put them on a diet, though I can't tell you how many tragic stories I've heard that have started with the sentence, "When I was eight, my mother took me to Weight Watchers." Since the 1970s, obesity in adolescents has increased by 75 percent. Researchers have found that "the very act of starting any diet increases the risk of eating disorders in adolescent girls." Obsessions with body image, low self-esteem, depression and suicide, and sudden cardiac death resulting from extreme weight-loss practices are increasingly common with teenagers.[342] The practices of dieting, fasting, extreme exercise, taking diet pills, bingeing, vomiting, and using laxatives will soon creep from high school and college to elementary-school-aged children if parents do not intervene. Starvation and vomiting both result in a pleasurable release of endorphins, which are our neurotransmitter equivalent to heroin, and if your child gets hooked on the pleasure associated with starvation and vomiting, you will have a much more difficult challenge on your hands in getting them to stop these behaviors.

On the other hand, studies demonstrate that kids can learn how to eat a healthy diet and will be much less likely to be overweight or obese if their parents provide them access to healthy foods and role models to emulate by developing good habits themselves.[343] In other words, no matter how old your children are and how programmed they are, you can still begin to educate them about the difference between factory food and real food. You can teach them that factory food erodes health and that real food will give their bodies and brains the building blocks of nutrition so that they can fully realize their genetic gifts—and their dreams. In addition to talking to your kids, you can form your children's lifelong attitudes about food by what you put on the table, what is in the refrigerator, and what you order or allow them to order in restaurants.

So it's a hassle to take along your own freshly prepared real food when you are, say, getting on an airplane. But when you're in poisonous food situations it's even more important to set an example to your children that you will not accept what is being foisted on you by the food industry just because it's more convenient or "free." That you'll go the extra step necessary to put real food into your body and into the bodies of your children will make a concrete impression on your children.

How trusting are kids? Do we really need multimillion-dollar studies to tell us? In the 1950s and 60s there was a zany kids' program on TV called *The Soupy Sales Show*. On one show, Soupy (Milton Supman) gazed with his doggie eyes into the camera and suggested that kids sneak into their sleeping parents' bedrooms and extract from their wallets and purses all the little green pieces of paper and send them to him at the Channel 5 in New York. Allegedly he received $80,000 from his fans, which his producer insisted was mostly Monopoly money. Soupy got in lots of hot water for that prank. But the point here is that kids are innocent. Right now kids are getting mostly one side of the story about factory food—what advertisers want them to hear.

In 2005, Bill Clinton teamed up with the AHA to create the Clinton/American Heart Association Initiative in an attempt to halt childhood obesity in the United States by the year 2010.[344] As of this writing in 2010, the goal has been extended to 2015. So I guess that speaks volumes.

One very alarming campaign is ridding schools of sodas containing high-fructose corn syrup and replacing them with "healthier" choices: beverages containing caffeine, aspartame, and Splenda that will not only contribute to obesity (as you know, stimulants and fake sugar encourage eating) but will erode the developing brains of America with excitotoxins.[345]

Removing factory food from our food supply and feeding children real food that fosters brain health would be a step in the right direction as neurotransmitter balance is of the utmost importance in halting the unnatural hunger, craving, and bingeing cycles that condition children to knee-jerk react to every stressful situation by eating catastrophic and fattening substances. Remember the analogy of creating the best quality grape—or the best quality human being? Americans are not going to create the best quality human beings out of our children unless we provide them with healthy real, living food.

The latest travesty against children has been initiated by schools that are sending humiliated kids home with body mass index score reports euphemistically referred to as "obesity report cards."[346] Instead of stigmatizing overweight kids as outsiders ("the fat one on a diet"), real change can occur by changing your eating habits as a family from factory food to real food—and campaigning in your kids' schools to rid them of factory food. Then we will make healthy, life-lasting impressions and quality human beings. Of course, you'll need to purge your kitchen of all factory food and replace it with real food, and you will need to get out your cookbooks, strap on the apron, and prepare meals for your family. But really, getting is healthy is such a fun ride, why not take your kids along with you?

Conclusion

I HOPE THAT READING this book has helped you understand how real food differs from factory food, as my mantra is to "get educated" about the food, diet, and drug industries. Our lives depend on it, even though that may sound melodramatic. Switching from a diet of factory food to an exclusive diet of real, whole, living food will change your life and allow you to experience who you really are. You'll start to see a different person emerge, and you'll discover what it's like to achieve your genetic gifts, such as is possible in whatever stage of life you're in.

I'm a real food advocate, but I also advocate eating organic. I've been told that suggesting people buy organic, especially "out there" food items like raw milk, is "elitist." And I couldn't agree more. It's shameful that in the richest country in the world you have to be wealthy to afford real food. It's disgraceful that Hurricane Katrina victims were given military Meals Ready to Eat rations that are so artificial that they can withstand a 1,250-foot drop from a helicopter, temperatures from minus 60 to 120 degrees Fahrenheit, and have a minimum three-year shelf life. I also cringe when people criticize the 40 million people who rely on food stamps to survive. New York is paving the way for the poverty-stricken recipients of food stamps to be prohibited from buying sodas with their stamps. I've heard a lot of hateful remarks about these so-called leeches on society. Well, try living in a food desert your entire life, where your mother put a baby bottle of Coke in your mouth when you were an infant, and tell me that you would make better choices. The poor people in this country deserve the greatest compassion and assistance from those of us who can afford to eat real food.

The only way to lower prices of organic foods—and to pave the way for all fifty states to allow the sale of raw milk—is for those who can afford organic to buy and consume real, living organic food. When there is enough demand, prices will come down. Then someday we may see real, organically produced food in food banks for the poor on news footage at Christmas and Thanksgiving instead of the noxious stuff they are typically forced to accept as "charity."

I've often heard people complain about the price of real food (including myself). Fifty years ago, Americans spent one-fifth of their disposable incomes on food, with one-fifth of that expense going to eating out. Today Americans spend one-tenth of their disposable incomes on food, with half of that expense going to eating out.[347] So it appears that at least some Americans have enough money to buy real food if they wanted to.

The United States spends $147 billion dollars a year on medical expenses related to obesity.[348] Even if factory food is currently cheaper than organically grown real food, the health problems we will ultimately suffer from by saving a few pennies now will most certainly be regretted later. In the immortal words of my grandma, Stella, "Saving pennies and spending dollars!" Consuming certified organic foods that are produced in an environmentally responsible way is an immediate expense that provides enduring, positive quality-of-life effects.

Organic foods are whole, non-genetically modified, nonirradiated foods that can (theoretically) be picked, gathered, milked, hunted, or fished from a natural, clean environment and within natural conditions. True organic foods do not contain additives or poisons or synthetic processing residues, and have not been subjected to any types of processing. Therefore, a box of cereal cannot reasonably be called organic. Milk from cows kept in dry lots and fed species-unnatural feed is not organic. Meat from cattle that were fed an unnatural diet cannot be called "grass fed." You must seek out the true among the counterfeit organic in your daily hunt for sustenance.

Although America missed its opportunity for utopia, and we're now poised upon a precarious precipice, one of our culture's greatest attributes is that we love a comeback story. It's not too late for America to become the utopia it was meant to be—individual by individual. My hope is that Americans—like the Pilgrims, colonial Americans, and pioneers of the West, and all the awe-inspiring American heroes and heroines—will rebel against the tyranny that's kept us blinded to the industries that are profiting at the expense of our health, reject the industrialized food diet offered to us by the powerful elite, break out of the bubble that has kept us unnaturally hungry, fat, and sick, and begin to forge new dietary paths by eating real food. This one simple change would allow us to achieve and enjoy our genetic gifts and would drastically reduce the number of patients who are now flocking to obesity clinics, ERs, and shrinks' offices.

Rejecting the socially acceptable industrialized food diet is challenging. As we discussed earlier, there are many strikes against us; powerful forces, influences, and obstacles assist us in resisting doing what we know we need to do to eat a healthy diet. When it comes to stopping eating all factory food and eating only real food, each one of us must conquer our resistance to change. We have to face off every single day with the resistance that makes us want to succumb to the seductive siren call of the food, diet, and drug industries. We have to fight both our own resistance and these powerful forces as individuals, as families, and as communities. But what else is worth fighting for, if not health and happiness, especially for our children?

It's the American way.

Acknowledgments

BOOKS GET WRITTEN FOR a compilation of reasons: One is influence, and another is inspiration; then there is passion for a subject, but it's the all-important ingredient of believing you can do it that pulls it all together. My first influence on health and real food was my grandma, Stella Grabowski, a humble Polish immigrant who would be unnerved if she were alive to see her name in print. Without my grandma, I would have likely succumbed to the factory-food fate that I'm now so passionate about helping others avoid. My second huge influence was Heini Baumgartner, the world hitchhiker who swept me off to India and Europe, and who reinforced Grandma's admonitions to eat real food. But I could have just left it at that if it hadn't been for John Davis, the best friend I have ever had, the most brilliant strategist, advisor, coach, and partner. I can say with all honesty that this book, and everything I've accomplished in my career, has John all over it.

Not to assign grades of importance, because every person who helped me along the way made a difference and was indispensable in my efforts to put this book together, but way at the top is my sister, Nadine Saubers, R.N., who is brilliant and often hilariously insightful, and not lacking in passion when it comes to revealing the truth about the food, diet, and drug industries. Truly, I couldn't have dealt with the never-ending research necessary if not for her. She is also the mega-creative talent who designed and manages my website, blog, and Facebook pages.

I also want to say thank you to my former agent Gary Heidt, who worked so hard on my behalf, and I hope that I will do justice to his belief in me.

This book would not exist ultimately without the backing of Clint Greenleaf and the entire team at Greenleaf Book Group, specifically Justin Branch, who initially ushered me into the company; Hobbs Allison, my liaison and sounding board; Lari Bishop, whose expertise and talent helped reshape this rewrite; Jay Hodges, who edits brilliantly without nitpicking; Daniela Richardson, for the gorgeous book jacket design; Wendy Swanson, for managing the entire production process and giving me much-needed reprieves; and thanks to editors Patricia Fogarty and Heather Jones. I've never had as much fun or felt as inspired and confident working on a book as with the Greenleaf Book Group team.

But I would never have connected with Greenleaf had it not been for Pamela Miles, whose generous introduction paved the way.

I have numerous experts to thank who graciously granted interviews and contributed quotes and otherwise helped me through the process of putting this book together: Christopher K. Germer, Ph.D.; Russell Blaylock, M.D.; Daniel E. Lieberman, Ph.D.; the late David Kritchevsky, Ph.D.; David R. Allen, M.D.; David Zava, Ph.D.; Henry Han, O.M.D.; John Komlos, Ph.D.; John W. Olney, M.D.; Joseph and Brenda Cochran; Kaayla T. Daniel, Ph.D., C.C.N.; Maoshing Ni, Ph.D., L.A.C., D.O.M.; Mark McAfee; Mary Dan Eades, M.D.; Mary Enig, Ph.D.; Michael Eades, M.D.; Mike Katke; Robin Marzi, R.D., M.A.; Ron Schmid, N.D.; Sally Fallon; Samuel Epstein, M.D.; Stephanie Gunning; Uffe Ravnskov, M.D., Ph.D; Vidu Gunaratna; and Tommy O'Malley.

I also can't forget my Facebook fans who inspired me along the way with their questions, insights, and enthusiasm. In a huge way, this book is for them.

Om Shanti,
Nancy Deville

Endnotes

1 "Obesity (most recent) by Country," accessed October 13, 2010, http://www.nationmaster.com/graph/hea_obe-health-obesity.

2 "World Health Statistics 2009," World Health Organization, accessed October 7, 2010, http://www.who.int/whosis/whostat/2009/en/index.html.

3 Burkhard Bilger, "The Height Gap: Why Europeans are Getting Taller and Americans Aren't," *The New Yorker*, June 3, 2004, accessed October 27, 2005, http://mailman1.u.washington.edu/pipermail/pophealth/2004-April/000855.html; John Komlos, "Anthropometric History: What Is It?" *OAH Magazine of History 6*, Spring 1992, acccessed July 4, 2004, http://www.oah.org/pubs/magazine/communication/komlos.html; John Komlos, e-mail message to author, July 1, 2004, 12:08 p.m.

4 "Depression in Children and Adolescents," Child Development Institute, accessed November 4, 2004, http://childdevelopmentinfo.com/disorders/depression_in_children_and_teens.htm; "ADHD—A Public Health Perspective," accessed October 31, 2004, http://www.cdc.gov; Bill Sardi, "How to Quell the Rising Rate of Autism," accessed November 1, 2004, http://www.knowledgeofhealth.com/pdfs/autism.pdf.

5 Adele Davis, *Let's Eat Right To Keep Fit: The Practical Guide to Nutrition Designed to Help You Achieve Good Health Through Proper Diet* (New York: Harcourt, Brace and Company, Inc., 1954), 256.

6 Mary Enig, *Know Your Fats: The Complete Primer for Understanding the Nutrition of Fats, Oils and Cholesterol* (Maryland: Bethesda Press, 2000), 249.

7 Mira B. Irons, "Cholesterol in Childhood: Friend or Foe?" *Pediatric Research*, vol. 56 (2004), 679-681.

8 Nadia Bennis-Taleb, "A Low-Protein Isocaloric Diet During Gestation Affects Brain Development and Alters Permanently Cerebral Cortex Blood Vessels in Rat Offspring," *Journal of Nutrition*, vol. 129 (1999), 1613-1619; W. Prasad, "Maternal protein deficiency in rat: effects on central nervous system gangliosides and their catabolizing enzymes in the offspring," *Lipids*, vol. 26 No. 7 (July 1991), 553-6.

9 Weston A. Price, *Nutrition and Physical Degeneration*, 6th ed. (La Mesa, CA: PricePottenger Nutrition Foundation, 1939-2003); Maureen Mulhern-White, "Brain Power Starts in the Womb: DHA: An omega-3 fatty acid that's critical for brain development," accessed October 31, 2005, http://www.wholehealth md.com/hk/articles/view/1,1471,950,00.html; Gerard Hornstra, "Essential fatty acids in mothers and their neonates,"*American Journal of Clinical Nutrition* 71, no. 5 (May 2000): 1262s-1269s; Guoyao Wu et al., "Maternal Dietary Protein Deficiency Decreases Amino Acid Concentrations in Fetal Plasma and Allantoic Fluid of Pigs," *The Journal of Nutrition* 128, no. 5 (May 1998): 894-902; Alan Parkinson et al., "Elevated concentrations of plasma Omega-3 polyunsaturated fatty acids among Alaskan Eskimos," *American Journal of Clinical Nutrition* 59 (1994): 384-8; Monique DM Al, Adriana C van Houwelingen, and Gerard Hornstra, "Long-chain polyunsaturated fatty acids, pregnancy, and pregnancy outcome," *American Journal of Clinical Nutrition* 71, no. 1 (January 2000): 285s-291s.

10 R.J. Wurtman and J.J. Wurtman, "Brain serotonin, carbohydrate-craving, obesity and depression," *Obes Res.* 3, suppl. 4 (1995): 477s-480s.

11 Sharon Begley, "The Depressing News About Antidepressants," *Newsweek*, accessed January 29, 2010, http://www.newsweek.com/2010/01/28/the-depressing-news-about-antidepressants.html.

12 Lisa W. Foderaro, "These Days, the College Bowl Is Filled With Milk and Cereal," *New York Times*, November 14, 2004, 1.

13 Ken C. Winters, "Adolescent Brain Development and Drug Abuse," *A Special Report Commissioned by the Treatment Research Institute,* November 2004, 1.

14 Michael Eades and Mary Dan Eades, *The Protein Power Lifeplan: A New Comprehensive Blueprint for Optimal Health* (New York: Warner Books, 2000), 3-4.

15 Davis, *Let's Eat Right To Keep Fit*, 107.

16 Mary Enig and Sally Fallon, *Eat Fat, Lose Fat: Three Delicious, Science-Based Coconut Diets* (New York: Hudson Street Press, 2005), 90; "Cereals production: from grain flour to crunchy delight," accessed October 30, 2005, http://www.buhlergroup.com/19889EN.htm?grp=60; "Canine Nutrition," accessed October 30, 2005, http://www.pamperedpawswimspa.com/html/canine_nutrition.html.

17 "Kellogg's Nutri-Grain Yogurt Bars Strawberry Yogurt," http://www.nutrigrain.com/ProductDetail.aspx?product=360.

18 "Video Love Stories," Cheerios Cereal, http://www.cheerios.com/Love/VideoStories.aspx?fbid=FH0NCZEpwKo.

19 Lance Armstrong, *It's Not About the Bike: My Journey Back to Life* (New York: Putnam, 2000), 28-29.

20 "Class action sought for 'Dr. Phil' diet suit," accessed November 5, 2005, http://www.cnn.com/2005/LAW/10/04/dr.phil/.

21 Sherri Day, "Dr. Phil, Medicine Man," *New York Times*, October 27, 2003, Media.

22 Betsy Schiffman, "The Doctor is Out," accessed October 27, 2005, http://www.forbes.com/2004/03/05/cx_bs_0305movers.html.

23 Phil McGraw, *The Ultimate Weight Solution: The 7 Keys to Weight Loss Freedom*, (New York: The Free Press, 2003), 108, 119.

24 "Class action sought for 'Dr. Phil' diet suit," accessed November 5, 2005, http://www.cnn.com/2005/LAW/10/04/dr.phil/.

25 "High Fructose Corn Syrup (HFCS): 'Two Bites' TV Original Ad," http://www.youtube.com/watch?v=W40yHDFxkAY.

26 "A sweet problem: Princeton researchers find that high-fructose corn syrup prompts considerably more weight gain," Princeton University, http://www.princeton.edu/main/news/archive/S26/91/22K07/; http://www.lef.org/magazine/mag2008/dec2008_Metabolic-Dangers-of-High-Fructose-Corn-Syrup_01.html.

27 Karen Ritchie, "Why Doctors Don't Listen," accessed October 30, 2005, http://www.cancerlynx.com/doctorlisten.html.

28 Ralph Selitzer, *The Dairy Industry in America* (New York: Dairy & Ice Cream Field, 1976), 37.

29 Mark Motivans, PhD, "Federal Justice Statistics, 2007—Statistical Tables," accessed October 3, 2010, http://bjs.ojp.usdoj.gov/index.cfm?ty=pbdetail&iid=2196.

30 Federal Bureau of Investigation, "Supplementary Homicide Reports for the years 1980–2006," accessed October 2, 2010, http://www.ojjdp.gov/ojstatbb/ezashr/.

31 "What Certification Means," accessed October 6, 2010, http://www.heart.org/HEARTORG/GettingHealthy/NutritionCenter/HeartSmartShopping/Heart-Check-Mark_UCM_300914_Article.jsp.

32 Rose Marie Robertson, MD, FAHA, FACC,FESC, "Food and Drug Administration Public Hearing Food Labeling: Use of Symbols to Communicate Nutrition Information," accessed October 5, 2010, http://www.americanheart.org/downloadable/heart/1190912885142AHA%20Testimony%20to%20FDA%20on%20Nutrition%20Icons.pdf.

33 Marion Nestle, "Food company sponsorship of nutrition research and professional activities: a conflict of interest?" *Public Health Nutrition*, 4(5), 1015–1022.

34 Scott Murphy, e-mail message to author, July 15, 2004, 4:07 p.m.

35 "My Grocery List," American Heart Association, accessed October 5, 2010, http://checkmark.heart.org/.

36 "The Food Pyramid Scheme," *New York Times*, September 1, 2004, accessed February 23, 2005, http://www.health.gov/dietaryguidelines/dga2005/document/.

37 "Dietary Guidelines for Americans," United States Department of Agriculture Center for Nutrition Policy and Promotion, accessed October 5, 2010, http://www.cnpp.usda.gov/dietaryguidelines.htm.

38 "The Fat of the Land," *New York Times*, February 2, 2004, A-24.

39 Kelly D. Brownell and Marion Nestle, "The Sweet and Lowdown on Sugar," *New York Times*, January 23, 2004, A-25.

40 "White House takes aim at obesity," accessed September 17, 2004, http://www.cnn.com.

41 "Take the Path to Good Health Daily," *Sun Journal*, September 2, 2004, accessed September 17, 2004, http://sunjournal.com/node/74343?quicktabs_2-1.

42 Amy Corderoy, "Obesity is now more deadly than smoking," *The Sidney Morning Herald*, April 9, 2010, accessed October 5, 2010, http://www.smh.com.au/lifestyle/wellbeing/obesity-is-now-more-deadly-than-smoking-20100408-rv5l.html.

43 "Corn subsidies in the United States totaled $73.8 billion from 1995-2009," accessed October 7, 2010, http://farm.ewg.org/progdetail.php?fips=00000&progcode=corn.

44 Erik R. Olson et al., "Inhibition of cardiac fibroblast proliferation and myofibroblast differentiation by resveratrol," *American Journal of Physiology - Heart and Circulatory Physiology* 288 (2005): H1131-H1138; Zou et al., 'Effect of red wine and wine polyphenol resveratrol on endothelial function in hypercholesterolemic rabbits,' *International Journal of Molecular Medicine* 11, no. 3 (2003): 317-320.

45 "John W. Olney, MD," Washington University in St. Louis, accessed October 7, 2010, http://psychiatry.wustl.edu/c/faculty/FacultyDetails.aspx?ID=282.

46 John Olney, e-mail message to author, June 18, 2004, 6:24 p.m.

47 Russell L. Blaylock, e-mail message to author, March 28, 2005, 12:45 p.m.

48 Russell L. Blaylock, e-mail message to author, March 28, 2005, 12:45 p.m.

49 Russell L. Blaylock, MD, *Excitotoxins: The Taste that Kills* (Santa Fe, New Mexico: Health Press, 1977), 255-256.

50 Ibid., 45.

51 Russell L. Blaylock, e-mail message to author, March 28, 2005, 12:45 p.m.

52 Ibid.

53 "Aspartame Controversy," Wikipedia, http://en.wikipedia.org/wiki/ Aspartame_controversy.

54 Russell L. Blaylock, e-mail message to author, August 23, 2005, 11:23 a.m.

55 *Brown Book: War and Nazi Criminals in West Germany* (Dresden, Germany: National Council of the National Front of Democratic Germany Documentation Centre of the State Archives Administration of the German Democratic Republic, 1965), 33-34. Dan J. Forrestal, *Faith, Hope & $5,000* (New York: Simon and Schuster, 1977), 149, 159-161. Erik Olson and Elliot Negin, "EPA Reverses Ban on Testing Pesticides on Human Subjects," National Resources Defense Council, November 28, 2001, accessed December 17, 2005, http://www.nrdc.org/media/pressReleases/011128a.asp.

56 *Adverse Effects of Aspartame-January '86 through December '90, 167 Citations*, National Institutes of Health, U.S. Department of Health and Human Services, National Library of Medicine pamphlet, 1991.

57 Morando Soffritti et al., "Aspartame induces lymphomas and leukaemias in rats," *European Journal of Oncology* 10, no. 2 (2005): 00-00; H. J. Roberts, "Does Aspartame Cause Human Brain Cancer?" *Journal of Advancement in Medicine* 4, no. 4 (Winter 1991): 232-240; C. Orange, "Effects of Aspartame on College Student Memory and Learning," *College Student Journal* 32, no. 1 (1998): 87-92; J. A. Konen et al., "Perceived Memory Impairment in Aspartame Users," (paper presented at the Society for Neuroscience 30th Annual Meeting, November 6, 2000); Ralph G. Walton, "Adverse Reactions to Aspartame: Double-Blind Challenge in Patients from a Vulnerable Population," *Biological Psychiatryn* 34 (1993): 13-17; H.J. Roberts, "Reactions Attributed to Aspartame-Containing Products: 551 Cases," *Journal of Applied Nutrition* 40 (1988): 85-94.

58 J. W. Olney et al., "Increasing brain tumor rates: is there a link to aspartame?" *Journal of Neuropathology and Experimental Neurology* 55, no. 11 (November 1996): 1115-23.

59 Blaylock, *Excitotoxins*, 214.

60 Russell L. Blaylock, e-mail message to author, March 28, 2005, 12:45 p.m.

61 Blaylock, *Excitotoxins*, 213.

62 R. J. Wurtman, "Neurochemical changes following high-dose aspartame with dietary carbohydrates," *The New England Journal of Medicine* 309, no. 7 (August 18, 1983): Correspondence.

63 H.J. Roberts, *Aspartame (Nutrasweet®) Is It Safe?* (Philidelphia, Pennsylvania: The Charles Press, 1990), 49, 142, 143, 144, 148, 149, 150. H.J. Roberts, "The hazards of very-low-calorie dieting," *American Journal of Clinical Nutrition* 41 (1985): 171-172. J.E. Blundell and A. J. Hill, "Paradoxical effects of an intense sweetener (aspartame) on appetite," *The Lancet* 1 (1986): 1092-1093.

64 Steven D. Stellman and Lawrence Garfinkel, "Patterns of artificial sweetener use and weight change in an American Cancer Society prospective study," *Appetite*, vol. II, supplement 1, 1988, 85-91.

65 J. W. Olney, "Brain Lesions, Obesity, and Other Disturbances in Mice treated with Monosodium Glutamate," *Science Magazine* 165 (1969): 719-271; John Olney, "Trying to get Glutamate out of Baby Food," *Clinical Medicine* 18, No. 34 (1990): 20; Jack L. Samuels, "The Obesity Epidemic: Should We Believe What We Read and Hear?" accessed November 7, 2005, http://www.westonaprice.org/msg/msgobesity.html; J.W. Olney, "Toxic Effects of Glutamate and Related Amino Acids on the Developing Central Nervous System," *Heritable Disorders of Amino Acid Metabolism* (New York: John Wiley, 1974).

66 "Carbohydrate Addiction," accessed December 1, 2005, http://www.americanheart.org/presenter.jhtml?identifier=4467; J. Barua and A. Bal, "Emerging Facts About Aspartame," *Journal Of The Diabetic Association Of India* 35, no.4 (1995): 92-107.

67 Olney et al., "Increasing Brain Tumor Rates," 1115-1123; Morando Soffritti et al., "First Experimental Demonstration of the Multipotential Carcinogenic Effects of Aspartame Administered in the Feed to Sprague-Dawley Rats," *Environmental Health Perspectives* 114, no. 3 (March 2006): 379-385; J.D. Smith et al., "Relief of fibromyalgia symptoms following discontinuation of dietary excitotoxins" *The Annals of Pharmacotherapy* 35, no. 6 (2001): 702-706; Rapid Responses to: EDITORIALS: Joseph M Mercola, "Aspartame Can Damage Your Health," John P Briffa, "It's not just misleading websites that the public should be protected from," Dr. Janet S Hull, "Aspartame Dangers ARE Real," John P Briffa," What Aspartame has in common with any artificial sweetener ("natural" or not) in effects on health," *BMJ* 329 (2004): 755-756; L Kovatsi and M Tsouggas, "The effect of oral aspartame administration on the balance of magnesium in the rat," *Magnesium Research Journal* 3 (September 14, 2001): 189-94; L.C. Newman and R.B. Lipton, "Migraine MLT-down: an unusual presentation of migraine in patients with Aspartame-triggered headaches," *Headache* 41, no. 9 (2001): 899-901; B. Christian et al., "Chronic Aspartame affects maze performance, brain cholinergic receptors and Na+, K+-ATPase in rats," *Pharmacology, Biochemistry, and Behavior* 78, no. 1 (2004): 121-127; Daniel DeNoon, "Rat Study Links Aspartame to Cancer," accessed November 7, 2005, http://www.medscape.com/viewarticle/509619.

68 Michael Friedman, MD, Deputy Commissioner for operations Food and Drug Administration, Department of Health and Human Services (statement made before the subcommittee on human resources and intergovernmental relations committee on government reform and oversight, U.S. House of Representatives, Washington D.C, May 10, 1996). accessed October 24, 2005, http://www.fda.gov/ola/1996/foodbor.html.

69 "Federal Food, Drug, and Cosmetic Act," accessed October 24, 2005, http://www.fda.gov/opacom/laws/fdcact/fdcact1.htm, http://www.fda.gov/opacom/laws/fdcact/fdcact1.htm; "FDA Backgrounder," October 1991, accessed October 24, 2005, http://www.geocities.com/HotSprings/2455/bak-msg.html.

70 Donald L. Bartlet and James B. Steele, "Deadly Medicine," *Vanity Fair*, January. 2011, 57–63, 113; M.M. Wolf, D.R. Lichtenstein, and G. Singh, "Gastrointestinal toxicity of nonsteroidal antiinflammatory drugs," *The New England Journal of Medicine* 340 (1999): 1888-1899.

71 "FDA implicated in conflict of interest for manufacturers of COX-2 inhibitor drugs," *Validation Times*, accessed July 2, 2005, http://www.fdainfo.com/vtonlinepages/valtimesweb041105.htm.

72 Gardiner Harris and Alex Berenson, "10 Voters on Panel Backing Pain Pills Had Industry Ties," *New York Times*, February 25, 2005, A-1.

73 Alex Berenson, "Evidence in Vioxx Suits Shows Intervention by Merck Officials," *New York Times*, April 24, 2005, National.

74 "Merck announces settlement to end Vioxx lawsuits," accessed October 7, 2010, http://www.lehighvalleylive.com/today/index.ssf/2010/02/merck_announces_settlement_to.html.

75 Dr. Joseph Mercola, "Finally, the FDA Decides to Curb Avandia – But Did the Agency Go Far Enough?" October 11, 2010, accessed October 12, 2010, http://www.foodconsumer.org/newsite/Non-food/Drug/avandia_0510101216.html.

76 Paul D. Thacker, "Glaxo's Avandia Cover-Up," September 29, 2010, accessed October 12, 2010, http://motherjones.com/politics/2010/09/glaxosmithkline-avandia.

77 Ibid.

78 "Avandia Lawsuit Settlement of $60M Will Resolve 700 Cases: Report," Aboutlawsuits.com, last modified May 11, 2010, accessed October 12, 2010, http://www.aboutlawsuits.com/avandia-lawsuit-settlement-reached-in-cases-10153/.

79 Interview with Dr. David Graham, "Prescription Drug Alert: Millions at risk from serious and possibly deadly side effects," *Crusader* (June/July 2005): 1-8.

80 Deborah Franklin, "Poisonings from a Popular Pain Reliever Are Rising," *New York Times*, November 29, 2005, http://wwwnytimes.com/2005/11/29/health/29cons.html?incamp=article_popula&pagewanted=print. John G. O'Grady, "Broadening the view of acetaminophen hepatotoxicity," *Hepatology* 42, no. 6 (2005): 1252-1254.

81 Center for Disease Control and Prevention, "How Many Children Have Autism?" accessed October 7, 2010, http://www.cdc.gov/ncbddd/features/counting-autism.html.

82 Robert F. Kennedy Jr., "Deadly Immunity," posted June 20, 2010, accessed June 27, 2005, http://www.rollingstone.com/politics/story/_/id/7395411; http://www.robertfkennedyjr.com/articles.html; http://www.youtube.com/watch?v=LP39qJLgNw; http://www.robertfkennedyjr.com/docs/ThimerosalScandalFINAL.PDF, accessed October 7, 2010.

83 U.S Food and Drug Administration, "Thimerosal in vaccines," accessed October 7, 2010, http://www.fda.gov/biologicsbloodvaccines/safetyavailability/vaccinesafety/ucm096228.htm.

84 "The FDA Versus The American Consumer," *Life Extension Magazine,* October 2002, accessed October 7, 2010, http://www.lef.org/magazine/mag2002/oct2002_awsi_01.html.

85 Peter R. Breggin, MD, "Violence and Suicide Caused by Antidepressants Report to the FDA," August 23, 2004, accessed October 7, 2010, http://www.breggin.com/index.php?option=com_content&task=view&id=197.

86 Bob Unruh, "Are meds to blame for Cho's rampage? Experts say psychiatric drugs linked to long list of school shooting sprees," WorldNetDaily, April 23, 2007, accessed October 7, 2010, http://www.wnd.com/?pageId=41218.

87 Gary G. Kohls, MD, "The Drugs May be the Problem: Inconvenient Truths about Psychotropic Drugs and the Pharmaceutical Industry," accessed October 7, 2010, http://www.mindbodymedicineduluth.com/mssa08/20_points.pdf.

88 Begley, "The Depressing News about Antidepressants."

89 Samuel Epstein, telephone interview with author, December 21, 2004.

90 Quote from *San Francisco Chronicle* (January 2, 1970), http://www.advancedhealthplan.com/fdafraud.html, accessed November 8, 2005.

91 Michael Culbert, *Medical Armageddon* (San Diego, California: C and C Communications, 1997), 333–334.

92 Gardiner Harris, "Top Democrat Finds F.D.A.'s Efforts Have Plunged," *New York Times*, June 27, 2006, accessed June 29, 2006, http://www.nytimes.com/2006/06/27/health/policy/27fda.html?ex=1152072000&en=151885b8ace9fb7e&ei=5070&emc=eta1.

93 Donald G. McNeil, Jr. "Review Finds Scientists with Ties to Companies," *New York Times*, July 15, 2005, A-15. Meredith Wadman, "One in three scientists confesses to having sinned," *Nature* 435 (June 9, 2005): 718-719.

94 U.S. Food and Drug Administration, "Consumer information about food ingredients and food packages," accessed November 8, 2005, http://www.cfsan.fda.gov/~dms/qa-adf9.html. "Aspartame is safe; the world agrees!" accessed October 7, 2010, http://www.fitnessandfreebies.com/fitness/aspartame.html.

95 Earl Mindell and Virginia Hopkins, *Prescription Alternatives 3rd Edition* (McGraw-Hill Companies: September 1, 1999), 6.

96 L. Tollefson, "Monitoring adverse reactions to food additives in the U.S. Food and Drug Administration," *Regulatory Toxicology and Pharmacology* 8, no. 4 (December 1988): 438-46.

97 Russell L. Blaylock, e-mail message to author, March 28, 2005, 12:45 p.m.

98 Christine Northrup, e-mail message to author, July 21, 2004, 3:13 p.m.

99 Bradley Willcox, e-mail message to author, August 23, 2004, 8:45 p.m.

100 "Weil: Your Trusted Health Advisor," accessed June 13, 2004, http://www.drweil.com.

101 Kaayla T. Daniel, e-mail message to author, August 16, 2004, 2:52 p.m.

102 Interested readers can take a look at pro and con research in the "Report on Phytoestrogens and Health" by the British government's Committee on Toxicity, accessed November 10, 2005, http://www.food.gov.uk/multimedia/pdfs/phytoreport0503.

103 Blaylock, *Excitotoxins*, 220; http://www.westonaprice.org, accessed March 14, 2005; Kaayla T. Daniel, *The Whole Soy Story: The Dark Side of America's Favorite Health Food* (Washington DC: New Trends, 2005); Carol Simontacchi, e-mail message to author, Wednesday, June 16, 2004, 8:44 a.m.; Robin Marzi, RD, MA, e-mail message to author, June 17, 2004, 10:32 a.m.; Maoshing Ni, PhD, LAc, DOM, e-mail message to author, August 20, 2004, 2:30 p.m.

104 "FDA scientists questions soy safety—but where is GM testing?" accessed November 10, 2005, http://www.netlink.de/gen/Zeitung/2000/000609.html.

105 FDA Talk Paper, "FDA Approves New Health Claim for Soy Protein and Coronary Heart Disease." accessed June 20, 2004, http://www.fda.gov/bbs/topics/ANSWERS/ANS00980.html.

106 Daniel, *The Whole Soy Story*, 295-310, 331-356.

107 Daniel, *The Whole Soy Story*, 363; M. Penotti et al., "Effect of soy-derived isoflavones on hot flashes, endometrial thickness and the pulsatility index of the uterine and cerebral arteries," *Fertility and Sterility* 79, no. 5 (2003):

1112-1117; E. Nikander et al., "A randomized placebocontrolled crossover trial with phytoestrogens in treatment of menopause in breast cancer patients," *Obstetrics and Gynecolocy* 101, no.6 (2003): 1213-1120; J.L. Balk et al., "A pilot study of the effects of phytoestrogen supplementation on postmenopausal endometrium," *Journal for the Society of Gynecologic Investigation* 9, no. 4 (2002): 238-242; D. Kotsopoulous et al., "The effects of soy protein containing phytoestrogens on menopausal symptoms in postmenopausal women," *Climacteric* 3, no. 3 (2000): 161-167; L.J. Lu, J.A. Tice, and F.L. Bellino, "Phytoestrogens and healthy aging: gaps in knowledge," *Menopause* 8, no. 3 (2001): 157-170; Editorial notes from Kaayla T. Daniel on manuscript (September 2005).

108 Kaayla T. Daniel, e-mail message to author, August 16, 2004, 2:52 p.m.

109 Marian Burros, "Eating Well: Doubts Cloud Rosy News on Soy," *New York Times,* January 26, 2000, Dining In, Dining Out/Style Desk.

110 Mike Fitzpatrick, "Soy Formulas and the Effects of Isoflavones on the Thyroid," *New Zealand Medical Journal* 113 (February 11, 2000): 24.

111 John C. Lowe, "Four 2003 Studies of Thyroid Hormone Replacement Therapies: Logical Analysis and Ethical Implications." accessed November 10, 2005, http://www.drlowe.com/frf/t4replacement/Critique.Replacement. Studies.pdf.

112 Bradley Willcox, e-mail message to author, August 23, 2004, 8:45 p.m.

113 Kaayla T. Daniel, e-mail message to author, December 18, 2005, 6:22 p.m.

114 David Zava, e-mail message to author, June 22, 2004, 6:35 a.m.

115 http://www.accesseonline.com/printstoryb.php?type=travel&id=3; http:// www.clearspring.co.uk/pages/site/products/macro/info1.html; http:// www.hi-net.zaq.ne.jp/yossy/global_education/example/note.html; http:// en.wikipedia.org/wiki/Japanese_cuisine, http://www.members.tripod. com/~Doc_In_The_Kitchen/japan, accessed November 11, 2005.

116 Daniel, *The Whole Soy Story*, 53.

117 Jeffrey M. Smith, *Seeds of Deception: Exposing Industry and Government Lies About the Safety of the Genetically Engineered Foods You're Eating* (Fairfield, IA: Yes! Books, 2002), 1.

118 Anon. "Health risks of genetically modified foods." *Lancet* 353, no. 9167 (1999): 181.

119 Ibid.

120 Ronnie Cummins, "Hazards of Genetically Engineered Foods and Crops: Why We Need A Global Moratorium," Organic Consumers Association, http://www.organicconsumers.org/ge/gefacts.pdf.

121 Steven Sprinkel, "When The Corn Hits The Fan," September 18, 1999, accessed October 9, 2010, http://www.mindfully.org/GE/Sprinkel-Corn-Hits-Fan.htm.

122 PureZing, "GMO / Genetically Modified Foods," accessed October 9, 2010, http://www.purezing.com/living/toxins/living_toxins_gmofoods.html.

123 J. J. Rackis, M. R. Gumbmann, and I. E. Liener, "The USDA trypsin inhibitor study. I. Background, objectives, and procedural details," *Plant Foods for Human Nutrition, (Formerly Qualitas Plantarum)* (Historical Archive) 35, no. 3 (September 1985): 213–242; "Evaluation of the Health Aspects of Soy Protein Isolates as Food Ingredients," Prepared for FDA by Life Sciences Research Office, *Federation of American Societies for Experimental Biology* (1979), Contract No. FDA 223-75-2004; Daniel, *The Whole Soy Story*, 93, 260–266.

124 Daniel, *The Whole Soy Story*, 95.

125 Enig and Fallon, *Eat Fat, Lose Fat*, 97, 99.

126 Joanne K. Tobacman, "Review of Harmful Gastrointestinal Effects of Carrageenan in Animal Experiments. *Environmental Health Perspective* 109, no.10 (October 2001): 983-94.

127 Kaayla T. Daniel, "Soy Milk Implicated in Sudden Deaths of Twins," News Release; Kaayla T. Daniel, e-mail message to author, October 27, 2005, 7:02 a.m.

128 "Rethinking Soy?" accessed May 9, 2005, http://www.drweil.com/u/QA/QA326575/.

129 Daniel, *The Whole Soy Story*, 307; Francine Grodstein, Richard Mayeux, and Meir J. Stampfer, "Tofu and Cognitive Function: Food for Thought," *Journal of the American College of Nutrition* 19, no. 2 (2000): 207-209.

130 Cases courtesy of Kaayla T. Daniel. All names and identifying characteristics have been changed.

131 V. Beral et al., "Breast cancer and breastfeeding: collaborative reanalysis of individual data from 47 epidemiological studies in 30 countries, including 50, 302 women with breast cancer and 96,973 women without the disease," *The Lancet* 360 (2002): 187-195.

132 Carol Simontacchi, *The Crazy Makers: How the Food Industry is Destroying Our Brains and Harming Our Children* (Tarcher/Putnam, 2000), 62.

133 C. Garza et al., "Special properties of human milk," *Clinics in Perinatology* 14, no. 1(March 1987): 11-32. Carol L Wagner, MD, " Human Milk and Lactation," accessed November 16, 2005, http://www.emedicine.com/ped/topic2594.htm#section~biochemistry_of_human_milk.

134 Sheila Innis, *Essential Fatty Acids in Growth and Development* (1991), 66-67.

135 Enig, *Know Your Fats*, 186.

136 Daniel, *The Whole Soy Story*, 144.

137 David Goodman, "Manganese madness," Wise Traditions. accessed March 27, 2005, http://www.westonaprice.org/soy/manganese.html.

138 Retha R. Newbold et al., "Uterine Adenocarcinoma in Mice Treated Neonatally with Genistein," *Cancer Research* 61 (June 1, 2001): 4325-4328; D.R. Doerge, "Goitrogenic and estrogenic activity of soy isoflavones," *Environmental Health Perspectives* 110, suppl. 3 (June 2002): 349-53; C.Y. Hsieh et al. "Estrogenic effects of genistein on the growth of estrogen receptor positive human breast cancer (MCF7) cells in vitro and in vivo," *Cancer Research* 58 (September 1, 1998): 3833; Gabe Mirkin, "Soy Causes Cancer?" accessed November 16, 2005, http://www.drmirkin.com/nutrition/9288.html; Joseph Mercola, "Newest Research On Why You Should Avoid Soy," accessed November 16, 2005, http://www.mercola.com/article/soy/avoid_soy2.htm.

139 P. Fort et al., "Breast and soy-formula feedings in early infancy and the prevalence of autoimmune thyroid disease in children," *Journal of the American College of Nutrition* 9, no. 2 (April 1990): 164-7; Y. Ishizuki et al., "The effects on the thyroid gland of soybeans administered experimentally in healthy subjects," *Nippon Naibunpi Gakkai Zasshi* 67, no. 5 (May 20 1991): 622-9; M. Fitzpatrick, "Soy formulas and the effects of isoflavones on the thyroid," *New Zealand Medical Journal* 113 (2000): 234-235; "Phytoestrogens—Antithyroid agents," accessed November 17, 2005, http://www.soyonlineservice.co.nz/04thyroid.htm.

140 Mary G. Enig, (from a summary of a presentation given at the 8th International Symposium of the Institute for Preventive Medicine, Vancouver, Canada, May 25, 2001); Weston A. Price Foundation, "The Soy Controversy," accessed November 17, 2005, http://www.westonaprice.org/soy-alert/672-soy-controversy.html; Katherine M. Flynn et al., "Effects of Genistein Exposure on Sexually Dimorphic Behaviors in Rats," *Toxicological Sciences* 55 (2000): 311-319; Amy B. Wisniewski et al., "Exposure to Genistein During Gestation and Lactation Demasculinizes the Reproductive System in Rats," *The Journal of Urology* 169, no. 4 (April 2003): 1582-1586; Fort P et al; "Breast feeding and insulin-dependent diabetes mellitus in children," *Journal of the American College of Nutrition* 5 (1986): 439-441.

141 Wendy Jefferson et al.,"Neonatal Genistein Treatment Alters Ovarian Differentiation in the Mouse: Inhibition of Oocyte Nest Breakdown and Increased Oocyte Survival," *Biology of Reproduction* 74, no. 1 (2006): 161-168; Kaayla T. Daniel, e-mail message to author, January 11, 2006, 7 p.m.

142 Weston A. Price Foundation, "Studies Showing Adverse Effects of Dietary Soy, 1939-2008," accessed October 9, 2010, http://www.westonaprice.org/soy-alert/667-studies-showing-adverse-effects-of-soy.html.

143 Ginanne Brownell, "Can't Buy Me Lard," *Newsweek* (December 6, 2004): 10.

144 Price, *Nutrition and Physical Degeneration 6th Edition*, 5.

145 Ron Schmid, "Raw Milk–history, health benefits and distortions," *Medical Veritas* 1 (2004): 278-286. "Dr. Francis M. Pottenger, Jr., MD," accessed November 18, 2005, http://www.price-pottenger.org/pottenger.htm.

146 "Heart Disease," accessed October 9, 2010, http://www.mamashealth.com/Heart_stat.asp.

147 Ancel Keys, "Atherosclerosis: A problem in newer public health," *Journal of Mount Sinai Hospital* 20 (1953): 118-139.

148 Uffe Ravnskov, *The Cholesterol Myth: Exposing the Fallacy That Saturated Fat and Cholesterol Cause Heart Disease* (Washington D.C.: New Trends Publishing, 2000), 101.

149 Uffe Ravnskov, "Is atherosclerosis caused by high cholesterol?" *Q J Med* 95 (2002): 397-403.

150 Ravnskov, *The Cholesterol Myth*, 122-123.

151 Telephone interviews with David Kritchevsky, January and March 2004.

152 Mary Enig and Sally Fallon, "The Oiling of America," *Nexus Magazine* (December 1998-March 1999); Weston A. Price Foundation, "Know Your Fats," accessed November 18, 2005, http://www.westonaprice.org/know-your-fats.html.

153 "2004-05 Statistical Abstract of the United States," accessed November 18, 2005, http://usa.usembassy.de/etexts/stab2004/health.pdf; "Fun Facts and Figures," accessed November 18, 2005, http://www.margarine.org/factsandtrivia.html, Cherie Calbom, "The Coconut Diet," accessed November 18, 2005, http://www.twbookmark.com/books/4/0446577162/chapter_excerpt19873.html.

154 Eades and Eades, *The Protein Power Lifeplan*, 66.

155 Enig, *Know Your Fats*, 249.

156 Trevor A. Mori et al., "Dietary fish as a major component of a weight-loss diet: effect on serum lipids, glucose, and insulin metabolism in overweight hypertensive subjects," *American Journal of Clinical Nutrition* 70, no. 5 (November 1999): 817-825; Julia Ross, *The Diet Cure* (New York: Viking, 1999), 106.

157 Stephanie Saul, "Gimme an Rx! Cheerleaders Pep Up Drug Sales," *New York Times,* November 28, 2005, http://www.nytimes.com/2005/11/28/business/28cheer.html?th&emc=th.

158 Marion Nestle, *Food Politics: How The Food Industry Influences Nutrition and Health* (Los Angeles: University of California Press, 2002), 117, 113-114.

159 Donald G. McNeil, Jr., "Review Cites Ethical Lapses By Scientists," *New York Times*, July 15, 2005, A-15.

160 Mary Enig et al, "Dietary Fat and Cancer Trends: A Critique," *Federation Proceedings* 37, no. 9 (July 1978): 2215-2220; Enig and Fallon, "The Oiling of America."

161 Edward R. Pinckney and Cathey Pinckney, *The Cholesterol Controversy* (Los Angeles: Sherbourne Press, 1973), 127-131.

162 Ibid.

163 Ravnskov, *The Cholesterol Myth*, 23.

164 Mary Enig, e-mail message to author, August 15, 2004, 3:49 p.m.

165 Mary Enig, *Trans Fatty Acids in the Food Supply: A Comprehensive Report Covering 60 Years of Research, 2nd Edition* (Silver Spring, MD: Enig Associates, Inc., 1995), 4-8; Enig, *Know Your Fats*, 86.

166 Bob Dylan, *Chronicles, Volume One* (New York: Simon & Schuster, 2004), 27.

167 John Robbins, *Diet for a New America: How Your Food Choices Affect Your Health, Happiness, and the Future of Life on Earth* (Tiburon, CA: HJ Kramer, 1987), 113-118.

168 Jo Robinson, "Grass-Fed Basics," accessed November 21, 2005, http://www.eatwild.com/Grass-Fed%20Basics.pdf.

169 Samuel S. Epstein, "The Chemical Jungle: Today's Beef Industry," *International Journal of Health Services* 20, no. 2 (1990): 277-280.

170 "Beware of Dangerous Meat Preservatives," foodrecap.net, (2009-2010), accessed October 11, 2010, http://www.foodrecap.net/safety/danger-meat-preservatives/.

171 Michael Moss, "Safety of Beef Processing Method Is Questioned," *New York Times*, December 31, 2009, accessed October 11, 2010, http://www.nytimes.com/2009/12/31/us/31meat.html?_r=1&pagewanted=print.

172 "The Framingham Heart Study," accessed May 13, 2004, http://www.framingham.com/heart/.

173 "Lipid Hypothesis," http://www.xetex.com/diabetes/Lipid_Hypothesis.html, accessed May 13, 2004.

174 Arthur Agatston, MD, *The South Beach Diet: The Delicious, Doctor-Designed, Foolproof Plan for Fast and Healthy Weight Loss* (Rodele Inc., 2003), 21-22.

175 Gerry Casanova, e-mail message to author, August 19, 2005, 10:15 a.m.; R.A. Vogel, "Effect of Single High Fat Meal on Endothelial Function in Healthy

Subject," *American Journal of Cardiology* 79, no. 3 (February 1, 1997): 350-54.

176 Sally Fallon, e-mail message to author, October 19, 2005, 10:55 a.m.; *Wise Traditions*, http://www.westonaprice.org, accessed Fall 2005.

177 Gary Taubes, "Nutrition: The Soft Science of Dietary Fat," *Science* 2001 291: 2536-2545; Ravnskov, *The Cholesterol Myth*, 46-47.

178 Telephone conversation with Mary Enig, Summer 2000.

179 Bruce Fife, *The Healing Miracles of Coconut Oil* (Colorado Springs, Colorado: Piccadilly Books, Ltd., 2001), 27-28.

180 Laurence Bergreen, *Over the Edge of the World: Magellan's Terrifying Circumnavigation of the Globe* (New York: Perennial, 2003), 240-241.

181 Bruce Fife, *The Healing Miracles of Coconut Oil* (Colorado Springs, Colorado: Piccadilly Books Ltd., 2001), 15.

182 Mary G. Enig, "Lauric Oils as Antimicrobial Agents: Theory of Effect, Scientific Rationale, and Dietary Applications as Adjunct Nutritional Support for HIV-infected Individuals in Nutrients and Foods in AIDS," ed. R.R. Watson (Boca Raton, FL: CRC Press, 1998), 81-97; Bruce Fife, ND, *The Healing Miracles of Coconut Oil* (Colorado Springs, Colorado: Piccadilly Books, Ltd., 2001), 162.

183 Mitsuyoshi Urashima et al., "Randomized trial of vitamin D supplementation to prevent seasonal influenza A in schoolchildren," *American Journal of Clinical Nutrition* 91, no. 5 (May 2010): 1255-1260.

184 T.R. Dhiman et al., "Conjugated linoleic acid content of milk from cows fed different diets," *Journal of Dairy Science* 82 (1999): 2146-56; S. K. Searles et al., "Vitamin E, Vitamin A, and Carotene Contents of Alberta Butter." *Journal of Diary Science* 53, no. 2 (1999): 150-154; S. K. Jensen, "Quantitative secretion and maximal secretion capacity of retinol, beta-carotene and alpha-tocopherol into cows' milk," *Journal of Dairy Research* 66, no. 4 (1999): 511-22; S. Banni et al., "Conjugated Linoleic Acid-Enriched Butter Fat Alters Mammary Gland Morphogenesis and Reduces Cancer Risk in Rats," *Journal of Nutrition* 129, no. 12 (1999): 2135-2142; Burton P. Koonsvitsky et al., "Olestra Affects Serum Concentrations of Alpha-Tocopherol and Carotenoids," *Jounral of Nutrition* 127 No. 8 (August 1997): 1636S-1645S; E. S. Ford and Anne Sowell, "Serum alpha-tocopherol status in the United States population: findings from the Third National Health and Nutrition Examination Survey," *American Journal of Epidemiology* 150 (August 1, 1999): 290-300; G. Jahreis et al., "Conjugated linoleic acid in milk fat: high variation depending on production system," *Nutrition Research* 17, no. 9 (1997): 1479-1484.

185 Ethan A. Huff, "Vitamin D really does prevent cancer, autoimmune diseases," NaturalNews.com, August 30, 2010, accessed November 11, 2010, http://

www.naturalnews.com/029605_vitamin_d_prevention.html#ixzz18OCvhlsY
http://www.naturalnews.com/029605_vitamin_d_prevention.html.

186 United States General Accounting Office, GAO Report to Congressional
Requesters, January 2002, Mad Cow Disease: Improvements in the Animal
Feed Ban and Other Regulatory Areas Would Strengthen U.S. Prevention
Efforts. GAO-02-183; Michael Greger, MD, "The Return of Mad Cow," ac-
cessed November 27, 2005, http://www.counterpunch.org/greger05232003.
html; USDA, Food Safety and Inspection Service, "USDA Begins Sampling
Program for Advanced Meat Recovery Systems," March 3, 2002, accessed
November 27, 2005, http://www.fsis.usda.gov/OA/news/2003/amrsampling.
html.

187 Sandra Blakeslee, "Jumble of Tests May Slow Mad Cow Solution," *New York
Times*, January 4, 2004, 10; Sandra Blakeslee, "Study Finds Broader Reach for
Mad Cow Proteins," *New York Times*, January 21, 2005, A18.

188 Donald G. McNeil, Jr., "Mad Cow Case Confirmed; U.S. Testing Will
Change," *New York Times*, June 25, 2005, 7; USDA Animal and Plant Health
Inspection Service, "Bovine Spongiform Encephalopathy (BSE) Ongoing Surveillance Plan," July 20, 2006, 6, 8; "USDA's BSE Surveillance Efforts (Factsheet)," accessed January 23, 2007, http://www.aphis.usda.gov/
publications/animal_health/content/printable_version/fs_BSE_
ongoing_vs.pdf.

189 "FAQs," accessed October 10, 2010, http://www.nodowners.org/faqs.html.

190 Donald G. McNeil, Jr., "Testing Changes Ordered After U.S. Mad Cow Case,"
New York Times, June 25, 2005, 7; Donald G. McNeil, Jr. and Alexei Barrion-
uevo, "For Months, Agriculture Department Delayed Announcing Result
of Mad Cow Test," *New York Times*, June 26, 2005, accessed November 27,
2005, http://www.nytimes.com/2005/06/26/national/26beef.html?ei=5070&e
n=0542e3793fdae07f&ex=1133240400&pagewanted=print.

191 John Robbins, *Diet for a New America: How Your Food Choices Affect Your
Health, Happiness, and the Future of Life on Earth* (Tiburon, CA: HJ Kramer,
1987), 73-96.

192 Ibid, 52-72.

193 Paul S. Mead et al, "Food-Related Illness and Death in the United States,"
Emerging Infectious Diseases Journal 5, no. 5 (September-October 1999); F.
Angulo et al., "Determing the Burden of Human Illness from foodborne
diseases: CDC's Emerging Infectious Disease Program Foodborne Disease
Active Surveillance Network (FoodNet)," accessed November 27, 2005,
http://www.cdc.gov/foodnet/pub/publications/1998/angulo_1998p.pdf;
"New Data on Incidence of Food-Borne Illness and Death in the United
States," *Safefood News* 4, no. 1 (Fall 1999), accessed November 30, 2004,
http://www.colostate.edu/Orgs/safefood/NEWSLTR/v4n1s01.html.

194 "Potential Health Hazards of Food Irradiation: Verbatim Excerpts from Expert Testimony," accessed November 28 ,2005, http://www.ccnr.org/food_ irradiation.html; "Food Irradiation Q&A's," accessed March 30, 2005, http:// www.citizen.org/cmep/foodsafety/food_irrad/articles.cfm?ID=12341.

194a Bill Maher, "I'm Swiss: and Other Treasonous Statements," HBO, July 30, 2005, 7 p.m.

195 References can be found on http://www.realmilk.com/indexpage.html and http://www.eatwild.com/references.html.

196 Ralph Seltzer, *The Dairy Industry in America* (New York: Dairy & Ice Cream Field, 1976), 3-8, 22-39.

197 Rose Marie Williams, MA, "Environmental Issues: What's Milk Got?" accessed November 28, 2005, http://www.townsendletter.com/Oct_2002/ milk1002.htm.

198 Weston A. Price, DDS, *Nutrition and Physical Degeneration, 6th Edition.* (La Mesa, CA: PricePottenger Nutrition Foundation, 1939-2003), 385.

199 Ron Schmid, *The Untold Story of Milk* (Washington, D.C.: New Trends Publishing, Inc., 2003), 32-37.

200 Ron Schmid, interview with author, November 14, 2004.

201 Edward Howell, *Food Enzymes for Health and Longevity, 2nd Edition* (Twin Lakes, Wisconsin: Lotus Press, 1994), 17-21.

202 F. Diez-Gonzalez et al., "Grain feeding and the dissemination of acid-resistant Escherichia coli from cattle," *Science* 281, no. 5383 (1998): 1666-8.

203 Elaine F. Weiss, "Thwarting Cancer Before it Strikes," *Johns Hopkins Magazine* (April 2000), accessed November 18, 2004, http://www.jhu. edu/~jhumag/0400web/48.html.

204 Schmid, *The Untold Story of Milk*, 203-204.

205 Ibid, 193-229.

206 K. Oster, J. Oster, and D. Ross, "Immune Response to Bovine Xanthine Oxidase in Atherosclerotic Patients," *American Laboratory*, August 1974, 41-47; K. Oster and D. Ross, "The Presence of Ectopic Xanthine Oxidase in Atherosclerotic Plaques and Myocardial Tissues," *Proceedings of the Society for Experimental Biology and Medicine*, 1973; K. A. Oster, "Plasmalogen diseases: a new concept of the etiology of the atherosclerotic process," *American Journal of Clinical Research* (1971): 2, 30-35; D. J. Ross, S.V. Sharnick, and K.A. Oster, "Liposomes as proposed vehicle for the persorption of bovine xanthine oxidase," *Proceedings of the Society of Experimental Biology and Medicine* (1980):163, 141-145; A.J. Clifford, C. Y. Ho, and H. Swenerton, "Homogenized bovine milk xanthine oxidase: a critique of the hypothesis relating

to plasmalogen depletion and cardiovascular disease," *American Journal of Clinical Nutrition* 38 (1983): 327-332.

207 Enig and Fallon, *Eat Fat, Lose Fat,* 97, 99.

208 Ron Schmid, interview with author, November 14, 2004.

209 "Mrs. Grubman," *Nip/Tuck,* FX, July 13, 2004.

210 Steven Mintz, John Moores, and Rebecca Moores, "Life Stages," University of Houston (2003), accessed December 16, 2010, www.usu.edu/anthro/childhoodconference/.../life_stages.doc.

211 Frank M. Biro et al., "Pubertal Assessment Method and Baseline Characteristics in a Mixed Longitudinal Study of Girls," *Pediatrics* 10, no. 1542 (August 9, 2010): 2009-3079, accessed October 11, 2010, http://pediatrics.aappublications.org/cgi/content/abstract/peds.2009-3079v1.

212 Sherrill Sellman, N.D., "Precocious Puberty," (Alive Publishing Group Inc., 2005), accessed October 11, 2010, http://www.alive.com/1958a5a2.php?subject_bread_cramb=153.

213 Marcia Herman-Gidens et al., "Secondary Sexual Characteristics and Menses in Young Girls Seen in the Office Practice: A Study from the Pediatric Research in Office Settings Network," *Pediatrics* 99, no. 4 (April 1997): 505-512; Marcia Herman-Giddens et al., "Secondary Sexual Characteristics in Boys," *Archives of Pediatrics & Adolescent Medicine* 155 (September 2001): 1022-28; Sandra Cabot, MD, "Toxins in food and the environment," accessed November 29, 2004, http://www.liverdoctor.com; Lindsey Tanner, "Study pointing to ealier puberty in boys," accessed November 29, 2004, http://www.mindfully.org.

214 P. E. Clayton and J. A. Trueman, "Leptin and puberty," *Archives of Disease in Childhood* (2000), accessed October 11, 2010, http://adc.bmj.com/content/83/1/1.extract.

215 Ibid.

216 Ferdhy Suryadi Suwandinata, "Endometriosis-Associated Pain, Social Impact, and Information Through Internet Survey," *Vvb Laufersweiler Verlag* (2006), accessed October 11, 2010, http://deposit.ddb.de/cgibin/dokserv?idn=981059775&dok_var=d1&dok_ext=pdf&filename=981059775.pdf.

217 Lawrence Wright, "Silent Sperm," *The New Yorker,* January 15, 1996, 42.

218 Peter Montague, "Milk Controversy Spills into Canada," accessed Novenber 28, 2005, http://www.garynull.com/Documents/erf/milk_controversy_spills_into_can.htm.

219 Jeffrey M. Smith, *Seeds of Deception: Exposing Industry and Government Lies About the Safety of the Genetically Engineered Foods You're Eating* (Fairfield, IA: Yes! Books, 2003), 79-81.

220 Samuel S. Epstein, *Got (Genetically Engineered) Milk?: The Monsanto BGH/BST Milk Wars Handbook* (New York: Seven Stories Press, 2001), 69; "Monsanto's Genetically Modified Milk Ruled Unsafe by the United Nations," *PR Newswire*, August 18, 1999; Telephone interview with Dr. Epstein (December 21, 2004); Epstein, *Got (Genetically Engineered) Milk?*, 79-80.

221 "The Tainted Milk Moustache—How Monsanto and the FDA Spoiled a Staple Food," reprinted from *Alternative Medicine Digest* (January 1999), accessed December 20, 2004, http:// www.afpafitness.com/articles/MilkMustache.htm.

222 "A New Study Warns Of Breast Cancer And Colon Cancer Risks From rBGH Milk," report on press conference by Cancer Prevention Coalition in Washington, D.C., January 23, 1996; "Monsanto's Biosynthetic Milk Poses Risks of Prostate Cancer, Besides Other Cancers," *PR Newswire*, March 15, 1998; "Monsanto's Hormonal Milk Poses Serious Risks of Breast Cancer, Besides Other Cancers," *PR Newswire*, June 21, 1998; S.E. Hankinson et al., "Circulating concentrations of insulin-like growth factor 1 and risk of breast cancer," *Lancet* 351, no. 93113 (1998): 1393-1396; Dr. Samuel S. Epstein, "Potential Public Health Hazards of Biosynthetic Milk Hormones," *International Journal of Health Services* 20, no. 1 (1990): 73-84.

223 Samuel Epstein, "FDA Is Ignoring Dangers of Bovine Growth Hormone," letter to the editor of *Austin American-Statesman*, June 2, 1990.

224 S.E. Hankinson et al., "Circulating concentrations of insulin-like growth factor 1 and risk of breast cancer," *Lancet* 351, no. 93113 (1998): 1393-1396; June Chan et al., "Plasma Insulin-Like Growth Factor-1 [IGF-1] and Prostate Cancer Risk: A Prospective Study," *Science* 279 (January 23, 1998): 563-566; R. Torris et al., "Time course of fenretinideinduced modulation of circulating insulin-like growth factor (IGF)-1, IGF-II and IGFBP-3 in a bladder cancer chemo-prevention trial," *International Journal of Cancer* 87, no. 4 (August 2000): 601-605.

225 Food and Drug Administration, "Interim guidance on the voluntary labeling of milk and milk products from cows that have not been treated with recombinant bovine somatotropin," *Federal Register* 59, no. 28 (1994): 6279-6280; Samuel S. Epstein, "Unlabeled Milk From Cows Treated With Biosynthetic Growth Hormones: A Case of Regulatory Abdication," *International Journal of Health Services* 26, no. 1 (1996): 173-185.

226 Jeffrey M. Smith, *Seeds of Deception: Exposing Industry and Government Lies About the Safety of the Genetically Engineered Foods You're Eating* (Fairfield, IA: Yes! Books, 2003), 82-83.

227 *The Agribusiness Examiner*, issue 38 (June 17, 1999); http:// www.electric arrow.com/CARP/agbiz/agex-38.html, accessed December 20, 2004. "The Tainted Milk Moustache—How Monsanto and the FDA Spoiled a Staple Food," reprinted from *Alternative Medicine Digest* (January 1999), accessed December 20, 2004, http://www.afpafitness.com/articles/MilkMustache. html; http://www.rockefeller.edu/lectures/friedman112700.html, accessed February 21, 2005.

228 Smith, *Seeds of Deception*, 81.

229 Epstein, *Got (Genetically Engineered) Milk?*, 66. "Monsanto's Genetically Modified Milk Ruled Unsafe by the United Nations," *PR Newswire*, August 18, 1999.

230 Epstein, *Got (Genetically Engineered) Milk?*, 460-490.

231 Mark McAfee, telephone interview with author, December 6, 2004; Mark McAffee, e-mail message to author, October 15, 2010, 2:05 a.m.

232 C. Ip et al., "Conjugated linoleic acid. A powerful anti-carcinogen from animal fat sources," *Cancer* 74, no. 3 (1994): 1050-4; A. Aro et al., "Inverse Association between Dietary and Serum Conjugated Linoleic Acid and Risk of Breast Cancer in Postmenopausal Women," *Nutrition and Cancer* 38, no. 2 (2000): 151-7; Z. Wu, L.D. Satter, and M.W. Pariza, "Paddocks containing red clover compared with all grass paddocks support high CLA levels in milk," US Dairy Forage Research Center (1997).

233 M.E. Jonsson et al., "Persistence of Verocytotoxin-Producing Escherichia Coli 0157:H7 in Calves Kept on Pasture and in Calves Kept Indoor," *International Journal of Food Microbiology* 66, no. 1-2 (2001): 5561.

234 U.S. Food and Drug Administration, "The Dangers of Raw Milk: Unpasteurized Milk Can Pose a Serious Health Risk," accessed October 11, 2010, http:// www.fda.gov/Food/ResourcesForYou/Consumers/ucm079516.html.

235 Eric Schlosser, *Fast Food Nation: The Dark Side of the American Meal* (New York: Perennial, 2002).

236 Jared Diamond, *Guns, Germs, and Steel: The Fates of Human Societies* (New York: Norton, 1999), 88.

237 Barbara Cohen, PhD, "The Psychology of Ideal Body Image as an Oppressive Force in the Lives of Women," 1984.

238 McGraw, *The Ultimate Weight Solution*, 120.

239 U.S. Dept. of Health, Education, and Welfare (1966) Obesity and Health, Wash., DC: US. DHEW, PHS Publication No. 1485; "Those Born During Biafra Famine are Susceptible to Obesity, Study Finds," *The New York Times*, November 2, 2010, D6.

240 A. Favaro, F.C. Rodella, and P. Santonastaso, "Binge eating and eating attitudes among Nazi concentration camp survivors," *Psychological Medicine* 30, no. 2 (March 2000): 463-6; M. M. Hagan, R. H. Whitworth, and D. E. Moss, "Semistarvation-Associated Eating Behaviors Among College Binge Eaters: A Preliminary Description and Assessment Scale—Statistical Data Included," *Behavioral Medicine* (Fall 1999), http://www.findarticles.com/p/articles/mi_m0GDQ/is_3_25/ai_58669772, accessed October 28, 2005.

241 M. M. Hagan, R. H. Whitworth, and D. E. Moss, "Semistarvation-Associated Eating Behaviors Among College Binge Eaters: A Preliminary Description and Assessment Scale - Statistical Data Included," *Behavioral Medicine,* (Fall 1999), http://www.findarticles.com/p/articles/mi_m0GDQ/is_3_25/ai_58669772, accessed October 28, 2005.

242 *Inside the Actor's Studio,* Bravo, September 2, 2004, 1 a.m.

243 F. Grün and B. Blumberg, "Environmental Obesogens: Organotins and Endocrine Disruption via Nuclear Receptor Signaling," *Endocrinology* 147, 6 Suppl. (June 2006): S50–5, doi:10.1210/en.2005-1129. PMID 16690801, http://endo.endojournals.org/cgi/reprint/147/6/s50.pdf; Sharon Begley, "Why Chemicals Called Obesogens May Make You Fat," *Newsweek,* September 21, 2009, accessed April 9, 2010, http://www.newsweek.com/id/215179; S. Kirchner et al., "Prenatal exposure to the environmental obesogen tributyltin predisposes multipotent stem cells to become adipocytes," *Molecular Endocrinology* 24, no. 3 (March 2010): 526–39, doi:10.1210/me.2009-0261. PMID 20160124; F. Grün and B. Blumberg, "Endocrine disrupters as obesogens," *Molecular and Cellular Endocrinology* 304, no. 1-2 (May 2009): 19–29, doi:10.1016/j.mce.2009.02.018, PMID 19433244; F. Grün and B. Blumberg, "Minireview: the case for obesogens," *Molecular Endocrinology* 23, no. 8 (August 2009): 1127–34, doi:10.1210/me.2008-0485, PMID 19372238; E. Diamanti-Kandarakis et al., "Endocrine-disrupting chemicals: an Endocrine Society scientific statement," *Endocrine Reviews* 30, no. 4 (June 2009): 293–342, doi:10.1210/er.2009-0002, PMID 19502515; B. Daley, "Is plastic making us fat?" *The Boston Globe*, January 14, 2008, accessed August 5, 2010, http://www.boston.com/news/health/articles/2008/01/14/is_plastic_making_us_fat/.

244 "Welcome to Diets FAQ," accessed December 13, 2005, http://www.dietsfaq.com/; "Why Diets Don't Work: The Myths that Make us Massive," accessed December 13, 2005, http://www.refityourself.com/refit/healthtopics_article5.html.

245 Davis, *Let's Eat Right To Keep Fit*, 246.

246 Gladys Block, "Foods contributing to energy intake in the US: data from NHANES III and NHANES 1999–2000,"*Journal of Food Composition and Analysis* 17, Issues 3-4 (June–August 2000): 439-447.

247 Atul Gawande, *Complications: A Surgeon's Notes on an Imperfect Science* (New York: Metropolitan Books of Henry Holt and Company, 2002), 183.

248 Joseph M. Dhahbi et al., "Temporal linkage between the phenotypic and genomic responses to caloric restriction," *Proceedings of the National Academy of Sciences* 101, no. 15 (April 13, 2004): 5524-5529; "Calorie restriction reduces risk of MI, stroke and diabetes," *Native American Cancer Research*, accessed June 10, 2005, http://natamcancer.org/page29.html.

249 Scott LaFee, "Eating less may mean a longer life if you can stand the hunger pangs," *San Diego Union Tribune*, November 24, 2004, accessed June 9, 2005, http://www.signonsandiego.com/uniontrib/20041124/news_lz1c24cr. html; Kim Pierce, "Disciplined and dedicated, they eat light for a long life," *The Dallas Morning News*, accessed June 9, 2005, http://www.imminst.org/forum/index.php?s=&act=ST&f=69&t=4701.

250 Daniel E. Lieberman, e-mail message to author, February 24, 2006, 1:53 a.m.

251 S. Gallistl et al., "Insulin is an independent correlate of plasma homocysteine levels in obese children and adolescents," *Diabetes Care* 23, no. 9 (2000): 1348-1352; D.S. Michaud et al., "Dietary sugar, glycemic load, and pancreatic cancer risk in a prospective study," *Journal of the National Cancer Institute* 94, no.17 (September 4, 2002): 1293-300; Anu Kareinen et al., "Cardiovascular Risk Factors Associated With Insulin Resistance Cluster in Families With Early-Onset Coronary Heart Disease," *Arteriosclerosis, Thrombosis, and Vascular Biology* 21, no. 8 (August 2001): 1346-52; Gerald Reaven, "Insulin Resistance, Hypertension, and Coronary Heart Disease," *Journal of Clinical Hypertension* 5, no. 4 (2003): 269-274.

252 Robert W. Stout, "Insulin and Atheroma 20-year Perspective," *Diabetes Care* 13, no. 6 (June 1990): 631.

253 Center for Disease Control and Prevention, "FastStats: Diabetes," accessed June 2, 2004, http://www.cdc.gov/nchs/fastats/diabetes.html; "2007 Diabetes Facts," accessed June 2, 2004, http://www.diabetes-tests.com/Diabetes_Facts. html; K. Gu, C.C. Cowie, and M.I. Harris, "Mortality in adults with and without diabetes in a national cohort of the US population," *Diabetes Care* 21 (1998): 1138-1145, 1971-93; Centers for Disease Control and Prevention, "National diabetes fact sheet: general information and national estimates on diabetes in the United States (2002)," (Atlanta, GA: U.S. Department of Health and Human Services, Centers for Disease Control and Prevention, 2003), accessed June 2, 2004, http://www.diabetes.org/diabetesstatistics/national-diabetes-fact-sheet.jsp.

254 "Diabetes FastStats," Centers For Disease Control and Prevention, http://www.cdc.gov/nchs/fastats/diabetes.htm, accessed October 11, 2010.

255 Patricia Reaney, "Obesity/Diabetes Could Hit Life Expectancy: Experts." *Reuters Health Information* (2004), accessed December 5, 2005, http://www.lap-band-surgery.org/obesity.cfm/39715398/Obesity/diabetes-could-hit-life-expectancy---experts/index.html; Lori Woosley, "Parents Outlive Children," accessed October 12, 2010, http://searchwarp.com/swa40618.htm.

256 Eades and Eades, *The Protein Power Lifeplan*, xix-xx.

257 Ravnskov, *The Cholesterol Myth*.

258 Uffe Ravnskov, e-mail message to author, November 5, 2005, 12:57 p.m.

259 "Interview: Gary Taubes," *Frontline*, http://www.pbs.org/wgbh/pages/frontline/shows/diet/interviews/taubes.html, accessed July 5, 2004.

260 Gina Kolata, "Low-Fat Diet Does Not Cut Health Risks, Study Finds," *New York Times*, February 8, 2006, http://www.nytimes.com/2006/02/08/health/08fat.html?ex=1140066000&en=4eb4d476df0744a2&ei=5070; Howard et al., "Low-Fat Dietary Pattern and Risk of Cardiovascular Disease: The Women's Health Initiative Randomized Controlled Dietary Modification Trial," *JAMA* 295, no. 6 (February 8, 2006): 655-666; Ross L. Prentice et al., "Low-Fat Dietary Pattern and Risk of Invasive Modification Trial," *JAMA* 295, no. 6 (February 8, 2006): 629-642; Shirley A. A. Beresford, "Low-Fat Dietary Pattern and Risk of Colorectal Modification Trial," *JAMA* 295, no. 6 (February 8, 2006): 643-654.

261 "You Can't Miss the Bear," *Weeds* pilot episode, Showtime, August 7, 2005.

262 Frederick F. Samaha et al., "A Low-Carbohydrate as Compared with a Low-Fat Diet in Severe Obesity," *The New England Journal of Medicine* 348, no. 21 (May 22, 2003): 2074-2081; D.L. Katz, "Competing dietary claims for weight loss: finding the forest through truculent trees," *Annual Review of Public Health* 26 (2005): 61-88.

263 Robert C. Atkins, *Dr. Atkins New Diet Revolution* (New York: Quill, 2002), 215.

264 "UK food agonises over Atkins," http://www.telegraph.co.uk/money/main.jhtml?xml=/money/2004/01/04/ccdiet04.xml; "Atkins launching education campaign to improve steak and bacon image," accessed June 13, 2004, http://www.medicalnewstoday.com/index.php?newsid=7400.

265 Kate Zernike and Marion Burros, "Low-Carb Boom Isn't Just for Dieters Anymore," *New York Times*, February 19, 2004, A16.

266 T. L. Davidson and S. E. Swithers, "Pavlovian Approach to the Problem of Obesity," *International Journal of Obesity* 28, no. 7 (2004): 933-935.

267 Daniel DeNoon, "Drink More Diet Soda, Gain More Weight?" accessed January 5, 2006, http://www.webmd.com/content/article/107/108476.htm.

268 Andy Coghlan, "Shrunken glands spark sweetener controversy," *New Scientist* 1796 (November 23, 1991).

269 B. A. John, S. G. Wood, and D. R. Hawkins, "The pharmacokinetics and metabolism of sucralose in the mouse," *Food Chemical Toxicology* 38, suppl. 2 (2000): S107-S110; Y.F. Sasaki et al., "The comet assay with 8 mouse organs: results with 39 currently used food additives," *Mutation Research* 519, no. 1-2 (August 26, 2002): 103-19.

270 Roger Ekirch, *At Day's Close: Night in Times Past* (New York: W.W. Norton & Company, 2005).

271 Ottar Nygard et al., "Coffee consumption and plasma total homocysteine: The Hordaland Homocystein Study," *American Journal of Clinical Nutrition* 65, no. 1 (1997): 136-43; C.K. Stanton and R.H. Gray, "Effects of caffeine consumption on delayed conception," *American Journal of Epidemiology* 142, no. 12 (1995): 1322; Claire Infante-Rivard et al., "Fetal Loss Associated with Caffeine Intake Before and During Pregnancy," *JAMA* 270 (December 22/29, 1993): 2940-2943; Mark A. Klebanoff et al., "Maternal Serum Paraxanthine, a Caffeine Metabolite, and the Risk of Spontaneous Abortion," *New England Journal of Medicine* 341, no. 22 (November 25, 1999): 1639-44; Stephen Cherniske, *Caffeine Blues* (New York: Warner Books, 1998), 7.

272 Diane Welland, "As caffeine controversy rages on, what's a coffee lover to do?" *Environmental Nutrition* 19 (1996): 1.

273 "Decaffeinating Coffee," accessed December 7, 2005, http://www.hi-tm.com/ Facts&tips/Decaf.html; R.G. Liteplo, G.W. Long, and M.E. Meek, "Relevance of Carinogenicity Bioassays in Mice in Assessing Potential Health Risks Associated with Exposure to Methylene Chloride," *Human and Experimental Toxicology* 17, no. 2 (February 1998): 84-87; E. Lynge, A. Anttila, and K. Hemminki, "Organic Solvents and Cancer," *Cancer Causes and Control* 8, no. 3 (May 1997): 406-19.

274 Marian Burros and Sherri Day, "Doubt Cast on Food Supplements for Weight Control," *New York Times*, October 27, 2003, http://query.nytimes. com/gst/fullpage.html?res=9C03E1DA1131F934A15753C1A9659C8B63, accessed May 16, 2005.

275 "Dr. Phil McGraw Facing Class-Action Suit," accessed December 30, 2005, http://www.casewatch.org/civil/drphil/classactioncomplaint.shtml.

276 Mike Katke, e-mail message to author, February 7, 2004, 11 a.m.

277 Sultan Muhammad, "Business with disease: The Scourge of prescription drugs," FinalCall.com News, accessed October 30, 2005, http://www.finalcall. com/artman/publish/article_1255.shtml.

278 S. L. Baker, "New study: 85% of Big Pharma's new drugs are 'lemons' and pose health risks to users," *Natural News*, August 18, 2010, accessed September 4, 2010, http://www.naturalnews.com/029506_Big_Pharma_lemons.html.

279 *Larry King Live*, November 15, 2006, accessed January 3, 2006, http://transcripts.cnn.com/TRANSCRIPTS/0611/15/lkl.01.html.

280 Kelly Patricia O'Meara, "Diagnosing Infants With Depression," accessed May 9, 2005, http://www.antidepressantsfacts.com/2004-05-03-infants-depression-antideps.htm.

281 Shankar Vedantam, "FDA Confirms Antidepressants Raise Children's Suicide Risk," *Washington Post*, September 14, 2004, A01.

282 "The FDA Exposed: An Interview With Dr. David Graham, the Vioxx Whistleblower," accessed on December 8, 2005, http://www.newstarget.com/z011401.html.

283 "Beloved Pharma TV Commercials," *Pixels and Pills*, May 4, 2010, accessed October 18, 2020, http://www.pixelsandpills.com/2010/05/04/beloved-pharma-tv-commercials/.

284 Associated Press, "Cruise Clashes with Lauer on 'Today' Show," June 24, 2005, accessed June 24, 2005, http://www.miami.com/mid/miamiherald/entertainment/11980135.html; http://www.drudgereport.com/flash3tc.html, accessed June 26, 2005.

285 Michael Smith, "Final Word May Not Come for a Year," accessed on July 1, 2006, http://www.webmd.com/content/biography/7/40428.htm.

286 "Tom Cruise Spars with Lauer on 'Today' Show," accessed June 26, 2005, http://www.ctv.ca/servlet/ArticleNews/story/CTVNews/20050624/cruise_lauer_050624?s_name=&no_ads=.

287 Alessandra Stanley, "Talk Show Rarity: A True Believer's Candor," *New York Times*, June 25, 2005, A15.

288 Nicholas D. Kristof, "Mike Huckabee Lost 110 Pounds. Ask Him How," *New York Times*, January 29, 2006, section 4, 17.

289 William A. Carlezon et al., "Antidepressant-like effects of uridine and omega-3 fatty acids are potentiated by combined treatment in rats," *Biological Psychiatry* 57, Issue 4 (February 15, 2005): 343-350.

290 C.B. Gesch et al., "Influence of supplementary vitamins, minerals and essential fatty acids on the antisocial behaviour of young adult prisoners," *The British Journal of Psychiatry* 181 (2002): 22-28; S.J. Schoenthaler and I.D. Bier, "The effect of vitamin-mineral supplementation on juvenile delinquency among American schoolchildren: a randomized, double-blind placebo-controlled trial," *Journal of Alternative and Complementary Medicine* 6, no. 1 (2000): 7–17; France Bellisle, "Effects of diet on behaviour and cognition

in children," *British Journal of Nutrition* 092, no. 0S2 (October 2004): S227-S232.

291 Begley, "The Depressing News About Antidepressants."

292 Davis, *Let's Eat Right To Keep Fit*, 249.

293 Bill Maher, "I'm Swiss: and Other Treasonous Statements."

294 Gillian Sanson, *The Myth of Osteoporosis: What Every Woman Should Know About Creating Bone Health* (Ann Arbor, Michigan: MCD Century Publications, 2003), accessed December 21, 2005, http://www.findarticles.com/p/articles/mi_m0ISW/is_245/ai_111496966.

295 "Fosamax Now Linked to Cancer of the Esophagus," accessed October 17. 2010, http://www.emaxhealth.com/1020/51/28157/fosamax-now-linked-cancer-esophagus.html; David Y. Graham, MD, and Hoda M. Malaty, MD, PhD, "Alendronate and Naproxen Are Synergistic for Development of Gastric Ulcers," *Archives of Internal Medicine* 161, no. 1 (2001): 107-110.

296 S. L. Ruggiero et al., "Osteonecrosis of the jaws associated with the use of bisphosphonates: a review of 63 cases," *Journal of Oral and Maxillofacial Surgery* 62, no. 5. (May 2004): 527-34.

297 C. V. Odvina et al., "Severely suppressed bone turnover: a potential complication of alendronate therapy," *Journal of Clinical Endocrinology and Metabolism* 90, no. 3 (March 2005): 1294-301.

298 G. Sanson, "The myth of osteoporosis," accessed December 20, 2005, http://www.healthyskepticism.org/library/ref.php?id=1166.

299 http://www.latimes.com/sns-ap-us-bone-drugs-fda,0,7034107.story, accessed October 18, 2010.

300 Ravnskov, *The Cholesterol Myth*, 2, 61, 206,

301 Ravnskov, *The Cholesterol Myth*, 143-224; "The Cholesterol Myths," accessed August 13, 2004, http://www.ravnskov.nu/cholesterol.htm.

302 Mary Enig, PhD, e-mail message to author, August 15, 2004, 3:49 p.m.

303 Ibid.

304 Ravnskov, *The Cholesterol Myth*, 130-131, 135, 238-239.

305 Russell L. Blaylock, MD, *The Blaylock Wellness Report* 1, no. 3 (August 2004): 3.

306 Gina Kolata, "New Conclusions on Cholesterol: Study Sees Gain for Heart in Levels Kept Very Low," *New York Times*, March 9, 2004, front page.

307 Michael and Mary Dan Eades, e-mail message to author, July 5, 2004, 4 p.m.; Loren Cordain et al., "Origins and evolution of the Western diet: health implications for the 21st century," *American Journal of Clinical Nutrition* 81, no. 2 (February 2005): 341-354.

308 Louis Menand, "Acid Redux: The life and high times of Timothy Leary," *The New Yorker*, June 26, 2006, 79.

309 www.generalmills.com, accessed October 18, 2010.

310 www.glucerna.com, accessed October 18, 2010.

311 "Horizon Organic, Now Dean Foods, Threatens Livelihood of Organic Farmers," accessed November 30, 2004, http://www.organicconsumers.org/organic/horizon_farmers.cfm. http://www.horizonorganic, accessed November 30, 2004.

312 Alex Avery, "Organic Fear Profiteers Milk Big Bucks from Shoppers," accessed December 20, 2004, http://www.cgfi.org/materials/articles/2003/june_18_03.html; "Is Horizon Organic truly Organic?" accessed January, 2007, http://www.accidentalhedonist.com/index.php/2005/02/28/is_horizon_organic_truly_organic; Cameron Scott, "Organic Milk Goes Corportate," accessed January 27, 2007, http://www.motherjones.com/news/update/2006/04/organic_milk.html.

313 Jessica Vanegeren, "Does Dean Foods have unfair advantage?" *The Capital Times*, accessed October 18, 2010, http://host.madison.com/ct/news/local/govt_and_politics/article_ac0574a4-893e-11df-8e61-001cc4c03286.html.

314 Organic Consumers Association, "Profit Over Organics: Dean Foods Sets Up New Competing Market Category—'Natural' Dairy Products," accessed October 18, 2010, http://www.organicconsumers.org/articles/article_18437.cfm.

315 Telephone interview with Joe and Brenda Cochran, December 10, 2004.

316 www.pgfoodingredients.com, accessed October 18, 2010.

317 Center for Science in the Public Interest, "New Olestra Complaints Bring Total Close To 20,000—More Than All Other Food Additive Complaints In History Combined," accessed October 20, 2010, http://www.cspinet.org/new/olestrapr_041602.html.

318 "New Olestra Complaints Bring Total Close To 20,000—More Than All Other Food Additive Complaints In History Combined," http://www.cspinet.org/new/olestrapr_041602.html, accessed March 20, 2004.

319 Brad Dorfman, "Companies Putting Olestra in Chips Can Remove Diarrhea Warnings," *Reuters*, August 1, 2003, accessed October 28, 2005, http://www.organicconsumers.org/foodsafety/olestra.cfm.

320 http://www.olean.com/products/snacks.html, accessed March 20, 2004.

321 Carl Hulse, "Vote in House Offers a Shield for Restaurants in Obesity Suits," *New York Times*, March 11, 2004, front page.

322 John Vidal, *McLibel: Burger Culture on Trial* (New York: New Press, 1997).

323 Pinckney and Pinckney, *The Cholesterol Controversy*, 4, 63.

324 http://www.honeynutcheerios.com, accessed October 18, 2010.

325 http://www.plavix.com/clopidogrel/blood-clots.aspx, http://content. healthaffairs.org/cgi/content/full/hlthaff.w4.234v1/DC1, accessed October 18, 2010.

326 http://www.actonel.com/index.jsp, accessed October 18, 2010.

327 Matthew Arnold, "Nexium ad campaign promises nighttime relief," February 03, 2010, October 18, 2010, http://www.mmm-online.com/nexium-ad-campaign-promises-nighttime-relief/article/163090/, accessed October 18, 2010.

328 Bill Maher, "I'm Swiss: and Other Treasonous Statements."

329 Karen Kersting, "Marketing encourages teens to tie brand choices to personal identity," accessed December 12, 2005, http://thestressoflife.com/ marketing_encourages_teens_to_ti.htm.

330 Dan DeLuca, "Maestros of misconduct: Creeps we love to envy," *Santa Barbara News Press*, March 22, 2004, D3.

331 Melanie Warner, "Is a Trip to McDonald's Just What the Doctor Ordered?" *New York Times*, May 2, 2005, accessed July 8, 2005, http://query.nytimes. com/gst/health/article-page.html?res=9C0DE2D61E31F931A35756C0A963 9C8B63.

332 Kelly Brownwell and Marion Nestle, "Are You Responsible for Your Own Weight?" *Time*, June 7, 2004, 113; Kelly D. Brownwell; *Food Fight: The Inside Story of the Food Industry, America's Obesity Crisis and What We Can Do about It* (New York: Contemporary Books, 2004), 48-51.

333 Sherri Day, "Dr. Phil, Medicine Man," *New York Times*, October 27, 2003, accessed May 16, 2005, http://www.nytimes.com.

334 Lilka Woodward Areton, "Factors In The Sexual Satisfaction Of Obese Women In Relationships," *Electronic Journal of Human Sexuality* 5 (January 15, 2002, accessed October 28, 2005, http://www.ejhs.org/volume5/ Areton/03Background.htm.

335 Norman Goodman et al., "Variant Reactions to Physical Disabilities," *American Sociological Review* 28 (1963): 429-435.

336 M. Roehling, "Weight-Based Discrimination in Employment: Psychological and Legal Aspects," *Personnel Psychology* 52 (1999): 969-1016.

337 R.C. Whitaker et al., "Predicting obesity in young adulthood from childhood and parental obesity," *New England Journal of Medicine* 337, no. 13 (1997): 869-873.

338 M.S. Treuth, N. F. Butte, and J.D. Sorkin, "Predictors of body fat gain in nonobese girls with a familial predisposition to obesity," *American Journal of Clinical Nutrition* 78, no. 6 (December 2003): 1051-2.

339 "Three-year-old dies from obesity," *BBC News*, May 27, 2004, accessed October 28, 2005, http://newsvote.bbc.co.uk/mpapps/pagetools/print/news.bbc. co.uk/1/hi/health/3752597.stm; Susan Reed, "Obese girl's mother guilty of misdemeanor child abuse," *U.S. News*, January 9, 1998, accessed on October 28, 2005, http://www.cnn.com/US/9801/09/obese.abuse/; http://abcnews. go.com/Health/obese-children-parents-abusive/story?id=11446364

340 McGraw, *The Ultimate Weight Solution*, 119.

341 KeShun Liu, *Soybeans Chemistry, Technology and Utilization* (Culinary and Hospitality Industry Publications Services), 297-347.

342 Allison Daee et al., "Psychologic and Physiologic Effects of Dieting in Adolescents," *Southern Medical Journal* 95, no. 9 (2002): 1032–1041.

343 Sally Squires, "Teaching Kids to Eat Well," *The Washington Post*, accessed October 29, 2005, http://www.washingtonpost.com/wp-dyn/content/ article/2005/06/06/AR2005060601671.html. "The Dietary Intervention Study in Children (DISC)," accessed October 29, 2005, http://www.nhlbi.nih.gov/ resources/deca/agreements/disc.pdf.

344 http://www.clintonfoundation.org/what-we-do/alliance-for-a-healthier-generation/

345 "Bottlers want to limit school soft drinks," cnn.com, accessed August 17, 2005, http://www.cnn.com/2005/HEALTH/diet.fitness/08/17/soda.in.school. ap/index.html.

346 Jodi Kantor, "As Obesity Fight Hits Cafeteria, Many Fear a Note From School," *New York Times*, January 8, 2007, accessed February 6, 2007, http:// query.nytimes.com/gst/fullpage.html?sec=health&res=9801E4DA1530F93 BA35752C0A9619C8B63; Stephen Smith, "State readies campaign to curb obesity epedemic," *The Boston Globe*, January 8, 2009, accessed October 19, 2009, http://www.boston.com/news/health/articles/2009/01/08/state_readies_campaign_to_curb_obesity_epidemic/.

347 Robert J. Samuelson, "The Afflictions of Affluence," http://www.newsweek. com/2004/03/21/the-afflictions-of-affluence.html, accessed October 30. 2005.

348 Steven Reinberg, "Almost 10 Percent of U.S. Medical Costs Tied to Obesity," ABC News, July 28, 2010, accessed October 19, 2010, http://abcnews. go.com/Health/Healthday/story?id=8184975&page=1.

Index